MORAL PROBLEMS

A Coursebook for Schools
and Colleges

Michael Palmer

The Lutterworth Press
Cambridge

FOR

Leighton Bohl   *Robert Lock*

Timothy Eustace   *Paul Ponder*

Christopher Johnson   *Robin Price*

The Lutterworth Press
P.O. Box 60
Cambridge CB1 2NT

British Library Cataloguing-in-Publication Data
Palmer, Michael
  Moral problems: a coursebook for schools and colleges
  1.Ethics. Theories, history.
  I. Title
  170'.9
  ISBN 0-7188-2791-0

First published in 1991, reprinted 1991

Line drawings by Marilyn Pedder
Cover design by Anna Bakhnova

Printed in Great Britain at the Alden Press, Oxford

Introduction

This book incorporates the major part of the general philosophy course currently taught in all the sixth forms at The Manchester Grammar School.

The development of philosophy in schools has been one of the more remarkable educational developments in recent years. We now have A and AS levels in the subject and it figures prominently in other associated examinations such as religious studies and politics. At a non-examinable level, more and more schools, in the quest to broaden their curricula, are extending their general studies timetables, and here too it is refreshing to see the extent to which a philosophical component is required.

With this rapid expansion, however, the teacher has been faced with the problem of finding material suitable for school rather than university use. This course is an attempt to fill the gap. Within the compass of one book it is, of course, impossible to cover the subject as a whole to any degree of depth. For that reason I have concentrated on the most frequently taught and examined area: Ethics. Experience has also shown that this provides the most readily accessible introduction to the subject and the most immediately enjoyable.

I have described elsewhere how this course came into being.[1] Suffice to say, during the many years it has been in place at The Manchester Grammar School, it has undergone many transformations, particularly since pupils and colleagues were encouraged to provide criticism of its weaknesses and advice on improvements. With publication I have broadened its scope somewhat in order to accommodate not only school but college use.

As its name suggests, this is not a compendium of ethical theories but a course book, providing the instructor, student and general reader with a step-by-step introduction to the major ethical theories, with each chapter leading on to the next. Since I am also aware of the limitations placed on teaching time in most educational establishments, the course is unavoidably selective. I realise that for some readers the omission of, for example, Existentialist, Marxist and Christian ethics will be a serious one. I can only reply that completeness has not been my first priority, and that for a better understanding of what ethical analysis involves it has always seemed to me better to increase the detail and reduce the scope.

What has, however, been a major priority is to provide the reader with original texts. Again, it has always seemed strange to me that a student can become familiar with, say, Utilitarianism, without ever having read Bentham or Mill. To that end, every theory analysed includes extensive extracts from primary sources.

A second priority has been to provide the teacher and student with as much help as possible in their analysis of individual theories. To that end I have not only provided a lengthy introduction and criticism of each theory but also included various exercises at points in the text where I think some clarification helpful. Each section also contains a number of essay questions and a bibliography.

---

1. See: Philosophy at Manchester Grammar School, *Cogito,* Vol.3 No.1(1989) pp.72 - 76.

A third priority has been to relate the ethical theory to a contemporary issue. This explains the so-called Discussion sections of the course. Here the ethical theory being examined is discussed in the light of particular moral dilemma. So to the theory of utilitarianism is appended the problem of punishment, to Kant's theory the problem of war, and so on. An introduction to each contemporary issue is provided, and the issue itself presented by three short extracts from the original sources. The purpose of this section is to set the theory in a familiar context and thereby to provide further clarification. Hopefully this will also offset the recurrent criticism of philosophy that it has little relevance to everyday affairs.

The structure of each chapter may therefore be summarised as follows:

The Ethical Theory

1 Introduction
2 Original text
3 Exercises
4 Criticism
5 Essay questions
6 Bibliography

Discussion: A contemporary issue

1 Introduction
2 Original texts
3 Essay questions
4 Bibliography

I have already indicated the extent to which this book is the product of classroom experience. I have been particularly encouraged by those colleagues in Manchester who, although often without any previous philosophical training, taught the course with remarkable success and enthusiasm. It is only fitting therefore that this book is dedicated to them.

MICHAEL PALMER

CONTENTS

Introduction   3

Chapter 1

  1.What is Ethics   9

  2.Principles of Moral Action: Normative Ethics   11

A Case Study: Socrates in Prison   15

Discussion: Civil Disobedience   22

    1.John Rawls   23

    2.Henry Thoreau   25

    3.Peter Kropotkin   27

Chapter 2

Egoism   33

    1.What is Egoism   34

    2.Psychological Egoism   37

    3.Ethical Egoism   40

Discussion: The Right to Life   47

  The Right to Life and Abortion   48

  The Right to Life and Euthanasia   49

  The Right to Life and Animal Rights   51

    1.Judith Thomson   52

    2.James Rachels   56

    3.Peter Singer   59

Chapter 3

Utilitarianism: The Theory of Jeremy Bentham   63

  1.The Principle of Utility   64

  2.The Hedonic Calculus   66

Utilitarianism: The Theory of John Stuart Mill   69

  1.Mill: The Greatest Happiness Principle   70

Some Criticisms of Utilitarianism   75

  The Problem of Consequences   75

  The Problem of Special Responsibilities   75

  The Problem of Justice   76

    1.Machiavelli   77

    2.Dostoyevsky   79

    3.Huxley   81

Discussion: Punishment   85

    1.Karl Menninger   87

    2.C. S. Lewis   89

    3.John Stuart Mill   91

Chapter 4

The Theory of Immanuel Kant   95
   1.The Good Will   97
   2.The Categorical Imperative   99

Some Criticisms and Amendments of Kant   105
   The Theory of W. D. Ross   108
   Rule-Utilitarianism   111

Discussion: The Morality of War   118
   1.Mohandas Gandhi   121
   2.Elizabeth Anscombe   123
   3.Douglas Lackey   125

Chapter 5

Determinism and Free Will   131
   1.Hard Determinism   132
   2.Libertarianism   135
   3.Soft Determinism   139

Discussion: Behaviourism   143
Psychological Behaviourism   143
Biobehaviourism   145
   1.B. F. Skinner   148
   2.Joseph Fletcher   151
   3.Aldous Huxley   153

Appendix

Meta-ethics   156
   1.Ethical Naturalism   156
   2.Ethical Neo-naturalism   157
   3.Ethical Non-cognitivism   158

Index   160

Chapter 1

1. What is Ethics?

All of us, at some time or other, are faced with the problem of what we ought to do. It is not difficult to think of examples. We accept we ought to help a blind person cross the road, or that we ought to tell the truth in a court of law. We also recognize that we ought not to cheat in examinations and ought not to drink and drive. These 'oughts' and 'ought nots' are clear to us: although this does not necessarily mean that we always act accordingly. Because of this we also attach praise and blame to our own actions and those of others.

In all these cases we are making **moral** or **ethical** judgements. In these judgements we decide that this action is right or wrong or that person is good or bad. Ethics is, therefore, usually confined to the area of human character or conduct, the word *ethics* deriving from the Greek *ethikos* (that which relates to *ethos* or character.) Men and women generally describe their own conduct and character, and that of others, by such general terms as 'good', 'bad', 'right' and 'wrong'; and it is the meaning and scope of these adjectives, in relation to human conduct, that the moral philosopher investigates. The philosopher is not, however, concerned with merely a *descriptive* account of the attitudes and values that people hold: that 'X believes that war is wrong' or that 'Y believes that abortion is right'. That X and Y believe these things may be of interest to the anthropologist or sociologist, but they are of little interest to moral philosophers. What concerns them is not *that* X and Y should believe these things but *why* they do. Ethics, in other words, is much more than explaining what you or I might say about a particular moral problem; it is a study of the reasoning behind our moral beliefs, of the *justification* for the particular moral positions we adopt.

The study of ethics is split into two branches. First, there is **normative ethics**. Here we consider what kinds of things are good and bad and how we are to decide what kinds of action are right and wrong. This is the main tradition of ethical thinking, extending back to Socrates, Plato and Aristotle, and the one we are most concerned with in this book.

Then there is **meta-ethics**, a detailed account of which is given in the Appendix (page 156). Meta-ethics deals with a philosophical analysis of the meaning and character of ethical language; with, for example, the meaning of the terms 'good' and 'bad', 'right' and 'wrong'. Meta-ethics is, therefore, *about* normative ethics and seeks to understand the terms and concepts employed there. For example, when I say 'Saving life is good' I might well begin a normative debate about when I should and should not do such a thing. Do I mean that all lives should be saved or only some? But in meta-ethics, I will be concerned much more with the meaning of the term 'good' within the sentence 'Saving life is good'. Is it something I can find in objects, so that I can easily detect it in some and not in others? Or, is it something I can see (like a colour) or something I can feel (like a toothache)?

In recent years, largely through philosophy's increasing preoccupation with the analysis of language, this branch of ethics has tended to dominate ethical discussion. It is held that one cannot even begin normative ethics without a prior analysis of the terms it uses. Certainly the overlap between the two is extensive, although whether meta-ethics is necessarily prior to normative ethics is an open question and the subject of considerable philosophical dispute.

From what has been said so far, it may be gathered that ethical statements are statements of a particular kind. They are not, for example, straightforward *empirical* statements, ie, statements of demonstrable fact. If we say 'Atomic weapons kill people', we are stating a simple observable fact; but if we say 'Atomic weapons should be banned', we are stating what we believe ought to happen.

In the first case, it is easy to establish whether the statement is true or false; but in the second, this is clearly impossible. In this instance, we are not stating facts so much as giving a *value* to certain facts - and a negative value at that. We are expressing a point of view about a particular circumstance, which we also know is not shared by everyone.

This is not to say that all propositions that give value to something are ethical propositions. We might say that 'Rolls-Royce make *good* cars' or 'That is a *bad* tyre', but we would not be attributing moral value to the cars or tyre. Similarly, in the area of art judgements (or *aesthetics*), we might speak of a '*good* painting' or '*bad* play', but usually we are not referring to the moral significance of the painting or play. All these, then, are *non-moral* uses of the words 'good' and 'bad'.

Exercise 1

How is the term 'good' being used in the following sentences? Which of these sentences are morally or ethically significant?

a	That music is good
b	Democracy is a good thing
c	He is a good footballer
d	He did me no good
e	This is a good report
f	He had a good life
g	He led a good life
h	It is good to tell the truth
i	Did you have a good holiday?
j	Take a good look
k	He has good manners
l	It is good to see you
m	God is good

2. The principles of moral action: Normative ethics

When we attempt to provide standards or rules to help us distinguish right from wrong actions or good from bad people, we are, therefore, engaged in normative ethics. In normative ethics, to repeat, we try to arrive, by rational means, at a set of acceptable criteria which will enable us to decide why any given action is 'right' or any particular person is called 'good'.

Take, for example, the rule 'Thou shalt not kill'. Opponents of the death penalty appeal to this rule to support their claim that no man, or group of men, has the right to take the life of another. Advocates of the death penalty, on the other hand, may refer to different standards: for example; that a man forfeits his life if he takes a life. Behind the question, 'Should Smith hang?' lies a debate between rival rules of moral behaviour. Having justified the rule, we then apply it to the case at hand, namely to Smith.

Normative ethics is generally split into two categories:
a) **teleological theories,**
b) **deontological theories.**
The philosopher C D Broad defined them in this way:

> *Deontological theories hold that there are ethical propositions of the form: 'Such and such a kind of action would always be right (or wrong) in such and such circumstances, no matter what its consequences might be . . .' Teleological theories hold that the rightness or wrongness of an action is always determined by its tendency to produce certain consequences which are intrinsically good or bad.*[1]

1. A **teleological theory** (from the Greek *telos*, meaning 'end') maintains, therefore, that moral judgements are based entirely on the effects produced by an action. An action is considered right or wrong in relation to its *consequences*. This view appeals to our common sense. Often, when considering a course of action, we ask: 'Will this hurt me?' or 'Will this hurt others?' Thinking like this is thinking teleologically: whether we do something or not is determined by what we think the consequences will be; whether we think they will be good or bad. Inevitably, of course, people have different opinions about whether a particular result is good or bad, and this accounts for the great variety of teleological theories. For some, an action is only right if it benefits the person performing the action. For others, this is too narrow, and the action's effects must apply to others besides the agent.

2. A **deontological theory** denies what a teleological theory affirms. The rightness of an action does not depend solely on its consequences since there may be *certain features of the act itself* which determine whether it is right or wrong. Pacifists, for example, contend that the act of armed aggression is wrong and always will be wrong, no matter what the consequences. Others believe we should take account of the 'motive' behind the act. If the intention of the person performing the act was to do harm, then that action is wrong quite apart from its effects, harmful or not. Or again, many argue that certain actions are right if they conform to certain absolute rules; like 'Keep your promises' or 'Always tell the truth'. It is quite possible that, in obeying these rules, you do not promote the greatest possible balance of good over evil; but for the deontologist this does not detract from the original good of your action in keeping your promise or telling the truth.

As we shall see, this difference between the teleologist and the deontologist is the most fundamental one in normative ethics. Simply put, the former looks ahead to the consequences of his or her actions; while the latter looks back to the nature of the act itself. It is not, however, always easy to pigeonhole our everyday decisions in this way, and invariably we find that they are compounded of both teleological and deontological elements.

---

1. *Five Types of Ethical Theory* (London: Kegan Paul, Trench, Trubner & Co, 1930) pp 206-207.

Exercise 2

Which of the following moral commands (which you may or may not agree with) are teleological, deontological, or both?

a	Do not drink and drive
b	Do not accept sweets from strangers
c	Do not take unnecessary risks
d	Always obey your superiors
e	Do not kill
f	Avenge wrongs done to you
g	Tell the truth
h	Never tell a lie except to an enemy
i	Love thy neighbour as thyself
j	Be ruled by your conscience
k	Never trust a traitor
l	Do not eat pork
m	Do not steal
n	Do not get caught stealing
o	Do as you would be done by

Exercise 3

Here are some examples of moral dilemmas. In each example: **1** justify your answer in relation to a particular moral principle; **2** determine whether this principle is teleological, deontological, or a mixture of both; **3** think of another situation (if you can) in which you would consider disobeying this principle.

1. Sanctions and South Africa

You are Prime Minister of a country which opposes apartheid in South Africa.

Should you impose sanctions against South Africa, even though you know these will seriously affect the already deprived black population?

2. The ruthless dictator

After a fair and legal election, a new President is elected in a central African state. Within a few months he reveals himself to be a ruthless and mentally unbalanced tyrant, merciless in liquidating all who oppose him. You have the power to assassinate him.

Should you?

3. The drowning men

Walking one day near the river, you hear frantic cries for help. Two men are struggling in the water and clearly drowning. With dismay you see that one is your father, whom you love dearly, and the other a famous scientist, whom the newspapers report is close to a cure for cancer.

Whom should you save?

4. The thief

Your schoolfriend says, 'I have something important to tell you, but you must keep it a secret'. You promise you will. Your friend then confesses that it was he who stole the money from the classroom. 'But this is terrible', you say. 'David has already been accused of this and is being expelled! You must tell the Headmaster at once!' Your friend refuses.

What should you do?

5. The doctor

A fifteen year-old girl comes to you as her doctor. She wants you to supply her with contraceptives. You discuss the matter with her and discover that she has never had sexual intercourse before and has never discussed the matter with her family.

Should you prescribe the contraceptives or inform her parents?

6. The sadist

The sadistic commandant of the camp shouts at you, 'Unless you hang your son, I'll hang him myself and these other prisoners as well!'.

What should you do?

7. The mayor

A shop selling pornography is about to open in your town. Local feeling is running high: some argue that you, as mayor, have the duty to prevent the sale of such corrupting literature, others that you do not have the right to censor what people read.

What is your decision?

Questions: Normative Ethics

1. How do ethical statements differ from ordinary empirical statements? Give examples.

2. List four qualities of human character that you think are good and four that are bad. Do you think them good and bad for deontological or teleological reasons?

3. Argue for a) pacifism and b) vegetarianism from both a deontological and teleological viewpoint.

4. Tom has lived alone on a desert island all his life. How would you explain to him the difference between right and wrong?

5. Are there any moral rules which you believe all societies, despite their cultural differences, should adopt? What are they, and how would you explain their universal acceptance?

Bibliography: Normative Ethics

* denotes text referred to or extracted in main text

Billington, Ray *Living Philosophy* (London & New York: Routledge, 1988) A wide-ranging discussion of normative theories, coupled with contemporary issues.

Brandt, R B *Ethical Theory: The Problem of Normative and Critical Ethics* (Englewood Cliffs, NJ: Prentice-Hall, 1959) Review of all major normative theories.

Broad, C D *Five Types of Ethical Theory** (London: Kegan Paul, Trench, Trubner & Co, 1930).

Frankena, William K *Ethics* (Englewood Cliffs, NJ: Prentice-Hall, 1973) A textbook, although not easy.

Gowans, Christopher W (ed) *Moral Dilemmas* (Oxford: Oxford University Press, 1987) Standard anthology.

Grassian, Victor *Moral Reasoning* (Englewood Cliffs, NJ: Prentice-Hall, 1981) Combines analysis of normative theories with discussion of contemporary moral problems.

Hospers, John *Human Conduct* (New York: Harcourt Brace Jovanovich, 1972) An excellent introduction to major theories.

MacIntyre, Alasdair *A Short History of Ethics* (London: Routledge & Kegan Paul, 1968) A history from the Homeric age to present day.

Purtill, Richard *Thinking about Ethics* (Englewood Cliffs, NJ: Prentice-Hall, 1976) A short but imaginative introduction.

Raphael, D D *Moral Philosophy* (Oxford: Oxford University Press, 1981) A short introduction.

Taylor, P W (ed) *Problems of Moral Philosophy* (Belmont, Calif: Dickenson, 1967) Substantial extracts, with introductions.

Case Study: Socrates in Prison

Before discussing further the various theories of normative ethics, it is useful to have an illustration of what is involved in an ethical debate and how a moral philosopher sets about dealing with a particular moral issue. The most famous example in the history of philosophy is found in Plato's dialogue, *Crito*. Plato's teacher, Socrates, is in prison, awaiting execution. His friend, Crito, visits him and urges him to escape. Socrates' reply is a model of ethical thinking, simultaneously brave and clear-headed. After reading this extract, let us consider, as our discussion topic, an issue that arises from this debate: *When has an individual the right to disobey the State?*

Socrates

Socrates was born in Athens in 469 BC, his father a sculptor, his mother a midwife. Little is known of his private life. We know that he was unhappily married, that he served as a 'hoplite' or foot-soldier in several campaigns, and that even his most implacable enemies admitted that he was a man of great physical courage. We know also that for most of his life he was virtually destitute, his poverty being so extreme that many contemporary writers made fun of it, as Aristophanes does in his play *The Clouds*. Nor did his actual appearance help matters: he was short, fat, and ugly; but he was also marvellous company, funny, a loyal friend, modest, devout, and, above all, possessed of quite extraordinary intellectual gifts. These latter, perhaps more than anything else, were to bring about his downfall.

A man of such prominence could hardly avoid becoming involved in politics. For one year, 406-405 BC, he was a member of the Council of 500, and, under the Reign of Terror of the Thirty Tyrants in 404 BC, he refused to agree to the arrest of Leon, and generally made himself so obnoxious to the 'Thirty' that a special ordinance was drawn up forbidding 'the teaching of the art of argument'. Had it not been for the counter-revolution of the Democrats, he would probably have been charged wth 'disobedience'.

Ironically enough, it was reserved for the reconstituted democracy to bring Socrates to trial. Upon their return to power, the Democrats proclaimed a general amnesty; but four years later, in 399 BC, and despite the fact that Socrates had always dissociated himself from the excesses of the old regime, they charged him with offences against public morality. His accusers were Meletus the poet, Anytus the tanner, and Lycon the orator - all members of the democratic party. The accusation ran: 'Socrates is guilty, firstly, of denying the gods recognized by the state and introducing new divinities, and secondly, of corrupting the young'.

What lay behind these allegations? According to Socrates' pupil, the historian Xenophon, the first of these charges rested on the notorious fact that Socrates believed himself to be guided by a mysterious power, a 'divine voice', which seems to have had a largely negative function: it always dissuaded him from certain courses of action but never urged him to act. The phenomenon dated from his early years and was, so far as he knew, peculiar to himself. Hearing this 'voice' - he called it his *daimonion* - Socrates believed he was charged with a divine mission to analyse and, if necessary, expose the wisdom of all those whom society called wise. Needless to say, this relentless inquisition created many enemies among the establishment - to them he was no better than an impecunious busybody, trampling on the cherished beliefs of others - while at the same time his radical views on religion, politics and education, coupled with his invincible skill in debate, attracted the young, and created the impression that he was the leader of a new iconoclastic and subversive movement. Today we see Socrates as the founder of philosophical enquiry and one of the indisputably great men of history; but for many of his contemporaries, he was little better than a criminal, a man betraying Athenic traditions, irreligious and corrupt. That a majority should pronounce him guilty is not therefore as strange as it appears.

The account of Socrates' trial is given in Plato's *Apology*. To the credit of the jury of 500, the initial vote was far from unanimous: Socrates was found guilty by 280 votes against 220. Meletus having demanded the death penalty, it now rested with the accused, according to Athenian law, to make a counter-proposition; and there is little doubt that had Socrates asked for some lesser penalty, his proposal would have been accepted. Instead, to the surprise of the judges and the dismay of his friends, he proudly maintained that, such had been his services to the State, he should be awarded a pension for life. As a 'token' fine, he suggested payment of *1 mina* (probably about £100). Socrates' condescending offer was quickly amended by his friends Plato, Critobulus and Appollodorus to thirty times that amount on their security. But it was too late: the judges returned a verdict of death by an increased majority. Then, in a powerful and moving speech, Socrates spoke of death and the fear of dying, concluding with the words, 'The hour of departure has arrived, and we go our ways - I to die, and you to live; but which is better only God knows'.

Normally sentence of execution was carried out within 24 hours. It so happened, however, that Socrates' trial coincided with the absence of the sacred ship to Delos - every year a ship sailed to Delos, commemorating the deliverance of Athens by Theseus - and it was the custom that the death penalty could not be inflicted during this period. Socrates was therefore kept in prison for thirty days. Perhaps even his enemies secretly hoped he would escape and leave the country. Certainly his friends urged him to do so. But would Socrates accept their advice and run? It is at this point that one of these friends, Crito, visits Socrates in prison.

Crito tells Socrates that the situation is now desperate: the ship from Delos has been sighted, which means that, unless Socrates does something, he will be executed the next day. In a last passionate appeal to persuade his friend, Crito puts forward various arguments:

1. Most people will simply refuse to believe that Socrates chose to remain in prison. Instead they will blame his friends for not helping him and consider Crito himself contemptible for not spending the money to get him out;

2. Perhaps Socrates thinks that his friends, if they help him, will be eventually betrayed by informers, and that they will then have to pay heavy fines or even lose their possessions? If so, his fears are groundless. There were men ready to rescue him for quite a modest sum, and informers could always be bought off cheaply;

3. If Socrates died, he would be wilfully orphaning his sons and depriving them of their education, which could be completed elsewhere;

4. Socrates was taking the easiest way out, contemplating an action that was neither brave nor good. Frankly his friends were ashamed and embarrassed by the whole business.

'Come, make up your mind', says Crito. 'There is no alternative; the whole thing must be carried through during this coming night. If we lose any more time, it can't be done, it will be too late. I appeal to you, Socrates, on every ground; take my advice and please don't be unreasonable'.

Socrates' Reply [1]

Socrates: My dear Crito, I appreciate your warm feelings very much - that is, assuming that they have some justification; if not, the stronger they are, the harder they will be to deal with. Very well, then; we must consider whether we ought to follow your advice or not . . . Suppose that we begin by reverting to this view which you hold about people's opinions . . . Consider, then; don't you think that this is a sound enough principle, that one should not regard all the opinions that people hold, but only some and not others? What do you say? Isn't that a fair statement?

Crito: Yes, it is.

Socrates: In other words, one should regard the good ones and not the bad?

Crito: Yes.

Socrates: The opinions of the wise being good, and the opinions of the foolish bad?

Crito: Naturally.

Socrates: To pass on, then: what do you think of the sort of illustration that I used to employ? When a man is in training, and taking it seriously, does he pay attention to all praise and criticism and opinion indiscriminately, or only when it comes from the one qualified person, the actual doctor or trainer?

Crito: Only when it comes from the one qualified person.

Socrates: Then he should be afraid of the criticism and welcome the praise of the one qualified person, but not those of the general public.

Crito: Obviously . . .

Socrates: Very good. Well now, tell me, Crito, we don't want to go through all the examples one by one, does this apply as a general rule, and above all to the sort of actions which we are trying to decide about: just and unjust, honourable and dishonourable, good and bad? Ought we to be guided and intimidated by the opinion of the many or by that of the one - assuming that there is someone with expert knowledge?   Or is this all nonsense?

Crito: No, I think it is true, Socrates . . .

Socrates: In that case, my dear fellow, what we ought to consider is not so much what people in general will say about us but how we stand with the expert in right and wrong, the one authority, who represents the actual truth. So, in the first place your proposition is not correct when you say that we should consider popular opinion in questions of what is right and honourable and good, or the opposite. Of course one might object 'All the same, the people have the power to put us to death.'

Crito: No doubt about that! Quite true, Socrates; it is a possible objection.

Socrates: But so far as I can see, my dear fellow, the argument which we have just been through is quite unaffected by it. At the same time I should like you to consider whether we are still satisfied on this point: that the really important thing is not to live, but to live well.

Crito: Why, yes.

Socrates: And that to live well means the same thing as to live honourably or rightly?

Crito: Yes.

Socrates: Then in the light of this agreement we must consider whether or not it is right for me to try to get away without an official discharge. If it turns out to be right, we must make the attempt; if not, we must let it drop. As for the considerations you raise about expense and reputation and bringing up children, I am afraid, Crito, that they represent the reflections of the ordinary public, who put people to death, and would bring them back to life if they could, with equal indifference to reason. Our real duty, I fancy, since the argument leads that way, is to consider one question only, the one which we raised just now: Shall we be acting rightly in paying money and showing gratitude to these people who are going to rescue me, and in escaping or arranging the escape ourselves, or shall we really be acting wrongly in doing all this? If it becomes clear that such conduct is wrong, I cannot help thinking that the question whether we are sure to die, or to suffer any other ill effect for that matter, if we stand our ground and take no action, ought not to weigh with us at all in comparison with the risk of doing what is wrong.

1. Plato, *The Last Days of Socrates*, trans Hugh Tredennick (Harmondsworth: Penguin Books, 1969) pp 84-96.

Crito: I agree with what you say, Socrates; but I wish you would consider what we ought to *do*.

Socrates: Let us look at it together, my dear fellow; and if you can challenge any of my arguments, do so and I will listen to you; but if you can't, be a good fellow and stop telling me over and over again that I ought to leave this place without official permission . . . Now give your attention to the starting point of this inquiry - I hope that you will be satisfied with my way of stating it - and try to answer my questions to the best of your judgement.

Crito: Well, I will try.

Socrates: Do we say that one must never willingly do wrong, or does it depend upon circumstances? Is it true, as we have often agreed before, that there is no sense in which   wrong-doing is good or honourable? . . . Surely the truth is just what we have always said. Whatever the popular view is, and whether the alternative is pleasanter than the present one or even harder to bear, the fact remains that to do wrong is in every sense bad and dishonourable for the person who does it. Is that our view, or not?

Crito: Yes, it is.

Socrates: Then in no circumstances must one do wrong.

Crito: No.

Socrates: In that case one must not even do wrong when one is wronged, which most people regard as the natural course.

Crito: Apparently not.

Socrates: Tell me another thing, Crito: ought one to do injuries or not?

Crito: Surely not, Socrates.

Socrates: And tell me: is it right to do an injury in retaliation, as most people believe, or not?

Crito: No, never.

Socrates: Because, I suppose, there is no difference between injuring people and wronging them.

Crito: Exactly.

Socrates: So one ought not to return a wrong or an injury to any person, whatever the provocation is. Now be careful, Crito, that in making these single admissions you do not end by admitting something contrary to your real beliefs . . .

Crito: . . . Go on.

Socrates: Well, here is my next point, or rather question. Ought one to fulfil all one's agreements, provided that they are right, or break them?

Crito: One ought to fulfil them.

Socrates: Then consider the logical consequence. If we leave this place without first persuading the State to let us go, are we or are we not doing an injury, and doing it in a quarter where it is least justifiable? Are we or are we not abiding by our just agreements?

Crito: I can't answer your question, Socrates; I am not clear in my mind.

Socrates: Look at it in this way. Suppose that while we were preparing to run away from here (or however one should describe it) the Laws and Constitution of Athens were to come and confront us and ask this question: 'Now, Socrates, what are you proposing to do? Can you deny that by this act which you are contemplating you intend, so far as you have the power, to destroy us, the Laws, and the whole State as well? Do you imagine that a city can continue to exist and not be turned upside down, if the legal judgements which are pronounced in it have no force but are nullified and destroyed by private persons?'

How shall we answer this question, Crito, and others of the same kind? . . . Shall we say 'Yes, I do intend to destroy the laws, because the State wronged me by passing a faulty judgement at my trial'? Is this to be our answer, or what?

Crito: What you have just said, by all means, Socrates.

Socrates: Then what supposing the Laws say . . . 'Come now, what charge do you bring against us and the State, that you are trying to destroy us? Did we not give you life in the first place? Was it not through us that your father married your mother and begot you? Tell us, have you any complaint against those of us Laws that deal with marriage?' 'No, none', I should say. 'Well, have you any against the laws which deal with children's upbringing and education, such as you had yourself? Are you not grateful to those of us Laws which were instituted for this end, for requiring your father to give you a cultural and physical education?' 'Yes', I should say. 'Very good. Then since you have been born and brought up and educated, can you deny, in the first place, that you were our child and servant, both you and your ancestors? And if this is so, do you imagine that what is right for us is equally right for you, and that whatever we try to do to you, you are justified in retaliating? You did not have equality of rights with your father, or your employer (supposing that you had had one), to enable you to retaliate; you were not allowed to answer back when you were scolded or to hit back when you were beaten, or to do a great many other things of the same kind. Do you expect to have such licence against your country and its laws that if we try to put you to death in the belief that it is right to do so, you on your part will try your hardest to destroy your country and us its Laws in return? And will you, the true devotee of goodness, claim that you are justified in doing so? . . . Both in war and in the law-courts and everywhere else you must do whatever your city and your country commands, or else persuade it in accordance with universal justice; but violence is a sin even against your parents, and it is a far greater sin against your country.' What shall we say to this, Crito? that what the Laws say is true, or not?

Crito: Yes, I think so.

Socrates: 'Consider, then, Socrates,' the Laws would probably continue, 'whether it is also true for us to say that what you are now trying to do to us is not right. Although we have brought you into the world and reared you and educated you, and given you and all your fellow-citizens a share in all the good things at our disposal, nevertheless by the very fact of granting our permission we openly proclaim this principle: that any Athenian, on attaining to manhood and seeing for himself the political organization of the State and us its Laws, is permitted, if he is not satisfied with us, to take his property and go away wherever he likes . . .

On the other hand, if any one of you stands his ground when he can see how we administer justice and the rest of our public organization, we hold that by doing so he has in fact undertaken to do anything that we tell him; and we maintain that anyone who disobeys is guilty of doing wrong on three separate counts: first because we are his parents, and secondly because we are his guardians; and thirdly because, after promising obedience, he is neither obeying us nor persuading us to change our decision if we are at fault in any way . . . These are the charges, Socrates, to which we say that you will be liable if you do what you are contemplating; and you will not be the least culpable of your fellow-countrymen, but one of the most guilty . . . You have never left the city to attend a festival or for any other purpose, except on some military expedition; you have never travelled abroad as other people do, and you have never felt the impulse to acquaint yourself with another country or constitution; you have been content with us and with our city. You have definitely chosen us, and undertaken to observe us in all your activities as a citizen; and as the crowning proof that you are satisfied with our city, you have begotten children in it. Furthermore, even at the time of your trial you could have proposed the penalty of banishment, if you had chosen to do so; that is, you could have done then with the sanction of the State what you are now trying to do without it . . . Now, first answer this question: Are we or are we not speaking the truth when we say that you have undertaken, in deed if not in word, to live your life as a citizen in obedience to us?' What are we to say to that, Crito? Are we not bound to admit it?

Crito: We cannot help it, Socrates.

Socrates: 'It is a fact, then,' they would say, 'that you are breaking covenants and undertakings made with us, although you made them under no compulsion or misunderstanding, and were not compelled to decide in a limited time; you had seventy years in which you could have left the country, if you were not satisfied with us or felt that the agreements were unfair . . . It is quite obvious that you stand by yourself above all other Athenians in your affection for this city and for us its Laws; - who would care for a city without laws? And now, after all this, are you not going to stand by your agreement? Yes, you are, Socrates, if you will take our advice; and then you will at least escape being laughed at for leaving the city.

'We invite you to consider what good you will do to yourself or your friends if you commit this breach of faith and stain your conscience. It is fairly obvious that the risk of being banished and either losing their citizenship or having their property confiscated will extend to your friends as well . . . Incidentally you will confirm the opinion of the jurors who tried you that they gave a correct verdict; a destroyer of laws might very well be supposed to have destructive influence upon young and foolish human beings . . . And will no one comment on the fact that an old man of your age, probably with only a short time left to live, should dare to cling so greedily to life, at the price of violating the most stringent laws? Perhaps not, if you avoid irritating anyone . . . But of course you want to live for your children's sake, so that you may be able to bring them up and educate them. Indeed! By first taking them off to Thessaly and making foreigners of them, so that they may have that additional enjoyment? Or if that is not your intention, supposing that they are brought up here with you still alive, will they be better cared for and educated without you, because of course your friends will look after them? Will they look after your children if you go away to Thessaly, and not if you go away to the next world? Surely if those who profess to be your friends are worth anything, you must believe that they would care for them.

Plato

'No, Socrates; be advised by us your guardians, and do not think more of your children or of your life or of anything else than you think of what is right; so that when you enter the next world you may have all this to plead in your defence before the authorities there. It seems clear that if you do this thing, neither you nor any of your friends will be the better for it or be more upright or have a cleaner conscience here in this world, nor will it be better for you when you reach the next. As it is, you will leave this place, when you do, as the victim of a wrong done not by us, the Laws, but by your fellow-men. But if you leave in that dishonourable way, returning wrong for wrong and evil for evil, breaking your agreements and covenants with us, and injuring those whom you least ought to injure - yourself, your friends, your country, and us - then you will have to face our anger in your lifetime, and in that place beyond when the laws of the other world know that you have tried, so far as you could, to destroy even us their brothers, they will not receive you with a kindly welcome. Do not take Crito's advice, but follow ours.'

That, my dear friend Crito, I do assure you, is what I seem to hear them saying, just as the mystic seems to hear the strains of music; and the sound of their arguments rings so loudly in my head that I cannot hear the other side. I warn you that, as my opinion stands at present, it will be useless to urge a different view. However, if you think that you will do any good by it, say what you like.

Crito: No, Socrates, I have nothing to say.

Socrates: Then give it up, Crito, and let us follow this course, since God points out the way.

With these arguments, Socrates condemned himself. The story of his final day is told, in simple and moving language, by Plato in his dialogue *Phaedo*. Socrates says goodbye to his wife and family, his friends gather about him, and the jailer enters, himself deeply upset by what he has to do and describing Socrates as 'the noblest and the gentlest and the bravest of all the men that have ever come here.' Despite Crito's efforts to delay matters, Socrates takes the cup of hemlock and 'quite calmly and with no signs of distaste', drinks the contents in a single draught. Seeing this, many of his friends break down and weep uncontrollably. Socrates paces the room and then lies down, covering his face. Pinching one of his feet, the jailer asks him whether he can feel anything. Socrates replies that he cannot. Then, just before the poison takes full effect, Socrates uncovers his face and murmurs, 'Crito, we ought to offer a cock to Asclepius. See to it, and don't forget.' - meaning that he wished to honour the God of healing and implying that death is the cure for life. 'It shall be done', answers Crito. 'Is there anything else?' There being no reply, his companions realized that Socrates was already dead.

In narrating these tragic events, the concluding words of the *Phaedo* form a fitting epitaph:

Such, Echecrates, was the end of our comrade, who was, we may fairly say, of all those whom we knew in our time, the bravest and also the wisest and most upright man.

Questions: Socrates in Prison

1. Make a list of the arguments employed by Socrates and Crito. To what extent are they teleological, deontological, or a mixture of both?

2. Socrates appeals to certain moral rules, which, he claims, are of universal application and should not be disobeyed. What are these rules and how far do you think they are justified?

3. To what extent is Socrates right in his condemnation of public opinion?

4. Are there experts in right and wrong? If there are, who are they? If there aren't, how can Socrates distinguish between right and wrong actions?

5. Do you think Socrates has an old-fashioned and outmoded view of the State?

6. In what circumstances do you think Socrates would disobey a State Law? When would you disobey one?

7. Are there any circumstances in which retaliation is justified?

8. Does a man, wrongly convicted of a crime, have the right to escape from prison? In your answer, take account of Socrates' reply to Crito.

9. What is the relationship between legality and morality? Give examples in which there is a conflict between them.

10. 'I'd rather be a coward for five minutes than dead for the rest of my life' (Irish saying). Discuss.

Bibliography: Socrates in Prison

---

* denotes text referred to or extracted in main text

Blum, Alan F *Socrates* (London: Routledge & Kegan Paul, 1978) Chapter 4 analyses Socrates' notion of Justice.
Ferguson, J *Socrates* (London: Macmillan, for the Open University, 1970) A source book of biographical information.
Guthrie, W K C *Socrates* (Cambridge: Cambridge University Press, 1971) A standard work.
Kraut, Richard *Socrates and the State* (Princeton: Princeton University Press, 1984) An extensive analysis of the arguments employed in *Crito*.
Parker, M *Socrates and Athens* (London: Macmillan, 1973) An informative booklet.
Plato, *The Last Days of Socrates*, * trans Hugh Tredennick (Harmondsworth: Penguin Books, 1969) The dialogues *Apology*, *Crito* and *Phaedo*.
Santas, G X *Socrates* (London: Routledge & Kegan Paul, 1979) Chapter 2 discusses Socrates' attitude to the laws of Athens.

Discussion: Civil disobedience

In his discussion with Crito, Socrates provides us with a classic statement of the problem of **civil disobedience**; whether the individual has the right to disobey the law if he or she believes it unjust. As we have seen, Socrates' argument is based on a kind of 'social contract' theory, which maintains that just as a citizen enjoys the benefits of the state, so he or she must obey the laws of that state. While it is, therefore, quite proper for people to try to change the law, they must always do so within the law and never commit any action that would do violence or injury to the law. To do so is to destroy the contract they have with the state and its laws. More specifically, then, individuals must accept the decisions of the courts, even though a particular verdict may be unjust. They may appeal against the verdict, but in the end, whatever the outcome, they must abide by that decision. Thus, even if an error of justice persists to the end and even if it results in the death of an innocent person, the sentence of the court must be upheld and carried out. For Socrates, the consequences of *not* doing this would be socially catastrophic and far outweighed all considerations of injustice in particular cases.

This is not to say that Socrates rules out all forms of civil disobedience. It is quite clear from his argument that if, for instance, a man believed that the laws of the state were corrupt, and if one of these laws prevented him from leaving the country, then the contract that bound him to obedience could be ignored and the law disobeyed. Unfortunately, however, matters are not always as straightforward as this. Often the problem is not whether the laws in general are unjust, but whether the injustice of a particular law outweighs the justice of the law in general. In other words, what should the law-abiding citizen do when he or she comes face to face with a law which they find quite intolerable?

In the following three extracts we find differing opinions about the issue of civil disobedience. The contemporary philosopher, John Rawls, introduces a 'social contract' theory similar to that of Socrates and based on his influential notion of 'fair play': if it is socially necessary that everyone should behave in a certain way, then it is unfair to the rest if someone gains an advantage by acting otherwise. To this extent, the injustice of a law is not a sufficient reason for not complying with it.

This view, however, is not supported by Henry Thoreau (1817-1862). In his celebrated essay - which, incidentally, Martin Luther King admits had a direct influence on his thinking - Thoreau contends that men's actions should be governed by justice, not legality. Accordingly, civil disobedience is justified if the law is seen to be the agent of injustice.

But the revolutionary Peter Kropotkin (1842-1921) will have none of this: it is not disobedience that requires justification but obedience! In an impassioned defence of anarchism, he denies the assumption that the rule of law can provide any benefits whatever.

1. John Rawls: The Duty of Fair Play [2]

. . . Fundamental to justice is the concept of fairness which relates to right dealing between persons who are co-operating with or competing against one another, as when one speaks of fair games, fair competition, and fair bargains. The question of fairness arises when free persons, who have no authority over one another, are engaging in a joint activity and amongst themselves settling or acknowledging the rules which define it and which determine the respective shares in its benefits and burdens. A practice will strike the parties as fair if none feels that, by participating in it, they or any of the others are taken advantage of, or forced to give in to claims which they do not regard as legitimate. This implies that each has a conception of legitimate claims which he thinks it reasonable for others as well as himself to acknowledge . . .

Now if the participants in a practice accept its rules as fair, and so have no complaint to lodge against it, there arises a . . . duty (and a corresponding . . . right) of the parties to each other to act in accordance with the practice when it falls upon them to comply. When any number of persons engage in a practice, or conduct a joint undertaking according to rules, and thus restrict their liberty, those who have submitted to these restrictions when required have the right to similar acquiescence on the part of those who have benefitted from their submission. These conditions will obtain if a practice is correctly acknowledged to be fair, for in this case all who participate in it will benefit from it . . . But one cannot, in general, be released from this obligation (to follow a rule) by denying the justice of the practice only when if falls on one to obey. If a person rejects a practice, he should, so far as possible, declare his intention in advance, and avoid participating in it or enjoying its benefits.

This duty I have called that of fair play, but it should be admitted that to refer to it in this way is, perhaps, to extend the ordinary notion of fairness. Usually acting unfairly is not so much the breaking of any particular rule, even if the infraction is difficult to detect (cheating), but taking advantage of loop-holes or ambiguities in rules, availing oneself of unexpected or special circumstances which make it impossible to enforce them, insisting that rules be enforced to one's advantage when they should be suspended, and more generally, acting contrary to the intention of a practice. It is for this reason that one speaks of the sense of fair play: acting fairly requires more than simply being able to follow rules; what is fair must often be felt, or perceived, one wants to say. It is not, however, an unnatural extension of the duty of fair play to have it include the obligation which participants who have knowingly accepted the benefits of their common practice owe to each other to act in accordance with it when their performance falls due; for it is usually considered unfair if someone accepts the benefits of a practice but refuses to do his part in maintaining it. Thus one might say of the tax-dodger that he violates the duty of fair play: he accepts the benefits of government but will not do his part in releasing resources to it; and members of labour unions often say that fellow workers who refuse to join are being unfair: they refer to them as 'free riders', as persons who enjoy what are the supposed benefits of unionism, higher wages, shorter hours, job security, and the like, but who refuse to share in its burdens in the form of paying dues, and so on . . .

The conception at which we have arrived, then, is that the principles of justice may be thought of as arising once the constraints of having a morality are imposed upon rational and mutually self-interested parties who are related and situated in a special way. A practice is just if it is in accordance with the principles which all who participate in it might reasonably be expected to propose or to acknowledge before one another when they are similarly circumstanced and required to make a firm commitment in advance without knowledge of what will be their peculiar condition, and thus when it meets standards which the parties could accept as fair, should occasion arise for them to debate its merits. Regarding the participants themselves, once persons knowingly engage in a practice which they acknowledge to be fair and accept the benefits of doing so, they are bound by the duty of fair play to follow the rules when it comes their turn to do so, and this implies a limitation on their pursuit of self-interest in particular cases . . .

2. 'Justice as Fairness'. *Philosophy, Politics and Society*, ed Peter Laslett and W G Runciman (Oxford: Basil Blackwell Ltd, 1962) pp 144-149; and (final paragraph) 'The Justification of Civil Disobedience', *Civil Disobedience: Theory and Practice*, ed H A Bedau (Indianapolis & New York: Pegasus, 1969) p 245.

The difficulty is that we cannot frame a procedure which guarantees that only just and effective legislation is enacted. Thus even under a just constitution unjust laws may be passed and unjust policies enforced. Some form of the majority principle is necessary but the majority may be mistaken, more or less wilfully, in what it legislates. In agreeing to a democratic constituiton . . . one accepts at the same time the principle of majority rule. Assuming that the constitution is just and that we have accepted and plan to continue to accept its benefits, we then have an obligation and a natural duty (or in any case the duty) to comply with what the majority enacts even though it may be unjust. In this way we are bound to follow unjust laws, not always, of course, but provided the injustice does not exceed certain limits. We recognize that we must run the risk of suffering from the defects of one another's sense of injustice; this burden we are prepared to carry as long as it is more or less evenly distributed or does not weigh too heavily. Justice binds us to a just constitution and to the unjust laws which may be enacted under it in precisely the same way that it binds us to any other social arrangement. Once we take the sequence of stages into account, there is nothing unusual in our being required to comply with unjust laws . . .

Questions: Rawls

1. What is the principle of 'fair play'? With the help of a practical example, how far do you think this principle justifies obedience to an unjust law?

2 . To what extent does Rawls allow disobedience to the law? Can you think of an actual instance in which you would feel morally bound to go against the principle of 'fair play'?

3. How would Rawls argue against tax evasion?

4. How would Rawls deal with the claim: Better to let the law be a victim than to be the victim of the law?

2. *Henry Thoreau: On the Duty of Civil Disobedience* [3]

I heartily accept the motto, 'That government is best which governs least;' and I should like to see it acted up to more rapidly and systematically. Carried out, it finally amounts to this, which also I believe, 'That government is best which governs not at all,' and when men are prepared for it, that will be the kind of government which they will have. Government is at best but an expedient; but most governments are usually, and all governments are sometimes, inexpedient. The objections which have been brought against a standing army, and they are many and weighty, and deserve to prevail, may also at last be brought against a standing government. The standing army is only an arm of the standing government. The government itself, which is only the mode which the people have chosen to execute their will, is equally liable to be abused and perverted before the people can act through it . . .

After all, the practical reason why, when the power is once in the hands of the people, a majority are permitted, and for a long period continue, to rule is not because they are the most likely to be in the right, nor because this seems fairest to the minority, but because they are physically the strongest. But a government in which the majority rule in all cases cannot be based on justice, even as far as men understand it. Can there not be a government in which majorities do not virtually decide right and wrong, but conscience? - in which majorities decide only those questions to which the rule of expediency is applicable? Must the citizen ever for a moment, or in the least degree, resign his conscience to the legislator? Why has every man a conscience, then? I think that we should be men first, and subjects afterward. It is not desirable to cultivate a respect for the law, so much as for the right. The only obligation which I have a right to assume is to do at any time what I think right. It is truly enough said, that a corporation has no conscience; but a corporation of conscientious men is a corporation *with* a conscience. Law never made men a whit more just; and, by means of their respect for it, even the well-disposed are daily made the agents of injustice. A common and natural result of an undue respect for law is, that you may see a file of soldiers, colonel, captain, corporal, privates, powder-monkeys, and all, marching in admirable order over hill and dale to the wars, against their wills, ay, against their common sense and consciences, which makes it very steep marching indeed, and produces a palpitation of the heart. They have no doubt that it is a damnable business in which they are concerned; they are all peaceably inclined. Now, what are they? Men at all? or small moveable forts and magazines, at the service of some unscrupulous man in power? . . .

The mass of men serve the state thus, not as men mainly, but as machines, with their bodies . . . In most cases there is no free exercise whatever of the judgement or the moral sense; but they put themselves on a level with wood and earth and stones; and wooden men can perhaps be manufactured that will serve the purpose as well. Such command no more respect than men of straw or a lump of dirt. They have the same sort of worth only as horses or dogs. Yet such as these are commonly esteemed good citizens . . .

Unjust laws exist; shall we be content to obey them, or shall we endeavour to amend them, and obey them until we have succeeded, or shall we transgress them at once? Men generally, under such a government as this, think that they ought to wait until they have persuaded the majority to alter them. They think that, if they should resist, the remedy would be worse than the evil. But it is the fault of the government itself that the remedy *is* worse than the evil. *It* makes it worse. Why is it not more apt to anticipate and provide for reform? Why does it not cherish its wise minority? Why does it cry and resist before it is hurt? Why does it not encourage its citizens to be on the alert to point out its faults and *do* better than it would have them? Why does it always crucify Christ, and excommunicate Copernicus and Luther, and pronounce Washington and Franklin rebels? . . .

If the injustice is part of the necessary friction of the machine of government, let it go, let it go: perchance it will wear smooth, - certainly the machine will wear out. If the injustice has a spring, or a pulley, or a rope, or a crank, exclusively for itself, then perhaps you may consider whether the remedy will not be worse than the evil; but if it is of such a nature that it requires you to be the agent of injustice to another, then, I say, break the law. Let your life be a counter friction to stop the machine. What I have to do is to see, at any rate, that I do not lend myself to the wrong which I condemn . . .

3. 'Civil Disobedience', *Civil Disobedience: Theory and Practice*, ed H A Bedau (Indianapolis & New York: Pegasus, 1969) pp 27-29, 34-35, 47-48.

There will never be a really free and enlightened State until the State comes to recognize the individual as a higher and independent power, from which all its own power and authority are derived, and treats him accordingly. I please myself with imagining a State at last which can afford to be just to all men, and to treat the individual with respect as a neighbour; which even would not think it inconsistent with its own repose if a few were to live aloof from it, not meddling with it, nor embraced by it, who fulfilled all the duties of neighbours and fellow-men. A State which bore this kind of fruit, and suffered it to drop off as fast as it ripened, would prepare the way for a still more perfect and glorious State, which also I have imagined, but not anywhere seen.

Questions: Thoreau

1. What is the role of 'conscience' in Thoreau's theory?

2. You are the President of a nation facing imminent attack. You need troops but many people in your country think war immoral and refuse to fight. What would Thoreau's advice to you be and would you agree with it?

3. Should soldiers retain the right to refuse to fight? How would Thoreau reply? How would you reply?

4. What are the objections to a standing army? Are these objections applicable to a standing government?

3. Peter Kropotkin: Law and Authority [4]

... In existing States a fresh law is looked upon as a remedy for evil. Instead of themselves altering what is bad, people begin by demanding a *law* to alter it. If the road between two villages is impassable, the peasant says: 'There should be a law about parish roads.' ... If the employer lowers wages or increases the hours of labour, the politician in embryo exclaims, 'We must have a law to put all that to rights.' In short, a law everywhere and for everything! A law about fashions, a law about mad dogs, a law about virtue, a law to put a stop to all the vices and all the evils which result from human indolence and cowardice.

We are so perverted by an education which from infancy seeks to kill in us the spirit of revolt, and to develop that of submission to authority; we are so perverted by this existence under the ferrule of a law, which regulates every event in life - our birth, our education, our development, our love, our friendship - that, if this state of things continues, we shall lose all initiative, all habit of thinking for ourselves ...

Indeed, for some thousands of years, those who govern us have done nothing but ring the changes upon 'Respect for law, obedience to authority.' This is the moral atmosphere in which parents bring up their children, and school only serves to confirm the impression. Cleverly assorted scraps of spurious science are inculcated upon the children to prove the necessity of law; obedience to the law is made a religion; moral goodness and the law of the masters are fused into one and the same divinity. The historical hero of the schoolroom is the man who obeys the law, and defends it against rebels ...

But times and tempers are changed. Rebels are everywhere to be found who no longer wish to obey the law without knowing whence it comes, what are its uses, and whither arises the obligation to submit to it, and the reverence with which it is encompassed. The rebels of our day are criticizing the very foundation of society which have hitherto been held sacred, and first and foremost amongst them that fetish, law ...

The millions of laws which exist for the regulation of humanity appear upon investigation to be divided into three principal categories: protection of property, protection of persons, protection of government. And by analyzing each of these three categories, we arrive at the same logical and necessary conclusion: *the uselessness and hurtfulness of law.*

Socialists know what is meant by protection of property. Laws on property are not made to guarantee either to the individual or to society the enjoyment of the produce of their own labour. On the contrary, they are made to rob the producer of a part of what he has created, and to secure to certain other people that portion of the produce which they have stolen either from the producer or from society as a whole. When, for example, the law established Mr So-and-So's right to a house, it is not establishing his right to a cottage he has built for himself, or to a house he has erected with the help of some of his friends. In that case no one would have disputed his right. On the contrary, the law is establishing his right to a house which is *not* the product of his labour; first of all because he has had it built for him by others to whom he has not paid the full value of their work, and next because that house represents a social value which he could not have produced for himself. The law is establishing his right to what belongs to everybody in general and to nobody in particular ... And it is precisely because this appropriation and all other forms of property bearing the same character are a crying injustice, that a whole arsenal of laws and a whole army of soldiers, policemen and judges are needed to maintain it against the good sense and just feeling inherent in humanity.

Half our laws, - the civil code in each country, - serves no other purpose than to maintain this appropriation, this monopoly for the benefit of certain individuals against the whole of mankind. Three-fourths of the causes decided by the tribunals are nothing but quarrels between monopolists - two robbers disputing over the booty ....

The remarks just made upon laws concerning property are quite as applicable to the second category of laws; those for the maintenance of government, ie, constitutional law.

It again is a complete arsenal of laws, decrees, ordinances, orders in council, and what not, all serving to protect the diverse forms of representative government, delegated or usurped, beneath which humanity

---

4. 'Law and Authority', *Civil Disobedience and Violence*, ed J G Murphy (Belmont, Calif: Wadsworth, 1971) pp 131-132, 134, 140-145. Cf also *Kropotkin's Revolutionary Pamphlets*, ed Roger Baldwin (New York: Benjamin Blom 1968).

is writhing. We know very well . . . that the mission of all governments, monarchical, constitutional, or republican, is to protect and maintain by force the privileges of the classes in possession, the aristocracy, clergy and traders. A good third of our laws - and each country possesses some tens of thousands of them - the fundamental laws on taxes, excise duties, the organization of ministerial departments and their offices, of the army, the police, the church, etc have no other end than to maintain, patch up, and develop the administrative machine. And this machine in its turn serves almost entirely to protect the privileges of the possessing classes. Analyze all these laws, observe them in action day by day, and you will discover that not one is worth preserving . . .

The third category of law still remains to be considered; that relating to the protection of the person and the detection and prevention of 'crime'. This is the most important because most prejudices attach to it; because, if law enjoys a certain amount of consideration, it is in consequence of the belief that this species of law is absolutely indispensable to the maintenance of security in our societies . . . Well, in spite of all the prejudices existing on this subject, it is quite time that anarchists should boldly declare this category of laws as useless and injurious as the preceding ones.

First of all, as to the so-called 'crimes' - assaults upon persons - it is well known that two-thirds, and often as many as three-fourths, of such 'crimes' are instigated by the desire to obtain possession of someone's wealth. This immense class of so-called 'crimes and misdemeanors' will disappear on the day on which private property ceases to exist. 'But,' it will be said, 'there will always be brutes who will attempt the lives of their fellow citizens, who will lay their hands to a knife in every quarrel, and revenge the slightest offense by murder, if there are no laws to restrain and punishments to withhold them.' This refrain is repeated every time the right of society to *punish* is called in question.

Yet there is one fact concerning this head which at the present time is thoroughly established; the severity of punishment does not diminish the amount of crime. Hang, and, if you like, quarter murderers, and the number of murders will not decrease by one. On the other hand, abolish the penalty of death, and there will not be one murder more; there will be fewer . . . Moreover, it is also a well-known fact that the fear of punishment has never stopped a single murderer. He who kills his neighbour from revenge or misery does not reason much about consequences; and there have been few murderers who were not firmly convinced that they should escape prosecution . . . We are continually being told of the benefits conferred by law, and the beneficial effect of penalties, but have the speakers ever attempted to strike a balance between the benefits attributed to laws and penalties, and the degrading effect of these penalties upon humanity? . . . Man is the cruelest animal upon earth. And who has pampered and developed the cruel instincts unknown, even among monkeys, if it is not the king, the judge, and the priests, armed with law . . . Finally, consider the corruption, what depravity of mind is kept up among men by the idea of obedience, the very essence of law; of chastisement; of authority having the right to punish, to judge irrespective of our conscience and the esteem of our friends; of the necessity for executioners, jailers, and informers - in a word, by all the attributes of law and authority. Consider all this, and you will assuredly agree with us in saying that a law inflicting penalties is an abomination which should cease to exist.

Peoples without political organization, and therefore less depraved than ourselves, have perfectly understood that the man who is called 'criminal' is simply unfortunate; that the remedy is not to flog him, to chain him up, or to kill him on the scaffold or in prison, but to help him by the most brotherly care, by treatment based on equality, by the usages of life among honest men. In the next revolution we hope that this cry will go forth:

'Burn the guillotines; demolish the prisons; drive away the judges, policemen and informers - the impurest race upon the face of the earth; treat as a brother the man who has been led by a passion to do ill to his fellow; above all, take from the ignoble products of middle-class idleness the possibility of displaying their vices in attractive colours; and be sure that but few crimes will mar our society.'

The main supports of crime are idleness, law and authority; laws about property, laws about government, laws about penalties and misdemeanors; and authority, which takes upon itself to manufacture these laws and to apply them.

No more laws! No more judges! Liberty, equality, and practical human sympathy are the only effectual barriers we can oppose to the anti-social instincts of certain among us.

Questions: Kropotkin

1. Do you agree with Kropotkin that the law is useless and hurtful?

2. To what extent do you agree with Kropotkin that present-day laws protect the social and political privileges of the possessing classes? Give examples.

3. According to Kropotkin, what social adjustments need to be made to reduce the amount of crime?

4. Do you agree with Kropotkin that education today stifles individuality?

Questions: Civil Disobedience

1. 'One man disobeying through conscience is commendable; a million men disobeying through conscience is rebellion.' How would Rawls, Thoreau and Kropotkin deal with this dilemma?

2. Your country has adopted the following policies, with which you disagree: a) apartheid; b) a tax levied for nuclear weapons. How would our three authors advise you, and whose advice would you take?

3. Perhaps the most famous exponent of civil disobedience in modern times was Martin Luther King. In the following passage he justifies the use of boycotts, sit-ins and marches. Analyse his argument and discuss what kind of action, if any, you would take against an unjust law.

Martin Luther King

An unjust law is a code that the majority inflicts on the minority that is not binding on itself. So that this becomes difference made legal. Another thing that we can say is that an unjust law is a code which the majority inflicts on the minority, which that minority had no part in enacting or creating, because that minority had no right to vote in many instances, so that the legislative bodies that made these laws were not democratically elected... Now the same token of just law would be just the opposite. A just law becomes saneness made legal. It is a code that the majority, who happen to believe in that code, compel the minority, who don't believe in it, to follow, because they are willing to follow it themselves, so it is saneness made legal. Therefore, the individuals who stand up on the basis of civil disobedience realize that they are following something that says that there are just laws and there are unjust laws. Now, they are not anarchists. They believe that there are laws which must be followed; they do not seek to evade the law. For many individuals who would call themselves segregationists and who would hold to segregation at any cost seek to defy the law, they seek to evade the law, and their process can lead on into anarchy. They seek in the final analysis to follow a way of uncivil disobedience, not civil disobedience. And I submit that the individual who disobeys the law, whose conscience tells him it is unjust and who is willing to accept the penalty by staying in jail until that law is altered, is expressing at the moment the very highest respect for law.[5]

5. Martin Luther King, 'Love, Law, and Civil Disobedience', *A Testament of Hope*, ed James Melvin Washington (New York: Harper & Row, 1986) pp 48-49. King's own account of the famous Montgomery bus boycott, and the moral problems it posed, is given in *Slide toward Freedom: The Montgomery Story* (New York: Harper & Row, 1958).

4. In 1948 the black activist A Philip Randolph refused to serve in the American forces. He defended his position before Senator Wayne Morse of Oregon. How far do you agree with Randolph's statement? What social policies, adopted by your Government, would require you to adopt a similar position?

Senator Morse: *But your proposal, and put me straight on this, your proposal is really based on the conviction that because your Government has not given you certain social, economic, and race protection from discrimination because of race, color, or creed, you feel that even in a time of national emergency, when your Government and the country itself may be at stake, you are justified in saying to any segment of our populace - whether it is the colored group or, as you say in your statement, the white group with like sympathies - that under those circumstances you would be justified then in saying, 'Do not shoulder arms in protection of your country in this national emergency'?*

Mr Randolph: *That is a correct statement, Mr Senator. I may add that it is my deep conviction that in taking such a position we are doing our country a great service. Our country has come out before the world as the moral leader of democracy, and it is preparing its defense forces and aggressive forces upon the theory that it must do this to protect democracy in the world.*

Well, now, I consider that if this country does not develop the democratic process at home and make the democratic process work by giving the very people whom they propose to draft in the Army to fight for them democracy, democracy then is not the type of democracy that ought to be fought for, and, as a matter of fact, the policy of segregation in the armed forces and in other avenues of our life is the greatest single propaganda and political weapon in the hands of Russia and international communism today.[6]

6. *Congressional Record*, Vol 94, pp 4312-4313 (80th Congress, 2d session, Senate, April 12, 1948). Reprinted in *Civil Disobedience in America: A Documentary History*, ed David R Weber (Ithaca & London: Cornell University Press, 1978) pp 207-208 .

Bibliography: Civil Disobedience

* denotes text referred to or extracted in main text.

Baldwin, R (ed) *Kropotkin's Revolutionary Pamphlets* (New York: Benjamin Blom, 1968)

Daniels, Norman (ed) *Reading Rawls: Critical Studies of a Theory of Justice* (Oxford: Basil Blackwell, 1975) An important collection of critical essays.

King, Martin Luther *A Testament of Hope** ed James Melvin Washington (New York: Harper & Row, 1986); *Slide toward Freedom: The Montgomery Story* (New York: Harper & Row, 1958) King's account of the Montgomery bus boycott.

Kropotkin, Peter 'Law and Authority',* *Civil Disobedience and Violence*, ed J G Murphy (Belmont, Calif: Wadsworth, 1971) pp. 131-145.

Rawls, John 'Justice as Fairness',* *Philosophy, Politics and Society*, Second Series ed Peter Laslett and W G Runciman (Oxford: Basil Blackwell, 1962) pp. 132-157.

'The Justification of Civil Disobedience', *Civil Disobedience: Theory and Practice*, ed H A Bedau (Indianapolis & New York: Pegasus, 1969) pp. 240-255.

'The Sense of Justice', *Moral Concepts*, ed Joel Feinberg (Oxford: Oxford University Press, 1970) pp. 120-140.

'Legal Obligation and the Duty of Fair Play', *Law and Philosophy*, ed Sidney Hook (New York: New York University Press, 1964) pp. 3-18 This volume contains a number of important discussions of Rawls.

Thoreau, Henry 'Civil Disobedience'* *Civil Disobedience: Theory and Practice*, ed H A Bedau (Indianapolis & New York: Pegasus, 1969) pp. 27-48.

Weber, David R (ed) *Civil Disobedience in America: A Documentary History** (Ithaca & London: Cornell University Press, 1978)

Chapter 2

Egoism

To the question, 'Should I take Crito's advice and escape?' Socrates replied by appealing to certain principles, principles which, he maintained, required that he stay in prison. In this respect Socrates' arguments are examples of ***deontological thinking*** - and extreme examples at that, given their repercussions for Socrates. They are deontological because they make no concessions to the consequences for Socrates in adopting them, and because they concentrate solely on the validity of certain rules and Socrates' obligation to obey them.

It would, however, be quite easy to alter Socrates' reply in such a way that it becomes an example of ***teleological thinking***:

Version A

My dear Crito, I must say your arguments are most compelling. I know I behaved rather foolishly at the trial, more bravado than sense, but even so, all were agreed that the evidence brought against me was clearly false. Besides, as you've made clear, if I do escape I shall be able to enjoy a longer life, see to the education of my children, still meet my friends, and above all continue with my work. Public opinion is behind me, and I suspect that even my enemies secretly hope I'll leave the country: my death would be too much of a political embarrassment for them. So, Crito, you make the arrangements and I'll do what you say.

This version is clearly teleological because Socrates' decision is determined solely by the consequences of his action, and these, he calculates, will be immediate, pleasurable and generally beneficial. However, another and more interesting version could be presented in which Socrates, while still arguing teleologically, chooses death rather than life:

Version B

My dear Crito, I appreciate what you are saying, but you have overlooked one possibility: that I may derive more satisfaction from my death than from my life. People are always apt to ignore this alternative because they tend to assume that anything is better than death. Now listen. You have already agreed that, if I follow your plan, I shall be guilty of breaking certain rules, rules that we both admit are valid and worthy of respect. But how could I live with myself, either in this world or the next, if I broke them? I should never have any peace of mind, and I would lose my reputation as a trustworthy and honourable man, both in my own eyes and in those of other people. Believe me, Crito, death is not easy; but it is easier and brings more satisfaction than disobeying these rules. As it is, I shall die happy in the knowledge that I did my duty and thereby earned the esteem of all those who, like me, believe these rules are just and worth dying for.

Both these versions are teleological, even though the outcome is very different. In neither case does Socrates decide by first establishing the moral principles to be obeyed; a deontological argument. Instead, he makes up his mind on the basis of what will be the *consequences* for him if he obeys or disobeys these principles; a teleological argument. In **Version A** this is obvious: if he obeys he dies, if he disobeys he lives; but it is no less apparent in **Version B**. If we look closer, we can see that, here too, Socrates is not deciding in relation to the rules themselves; nor is he even calculating whether his decision will act for the greatest general good. What matters to him now is whether the action being considered will be the most pleasing to *him* and for *his* own good. Once again, therefore, it is the *effect on him personally* in obeying or disobeying these rules that concerns Socrates, not the rules themselves. Since he believes that, in obeying them, he will retain his self-respect and even gain some posthumous fame, he chooses death.

There is, however, another point of contact between these two versions: it will probably be agreed that neither presents a Socrates quite as noble or heroic as Plato's original. After all, we would not be far wrong in saying that, in one version, we have a man out to save his skin, and, in the other, a man out to save his reputation; and, generally speaking, we do not find such people particularly edifying. But why is this? Primarily it is because we tend to deplore the attitude of mind they are displaying: the attitude which says 'Look after Number One' or 'Do what you want to do'. Many people find this attitude devoid of moral worth, and close to what we commonly call 'selfishness'.

Many thinkers and philosophers have profoundly disagreed with this judgement. What we have here, they contend, is not something immoral but something quite natural and understandable; something, indeed, which contains a fundamental insight into the nature of human motivation; namely, that a human being, however much he or she may wish or seek to do otherwise, cannot do other than serve their own best interests. Upon this insight rests one of the most popular and pervasive normative theories of moral behaviour. It is known as **Egoism**.

1. What is Egoism?

Egoism maintains that *each person ought to act to maximize his or her own long-term good or well-being*. An egoist, in other words, is someone who holds that their one and only obligation is to *themselves* and their only duty is to serve their own *self-interest*. Of course, different people have different ideas about what is or is not in their own interests. For a thief it might be to avoid capture, for a sailor to be able to swim. We have already seen, in **Versions A** and **B**, how different decisions were reached by Socrates: not because the arguments were different, in fact we noted how similar they are, but because in each case Socrates had a different idea about what *was* in his own best interest. The fact, however, that people do have different ambitions is quite beside the point for egoists, and in no way affects the general theory they are propounding. They are not saying that everybody should have identical aims; all they are claiming is that each person should act *if* and *only if* that action serves to promote their own long-term interests. If an action produces benefits for them, they should do it; if it doesn't, then it is morally acceptable for them not to do it.

It follows from this that an egoist is *not* necessarily someone who is always seeking pleasure and excitement without a thought for the future. To suppose otherwise is to overlook the careful inclusion of the words 'long-term' in the previous definitions. Egoists are not necessarily short-sighted: they know very well that self-interest depends not only on immediate aims but also on long-term effects. After all, Smith may like to get drunk everyday, but this would hardly be serving his long-term interests, such as leading an active and healthy life. A egoist, then, is not what he or she appears to be at first: they do not believe that you should always do what you like when you like, for the simple reason that doing what you like may not, in the end, serve your own best interests.

Historically speaking, the clearest evidence that egoists are not straightforward pleasure-seekers is to be found in the career and teaching of the Greek philosopher Epicurus (341-270 BC). Epicurus was perhaps the most influential exponent of egoism in the late classical world, and from his name we derive the word 'epicure', ie a lover of good food and drink. Epicurus was also a **hedonist** (from the Greek *hedone*, meaning pleasure'): that is, he believed that pleasure alone was good and worth pursuing. From this, one might conclude that Epicurus was a man who dedicated himself to a life of pleasure, indulgence and excess. But the contrary was the case. He lived very simply and is said to have suffered from stomach trouble, requiring the blandest of food and drink ('Send me a cheese,' he wrote to a friend, 'that I may fare sumptuously'). In his teaching he was uncompromising. He condemned the pursuit of sensual desires and believed instead that long-term pleasure could best be achieved by philosophical and artistic contemplation,

Epicurus

by a virtual absence of the physical appetites, and by a general freedom from worry or distress. Indeed, his own retiring style of life, simple and frugal as it was, suggests a total repudiation of the pursuit of pleasure at any cost. For Epicurus, the more violent a pleasure, the more likely were the unpleasant after-effects. So, in his *Letter to Menoeceus*, he writes:

Pleasure is our first and kindred good. It is the starting-point of every choice and of every aversion, and to it we come back, inasmuch as we make feeling the rule by which to judge of every good thing. And since pleasure is our first and native good, for that reason we do not choose every pleasure whatsoever, but oft-times pass over many pleasures when a greater annoyance ensues from them. And oft-times we consider pains superior to pleasures when submission to the pains for a long time brings us as a consequence a greater pleasure. While, therefore, all pleasure, because it is naturally akin to us, is good, not all pleasure is choiceworthy, just as all pain is an evil and yet not all pain is against another, and by looking at the conveniences and inconveniences, that all these matters must be judged. Sometimes we treat the good as an evil, and the evil, on the contrary, as a good . . .

When we say, then, that pleasure is the end and aim, we do not mean the pleasures of the prodigal or the pleasures of sensuality, as we are understood to do by some through ignorance, prejudice, or willful misrepresentation. By pleasure we mean the absence of pain in the body and of trouble in the soul. It is not an unbroken succession of drinking-bouts and of revelry, not the sexual love, not the enjoyment of the fish and other delicacies of a luxurious table, which produces a pleasant life; it is sober reasoning, searching out the ground of every choice and avoidance, and banishing those beliefs through which the greatest good is prudence. Wherefore prudence is a more precious thing even than philosophy; from it spring all other virtues, for it teaches that we cannot lead a life of pleasure which is not also a life of prudence, honour, and justice; nor lead a life of prudence, honour, and justice, which is not also a life of pleasure. For the virtues have grown into one with a pleasant life, and a pleasant life is inseparable from them.[1]

In modern philosophical terms, Epicurus is here making a distinction between **intrinsic good** and **instrumental good.** Something is *intrinsically good* if it is worth having for its own sake; something is *instrumentally good* if, while not necessarily being good in itself, it leads to goodness. For Epicurus pleasure is the sole intrinsic good and everything else is a possible

---

1. Diogenes Laertius, *The Lives of the Eminent Philosophers*, trans R D Hicks (Cambridge, Mass: Harvard University Press, 1950), Vol II, pp 123-124.

instrumental good. This is not to say, however, that pleasure itself is always instrumentally good because there may be cases in which an immediate pleasure does not lead to a long-term pleasure. For example, alcohol brings an intrinsic good in that it brings pleasure, but it does not bring instrumental good because of its ultimate consequences. Amputation, on the other hand, brings no intrinsic good in itself but it may lead to it in bringing about the pleasures of recovery and health.

Exercise 1

How would you classify the following? Are they intrinsically good or bad or instrumentally good or bad? Give your reasons.

a	Kindness
b	Vaccination
c	Freedom
d	Beauty
e	Murder
f	Doing one's duty
g	Punishment
h	Revenge
i	Wealth
j	Envy
k	Knowledge
l	Loyalty
m	Obedience
n	Sadism
o	Courage
p	Disease
q	Truth-telling

2. Psychological Egoism

Many people are egoists because they believe that egoism is the only ethical theory which presents an accurate account of what human beings are like. It rests, they claim, on a fundamental insight into the nature of man, or, to be more specific, on a psychological theory of human behaviour which is true. This theory is known as **psychological egoism.** It states that a *human being is psychologically incapable or doing anything that does not promote his or her own self-interest.*

Psychological egoism is not itself an ethical doctrine but a theory of human motivation: it is telling us how men are constructed, not whether their actions are right or wrong. For if psychological egoism is *true*, then any ethical system that suggests that we ought to do something which does not further our own self-interests will be *false*. Such a system is flying in the face of facts: it is asking people to do things they cannot do. The significance of psychological egoism is, therefore, that it requires the rejection of all ethical theories that are not themselves egoistic.

This connection between psychological egoism and ethics in general is best expressed in the saying 'Ought implies can'. If we say that somebody *ought* to perform a certain action, we are clearly implying that this person could do it if they wished: it is an action *possible* for them; they have a choice - to do it or not. But if this person simply cannot perform this action, no matter how hard they may try, then there is clearly no sense in our still saying that they ought to do it. After all, no one can be expected to do what they cannot do. If Smith cannot swim, he cannot save the drowning child. Should someone complain that Smith ought to have saved the child, Smith can reasonably reply that this accusation is absurd: he cannot be blamed for what he cannot do but only for not doing what he could do. Similarly, then, to say with psychological egoism that a man is psychologically able to perform only those actions which further his own self-interest implies that he cannot do otherwise, cannot be expected to do otherwise, and cannot be blamed if he does not do otherwise. So:

> **a.** If what we ought to do is what we are capable of doing.
> **b.** And, if all we are capable of doing is furthering our own self-interest.
> **c.** Then all that we ought to do is further our own self-interest.
> **d.** Thus egoism is true.

We should be clear what is not being said here. Psychological egoism is not claiming that all people *behave* selfishly: the theory would not deny, for example, that some people devote their lives to helping others. What is being said, however, is that the *motive* behind such actions is always and ultimately selfish. In other words, while people often do benevolent acts (ie acts which help others), they cannot act benevolently (ie act for the sake of those being helped). Human beings are so constructed that they cannot help acting in their own interests even when they are helping others. Psychological egoism, therefore, does not exclude unselfish acts, only unselfish *desires*. This point is well illustrated by the following story:

> *Mr Lincoln once remarked to a fellow-passenger on an old-time mud coach that all men were prompted by selfishness in doing good. His fellow-passenger was antagonizing this position when they were passing over a corduroy bridge that spanned a slough. As they crossed this bridge they espied an old razor-backed sow on the bank making a terrible noise because her pigs had got into the slough and were in danger of drowning. As the old coach began to climb the hill, Mr Lincoln called out, 'Driver, can't you stop just a moment?' Then Mr Lincoln jumped out, ran back and lifted the little pigs out of the mud and water, and placed them on the bank. When he returned, his companion remarked: 'Now, Abe, where does selfishness come in on this little episode?' 'Why, bless your soul, Ed, that was the very essence of selfishness. I should have had no peace of mind all day had I gone on and left that suffering old sow worrying over those pigs. I did it to get peace of mind, don't you see?'*[2]

---

2. Quoted by Victor Grassian, *Moral Reasoning* (Englewood Cliffs, NJ: Prentice-Hall, 1981) p 151.

Exercise 2

Consider whether the following situations are or are not examples of psychological egoism. Is it possible to regard them all as examples of it?

> **a.** A man hurries to the scene of an accident, thinking 'One day it might be me!'
> **b.** A doctor hurries to the scene of an accident, thinking 'Here is an opportunity to use my skill.'
> **c.** A clergyman hurries to the scene of an accident, thinking 'God commands me to do this.'
> **d.** A man sees a brick on the road and removes it, thinking 'There might have been an accident.' He does not drive himself and is leaving the country the next day.
> **e.** The driver says to the policeman, who did not see the accident, 'It was my fault, officer!'

At one time psychological egoism was almost universally accepted by philosophers: now it is almost universally condemned. To understand why this is, let us look again at its central claim that 'All men serve their own self-interest.'

The first thing to remember about this is that it is not concerned with ethics but with human motivation: it is not commending certain courses of action so much as telling us what human beings are like and how they will inevitably act. A claim like this is called an **empirical** claim; that is to say, it gives information about the world, based on our experience of it ('empirical' comes from the Greek word for 'experience'). Thus an empirical proposition is considered true if it conforms to experience and observation, and false if it does not. The following are all empirical statements:

> **a.** I have a nose
> **b.** Norway has fjords
> **c.** Some men have beards
> **d.** All cats have whiskers

All these statements are considered true on the basis of available evidence; and the same evidence would make the following empirical statements false:

> **a.** I have a beak
> **b.** Norway has deserts
> **c.** Some men have fins
> **d.** All cats have wings

If, however, we look more closely at our four true statements, we see that they are not all *equally* verifiable according to the evidence. For while we would say of the first three propositions that they are conclusively verifiable - that is, there is sufficient evidence to demonstrate that they are true beyond rational doubt - we cannot say this of 'All cats have whiskers'. If we are to say that it is empirically true, then we must mean that it is true universally, that it is true of every single cat. But what *observations* could possibly verify such a claim? Clearly, none. However many cats we did observe, the possibility would always remain that we had not observed *all* cats. Some cats, indeed, we could not observe. What we have here, then, is an assumption about cats based on what has *so far been observed to be the case*. Thus, we must always allow for the possibility that around the corner lurks a whiskerless cat!

Once we realize that the central claim of psychological egoism is like the statement 'All cats have whiskers', we can see where its fatal weakness lies: The statement 'All men serve their own self-interest' is also an empirical generalization - a generalization about the nature of human conduct - and as such it is based on experience and observation. But how can this be? This claim is true only if there is evidence that there never has been and never could be any unselfish action; and this is evidence psychological egoists cannot provide. How can they be *certain* that the man who sacrifices his life for a friend is acting selfishly, or that the doctor running a leper colony does so through self-interest? Do they know these people that intimately? Is their knowledge of them sufficiently comprehensive? We cannot, of course, exclude the possibility that these people are selfishly motivated. But if the psychological egoist cannot provide evidence that they are, then he must allow for the possibility that they are not - and this possibility alone is sufficient to refute his proposition that *all* human beings serve their own self-interest.

Indeed, we may go further and say that this proposition, although claiming to be empirical, *is not an empirical proposition at all*. Empirical propositions are considered true or false on the basis of available evidence. The claim of psychological egoism, however, does not allow for its possible falsification.

Let us take an example. Suppose X has to choose between two actions, A and B, where A is what we would ordinarily call a 'selfish' act and B an 'unselfish' act. If X chooses A, the psychological egoist will say that simply demonstrates the truth of his theory; but if X chooses B, the psychological egoist will not see this as contrary evidence and change his theory, but merely repeat that this choice must be selfish because X is a human being and all human beings act in this way. On this reasoning, therefore, it is not *evidence* which determines the theory but a *definition* of mankind, and a definition, moreover, that precludes any denial of its truth. To this extent, the claim that 'All human beings serve their own self-interest' is not empirical: it does not conform to the evidence but makes the evidence conform to it.

The criticisms offered here have done no more than point to the difficulties involved in general propositions of the sort 'All crows are black', 'All cats have whiskers' or 'All human beings serve their own self-interest'; or indeed in any unqualified empirical proposition that includes words like 'any' or 'every'. If, as psychological egoists suppose, this quality of selfishness is inescapable, then men and women must be said to possess it *in all circumstances*. Psychological egoists are thus forced into the untenable position of having to affirm, firstly, that they have here completed a description of a particular object (man) which foresees completely all the possible circumstances in which that description is true and in which it is false. Secondly, that their own factual knowledge of man is complete to the point that there is no chance of something unforeseen occurring (eg a person acting non-egoistically) that could upset or modify their description. This, however, is to assign to empirical knowledge an absoluteness it cannot possess.

3. Ethical Egoism

While there are good reasons for supposing that psychological egoism is false, this does not mean that we should reject egoism out of hand. Indeed, there are many egoists who are equally critical of psychological egoism, who deny its claim to present an accurate analysis of man, and who are therefore quite ready to accept that people often do act against their own self-interest. Their point is rather that egoism, when properly understood, is not concerned with what motives men and women actually have but with those that they ought to have. In other words, the true strength of egoism lies in its ethical, not psychological, form and is thus best seen in that version of it known as **Ethical Egoism.** Ethical egoism maintains that *each person ought to act to serve his or her own self-interest*. This proposition, while agreeing that some people may act against their own interests, condemns such action when it occurs.

If ethical egoists do not depend on psychological egoism to justify their position, upon what do they depend? Undoubtedly part of their case is based on the belief that such a doctrine will produce a happier world. If greater happiness and reward come to those pursuing their own interest, then the more people do this the better. Such reasoning does not exclude actions ordinarily called 'moral' - for example, being honest, not stealing, helping your neighbour, - but such actions are acceptable to the egoist only because they produce dividends for the agent, not because they are good or laudable in themselves: if you help others they will help you, if you don't steal neither will they, and so on. Most of us are familiar with this type of argument and it is one often presented by both ancient and modern philosophers. Its classic form is found in the ethical teaching of Epicurus, to which we have already referred, and according to which the sole valid standard of right action is the avoidance of painful or unpleasant experiences. Its most famous proponent in modern philosophy is Thomas Hobbes (1588-1679). In his book *Leviathan* (1651) Hobbes writes that 'Good and evil are names that signify our appetites and aversions' - namely, that what we like or desire is good and what we dislike or wish to avoid is evil. This explains why the citizen places himself under an obligation to obey the law: it is not because the law is something good in itself but because it maintains the security of the individual by protecting him from the injury others might do him. Hence the obligation to obey the law is itself grounded on self-interest.

Exercise 3

You are the Managing Director of a pharmaceutical company. What is your decision in the following cases and on what grounds would you make them? Would you call these decisions egoistic? If not, why not?

> **Case 1.** You discover that your product Y has unpleasant and even harmful side-effects, while your rival's product has none. Do you stop production of Y?
>
> **Case 2.** Your product Y is the only drug of its type available on the market, and many patients have benefited from it: some, however, have contracted cancer. Do you stop production of Y?
>
> **Case 3.** Your product Y is being tested for harmful side-effects. None have so far been found, but it cannot be sold at home until these tests are completed. Meantime, do you market the drug abroad?
>
> **Case 4.** You accept that your product Y is a potential cause of cancer. However, safety regulations in foreign countries are not so stringent. Do you market the drug abroad?
>
> **Case 5.** Your product Y, while safely used at home, is positively dangerous in underdeveloped countries, where often the standard of hygiene is low. Do you market the drug in these countries?

Ethical egoism is not without its difficulties. A major criticism is that it contains an inner contradiction; it being contradictory to claim that *all* men should look after themselves if this results in my *not* looking after myself. For example, suppose both Jones and I have a particular disease and that we shall both die unless treated with a specific vaccine. Suppose further that there is only one phial of vaccine available. If I am an ethical egoist I must not only attempt to get the vaccine exclusively for myself but also recommend, should I be asked, that Jones do the same: I must recommend, in other words, that Jones serve his interests but not mine. But if I do this I contradict the basic principle of ethical egoism since I clearly would not be serving my best interests if I gave Jones this advice. It clearly cannot be to my advantage to convince him to serve his own interests when these interests destroy mine. Indeed, in this patricular case, my best ploy would be to persuade him to forego his egoistic principles and adopt a more altruistic approach. Thus we arrive at the peculiar situation in which my interests as an ethical egoist are best served if I proclaim that ethical egoism is a *false doctrine*!

This line of attack on ethical egoism has been developed by the philosopher Kurt Baier. Ethical egoism, he says, cannot decide in cases where there is a *conflict of interests*. Consider the following case:

> *Let A and B be candidates for the presidency of a certain country and let it be granted that it is in the interest of either to be elected, but that only one can succeed. It would then be in the interest of B but against the interest of A if B were elected, and vice versa, and therefore in the interest of B but against the interest of A if A were liquidated, and vice versa. But from this it would follow that B ought to liquidate A, that it is wrong for B not to do so, that B has not 'done his duty' until he has liquidated A; and vice versa. Similarly A, knowing that his own liquidation is in the interest of B and therefore anticipating B's attempts to secure it, ought to take steps to foil B's endeavours. It would be wrong for him not to do so.*

He would 'not have done his duty' until he had made sure of stopping B. It follows that if A prevents B from liquidating him, his act must be said to be both wrong and not wrong - wrong because it is the prevention of what B ought to do, his duty, and wrong for B not do do it; not wrong because it is what A ought to do, his duty, and wrong for A not to do it. But one and the same act (logically) cannot be both morally wrong and not morally wrong.

This is obviously absurd. For morality is designed to apply in just such cases, namely, those where interests conflict. But if the point of view of morality were that of self-interest, then there could never be moral solutions of conflicts of interest.[3]

The strength of Baier's criticism can be seen if we place ourselves in the position of a judge deciding a conflict of interest, in which A and B want the same thing (be it the presidency, the custody of a child,some land or whatever). If the judge is an ethical egoist, he will never be able to resolve the issue between A and B because both of them are, in his eyes, right to pursue their own interests and, moreover, right to pursue them by any means available; the means being justified by their self-interest. In this way the principle of ethical egoism not only makes it impossible to decide who has the rightful claim, but also legitimates any action - legal or illegal - which will be the method by which the person concerned attains their end.

As a further variation on this argument, it is worth noting that ethical egoists give advice irrespective of the particular worth or merit of the individual they are advising; ie they make no moral judgment as to whether it would be *good* or *bad* if this individual did in fact achieve his aim - provided, of course, that this person's interest does not conflict with theirs. To take Baier's example: suppose you, as an ethical egoist, are advising A and B about obtaining the presidency, and suppose that it makes no personal difference to you who becomes president. Thus you advise A to liquidate B and B to liquidate A. When you are with A, his interests count; when with B, his interests count; but no judgement is here made as to whether it would be *better* if A and not B became president, and vice versa, for each man has an equal right to aim for the presidency, and this right is justified by the self-interest displayed. Thus you are deprived of the ability to decide who *ought* to be president. Hence there is an absence of moral decision. For as long as their interests do not disadvantage yours, you must remain neutral as to the rightness or wrongness of each man's candidacy, be he saint or sinner.

If the doctrine of self-interest cannot either judge or advise in cases of conflicting interest, then it is time to ask whether ethical egoism is an ethical system at all. Egoists, as we have seen, only have one principle - the promotion of their self-interest - so that what they *ought* to do is always what they think is best for them. Their understanding of what is right or wrong changes as their interest changes: at one moment a certain action will be applauded but at the next condemned. Such fluctuations in attitude render ethical egoism, as a theory of normative ethics, highly unsatisfactory. If an egoist thinks breaking the law is to his advantage, he will break it, even if this involves theft and murder; but this does not mean that he approves of crime but only that he approves of it *in this instance*. No consistency of moral judgement can therefore be guaranteed. Finally, the reason why we invariably regard such actions as reprehensible, and thus find it hard to subscribe to any ethical system that permits them, is that they take no account of the happiness of those they affect. In a word, the theory of ethical egoism seems misguided because it ignores one apparently essential ingredient of morality: namely, that the normative principles of moral action are meant for everybody, equally and alike; that individuals have no privileges other than those which belong to the rest of mankind, and cannot accordingly set aside the interests of others in the pursuit of their own.

---

3. *The Moral Point of View* (Ithaca, NY: Cornell University Press, 1958) pp 189-190.

Exercise 4

One of the most famous arguments against morality is given in Plato's *Republic*. In this dialogue, Glaucon and Adeimanthus challenge Socrates to justify why a man should live a moral life. Their challenge is presented in the form of a story, known as the Myth of Gyges.

1. The Myth of Gyges

> Read the story and decide:
>
> **a.** What you would do if you had Gyges' ring;
>
> **b.** Give reasons for not using the ring.

According to the tradition, Gyges was a shepherd in the service of the King of Lydia; there was a great storm, and an earthquake made an opening in the earth at the place where he was feeding his flock. Amazed at the sight, he descended into the opening, where, among other marvels, he beheld a hollow brazen horse, having doors, at which he, stooping and looking in, saw a dead body of stature, as appeared to him, more than human, and having nothing on but a gold ring; this he took from the finger of the dead and reascended. Now the shepherds met together, according to custom, that they might send their monthly report about the flocks to the king; into their assembly he came having the ring upon his finger, and as he was sitting among them he chanced to turn the collet of the ring inside his hand, when instantly he became invisible to the rest of the company and they began to speak of him as if he were no longer present. He was astonished at this, and again touching the ring he turned the collet outwards and reappeared; he made several trials of the ring, and always with the same result - when he turned the collet inwards he became invisible, when outwards he reappeared. Whereupon he contrived to be chosen one of the messengers who were sent to the court; where as soon as he arrived he seduced the queen, and with her help conspired against the king and slew him and took the kingdom. Suppose now that there were two such magic rings, and the just put on one of them and the unjust the other; no man can be imagined to be of such an iron nature that he would stand fast in justice. No man would keep his hands off what was not his own when he could safely take what he liked out of the market, or go into houses and lie with any one at his pleasure, or kill or release from prison whom he would, and in all respects be like a God among men. Then the actions of the just would be as the actions of the unjust; they would both come at last to the same point. And this we may truly affirm to be a great proof that a man is just, not willingly or because he thinks that justice is any good to him individually, but of necessity, for wherever any one thinks that he can safely be unjust, there he is unjust. For all men believe in their hearts that injustice is far more profitable to the individual than justice, and he who argues as I have been supposing will say that they are right. If you could imagine any one obtaining this power of becoming invisible, and never doing any wrong or touching what was another's, he would be thought by the lookers-on to be a most wretched idiot, although they would praise him to one another's faces, and keep up appearances with one another from a fear that they too might suffer injustice.[4]

4. Plato, The Republic, in *Five Great Dialogues*, trans Benjamin Jowett (New York: Walter J Black, 1942) pp 256-257.

2. Howard Roark's Speech [5]

Another argument for egoism is presented by the contemporary philosopher Ayn Rand (1905-1982). In her novel *The Fountainhead*, the architect Howard Roark agrees to design a government housing project, Cortlandt Homes, for another architect, Peter Keating: his only requirement is that the project must be built exactly as he designed it. This agreement is broken and Roark dynamites the project. At his trial Roark defends his action

To what extent do you consider Roark's arguments legitimate?

The first right on earth is the right of the ego. Man's first duty is to himself. His moral law is never to place his prime goal within the persons of others. His moral obligation is to do what he wishes, provided his wish does not depend primarily upon other men. This includes the whole sphere of his creative faculty, his thinking, his work. But it does not include the sphere of the gangster, the altruist and the dictator.

A man thinks and works alone. A man cannot rob, exploit or rule - alone. Robbery, exploitation and ruling presuppose victims. They imply dependence. They are the province of the second-hander.

Rulers of men are not egoists. They create nothing. They exist entirely through the persons of others. Their goal is their subjects, in the activity of enslaving. They are as dependent as the beggar, the social worker and the bandit. The form of dependence does not matter.

But men were taught to regard second-handers - tyrants, emperors, dictators - as exponents of egoism. By this fraud they were made to destroy the ego, themselves and others. The purpose of the fraud was to destroy the creators. Or to harness them. Which is a synonym.

From the beginning of history, the two antagonists have stood face to face: the creator and the second-hander. When the first creator invented the wheel, the first second-hander responded. He invented altruism.

The creator - denied, opposed, persecuted, exploited - went on, moved forward and carried all humanity along on his energy. The second-hander contributed nothing to the process except the impediments. The context has another name: the individual against the collective . . .

Now, in our age, collectivism, the rule of the second-hander and second-rater, the ancient monster, has broken loose and is running amuck. It has brought men to a level of intellectual indecency never equalled on earth. It has reached a scale of horror without precedent. It has poisoned every mind. It has swallowed most of Europe. It is engulfing our country . . .

Now you know why I dynamited Cortlandt.

I designed Cortlandt. I gave it to you. I destroyed it.

I destroyed it because I did not choose to let it exist. It was a double monster. In form and in implication. I had to blast both. The form was mutilated by two second-handers who assumed the right to improve upon that which they had not made and could not equal. They were permitted to do it by the general implication that the altruistic purpose of the building superseded all rights and that I had no claim to stand against it.

I agreed to design Cortlandt for the purpose of seeing it erected as I designed it and for no other reason. That was the price I set for my work. I was not paid . . .

I came here to say that I do not recognize anyone's right to one minute of my life. Nor to any part of my energy. Nor to any achievement of mine. No matter who makes the claim, how large their number or how great their need.

I wished to come here and say that I am a man who does not exist for others.

It had to be said. The world is perishing from an orgy of self-sacrificing.

5. Ayn Rand, *The Fountainhead* (New York & Indianapolis: The Bobbs-Merril Co, 1943) This passage reprinted in Rand, *For the New Intellectual* (New York: Random House, 1961) pp 82-85.

I wished to come here and say that the integrity of a man's creative work is of greater importance than any charitable endeavor. Those of you who do not understand this are the men who're destroying the world.

Questions: Egoism

1. What do you consider the three most important long-term pleasures?

2. What are the moral objections, if any, to the 'playboy'?

3. For Epicurus, the avoidance of pain is more important than the acquisition of pleasure. In that case, why not advocate (like the hedonist Hegesias) suicide on the grounds that it guarantees a state with no pain at all? Discuss.

4. Construct a moral situation to which you believe psychological egoism does not apply. Give your reasons.

5. Why is it claimed that the statement 'All men serve their own self-interest' is not an empirical statement.

6. Discuss and illustrate the conflict of interest within ethical egoism. Do you consider this conflict a decisive objection to the theory?

7. In what circumstances would you act immorally if you knew you couldn't be caught or punished?

8. 'To pursue one's own self-interest is good business practice: It creates jobs and raises the standard of living.' Discuss.

9. The company, of which you are Chairman, has discovered valuable mineral deposits. Would you purchase the land at the current market value, saying nothing to the present owner of its real worth?

10. Consider the following case. What other method of selection (if any) would you adopt? Would it make any difference if one crew-member had navigational experience?

The private yacht Mignonette sailed from Southampton on May 19 1884, bound for Sydney, Australia, where it was to be delivered to its owner. There were four persons aboard, all members of the crew: Dudley, the captain; Stephens, mate; Brooke, seaman; and Parker, a 17 year-old cabin boy and apprentice seaman. The yacht went down in the South Atlantic and all put off in a 13 foot lifeboat. After twenty days in the boat, during which they had no fresh water except rain water and during the last eight of which they had no food, Dudley, with Stephen's assent, killed the boy. Brooks objected. Thereafter all three fed on the body of the boy for four days. On the fifth day they were rescued. According to the jury's verdict, there was no likelihood that any of them would have survived unless one were killed and eaten, and it so appeared to the men.[6]

6.From *Ethics in Medicine*, ed S J Reiser, A J Dyck and W J Curran (Cambridge, Mass; The MIT Press, 1977) p.663.

Bibliography: Egoism

* denotes text referred to or extracted in the main text

Baier, Kurt *The Moral Point of View** (Ithaca, NY: Cornell University Press, 1958) Chapter 8 contains an influential criticism of the theory.
Beauchamp, T L & Bowie, N E (eds) *Ethical Theory and Business* (Englewood Cliffs, NJ: Prentice-Hall, 1983) Important collection of essays on business ethics.
Gauthier, D P *The Logic of Leviathan* (Oxford: Clarendon Press, 1969) Chapter 2 discusses Hobbes' moral theory.
Grassian, Victor *Moral Reasoning** (Englewood Cliffs, NJ: Prentice-Hall, 1981) Chapter 7.
Laertius, Diogenes *The Lives of the Eminent Philosophers** trans R D Hicks (Cambridge, Mass: Harvard University Press, 1950)
Norman, Richard *The Moral Philosophers* (Oxford: Clarendon Press, 1983) Especially Chapter 4.
Plato, The Republic* in *Five Great Dialogues*, trans Benjamin Jowett (New York: Walter J Black, 1942)
Rand, Ayn *Atlas Shrugged* (New York: Random House, 1957);
 For the New Intellectual (New York: Random House, 1961);
 *The Fountainhead** (New York & Indianapolis: The Bobbs-Merril Co, 1943);
 The Virtue of Selfishness (New York: New American Library, 1964) Rand's most extended discussion of her theory.
Raiser, S J, Dyck, A J & Curran, W J (eds) *Ethics in Medicine** (Cambridge, Mass: The MIT Press, 1977)

Discussion: The Right to Life

It might be supposed that egoists, having once declared that everyone should further their long-term interests, go on to say that everyone has a **right to life**. For if one's principal duty is to serve oneself, then self-preservation must be a priority since without life there would be no self-interest to serve. This supposition, however, is false. Because egoism is a teleological theory of normative ethics, the egoist's attitude to his own right to life, and to that of other people, will depend on whether he believes this right brings him benefit. If it does not, this right should be withdrawn. Egoists may therefore require another's death to further their interests, or indeed their own death, if they believe that life is intolerable and brings them no advantage . . . So if I know that I am going to Auschwitz, I have the right to commit suicide. I even have the right to assist the suicide of someone else going there. Similarly, if I know that the death of an evil dictator will end the torture of innocent people, I have the right to assassinate him; and so on. In all these cases the morality of withdrawing any person's right to life, including my own, is being judged in terms of future benefit; and it is worth adding that governments tend to argue along similar lines. For the state does not regard the citizen's right to life as an absolute moral right but as a legal right, as something that can be withdrawn by legislation. Here one thinks of those cases in which individuals may be deprived of their lives for committing murder or in which their lives may be at risk in battle. Whether the state is justified in doing these things is another matter and will be discussed in later chapters.

For the deontologist, on the other hand, the right to life is an inalienable right: it is something that cannot legitimately be taken away by another individual or group. Saying therefore that people have this right means that one is never morally justified in killing them and that the absolute wrongfulness of so doing is established independently of what may result. Thus a man may neither commit suicide, nor help another to kill himself, nor sacrifice himself for others, nor expect others to do the same for him, no matter how much he may desire it. This absolute right to life helps explain why so many of us think that killing people is wrong and always wrong; and why even those who do not think like this require very special reasons for approving it; for example war and self-defence. Both may well share the view that killing in itself is wrong, an evil, and contrary to the most basic instincts of man.

Not surprisingly, the question of whether man has or has not a right to life raises many serious moral problems. Three in particular deserve special attention. These are the problems of **abortion, euthanasia** and **animal rights**, and in the following extracts they are examined by three contemporary philosophers: Judith Thomson, James Rachels and Peter Singer. As a prelude to their discussions, let us look more closely at some of the issues involved.

The Right to Life and Abortion

Many opponents of abortion argue as follows: All human beings have a right to life; the foetus is a human being; therefore the foetus has a right to life. Abortion, as a denial of this right, is accordingly morally wrong. Those who support abortion maintain, however, that the foetus is not a human being but a clump of cells, and that, even if it were a human being, its right to life may be outweighed by certain other rights possessed by the mother. These rights, as described by Judith Thomson in her celebrated essay, are the woman's right to self-defence and her right to control her own body. We shall return to these presently.

When exactly does human life begin? There have been many divergent opinions. In the past there was strong support for the ancient Stoic view that life begins at birth, an opinion largely supported by contemporary Judaism, but this view has become increasingly unpopular the more our knowledge of foetal development has increased and the more the distinction between the born and the unborn has been blurred by advances in foetal photography. Others have found greater significance in 'quickening', the moment when the mother feels her baby move; but this event, although doubtless of great emotional significance for the mother, is not regarded as significant for the growth of the foetus. A more common argument is to say that human life begins at conception. It is held that, since development from foetus to baby is continous, it is purely arbitrary to choose any point other than conception as the moment when one becomes a person. But this conclusion does not follow. One could say the same thing about the development from acorn to oak, but this does not mean that acorns are oaks: a distinction can be made between them. Similarly, a fertilized egg is so unlike a person that, to suppose otherwise, is to stretch the meaning of 'person' beyond all normal usage. Hence the most accepted view, particularly among physicians, is to focus upon some interim point at which the foetus becomes 'viable', that is, potentially able to live outside the mother's womb, albeit with artificial aid. But this argument has its own weaknesses, the most glaring being that the date of viability changes: in English law it has recently been reduced from twenty-eight weeks to twenty-four, though some argued for eighteen weeks. Many find it offensive that whether one counts as a person depends on the shifting state of medical research.

Judith Thomson accepts that the foetus is a person at conception. Anti-abortionists, as we have seen, claim that it follows from this that the foetus, like all human beings, has the right to life, and that no other right can outweigh this right. Thomson challenges this view by saying that there are in fact two rights which may override the right to life. The first is the woman's right of self-defence, in which the mother may end the life of the foetus if it threatens her own; and the second is the right of ownership to her own body, according to which she has the right to use her body in the way she wants and which may or may not include carrying a foetus to term. Unlike the right of self-defence, the right of ownership extends to cases where the mother's life is not in danger. For example, if the woman has taken no contraceptive precautions, she has assumed responsibility for the unborn foetus and ought not to withdraw support; but if she has taken all possible precautions, she cannot be held responsible and may thus legitimately deny the foetus the use of her body. To continue the pregnancy in these circumstances is an act of charity on her part, but not a duty, and one which she cannot reasonably be expected to perform if the disadvantages to herself are considerable.

The Right to Life and Euthanasia

The right to life generates certain duties in others. Two in particular should be mentioned: the duty of non-interference and the duty of service. The duty of non-interference requires that no one should interfer in another's life in a way that may threaten it. So, if somebody is trying to shoot me, I have the right to stop him. My right to life also allows me to claim certain duties from others, the duties of service, and these may be claimed of those who are in the business of seeing that my life is sustained (doctors, firemen, lifesavers). Both duties presuppose that being alive is in itself valuable and worth preserving, and that to save someone's life, or at least not to shorten it, is to benefit them.

Normally this is true; but not always. Death from a bullet is probably preferable to death by starvation, and it is unlikely that a prisoner being tortured to death would accept a life-prolonging drug. Saving or prolonging someone's life is not therefore always to their advantage: in certain circumstances it might have been better if they had died earlier rather than later. Or, to put the matter another way, to say that someone has a right to life, while true, does not necessarily mean that exercising that right will bring them benefit or that those who safeguard it are their benefactors. What matters is the quality of their life and their attitude towards it, and both may challenge the duties of non-interference and service. For cases may arise in which not only should the duty of non-interference be witheld in the interests of certain individuals - their lives are deliberately terminated - but witheld by the very people who have a duty of service towards them.

Such cases introduce the problem of **euthanasia.** The original meaning of the word, derived from the Greek *eu* (good) and *thanasia* (death), is 'a quiet and easy death' as opposed to a violent or painful one. More recently it has come to mean 'the action of inducing a gentle and easy death' and so refers *mainly* to those actions, usually performed by a doctor, in which a person's life is deliberatly terminated or shortened. These actions are also known as 'mercy killings' since the death involved must in some way end suffering and therefore be in the person's own interest. This altruistic concern distinguishes these cases from, say, the euthanasia programme introduced by Hitler in 1939 which gassed 275,000 people, mostly the physically or mentally sick and elderly. They were not killed to relieve their suffering but because they were no longer able to work.

These sinister possibilities continue to haunt discussions of euthanasia. Many believe that, once this form of killing is legalized, it will lead to others, to infanticide or euthanasia for the socially maladjusted or politically deviant. Others point to the risk of abuse by members of the family and by all those who stand to gain by the death of someone old or sick. For members of the medical profession the problems are more immediate and acute. Some doctors will have nothing to do with euthanasia, saying that their job is to save life and not to kill and pointing to the constant possibility of a wrong diagnosis or a new treatment. Others, meanwhile, have argued that, since medical science can prolong life almost indefinitely, what must now be protected is not so much a person's right to life but his right to die, and that to subject a patient to an unnaturally slow and often painful deterioration, simply because it is technically possible, is not only uncivilized and lacking in compassion for patient and family alike, but also an infringement of individual liberty.

This debate is further complicated by the fact that euthanasia applies to two different groups of person: those who can exercise their right to die and those who, because of their mental or physical condition, cannot. In the first group are all those who are terminally ill but mentally alert: since they know they are dying, often in acute pain, should they be allowed to die sooner rather than later? This group also includes those who are not terminally ill but have become, perhaps through some serious accident, totally paralysed or dependent on machines: they are not about to die and may suffer no pain, but they too are aware of their own deterioration. Should they be allowed to bring their suffering to an end? In the second group we find all those in irreversible coma, kept alive by a life-support machine, but for whom the technical definition of death as brain death does not apply. Here too are elderly people suffering from extreme senile dementia and new-born infants with incurable genetic defects. Since these people cannot exercise their right to die, should somebody else do so on their behalf? And if so, who?

Given the complexity of the issues involved here, and given that no two cases are the same, a simple theory of euthanasia, covering all eventualities, is impossible. Philosophers have, however, introduced a number of useful distinctions between types of euthanasia, which have been generally recognized if not universally accepted. The first is between **voluntary** and **involuntary** euthanasia. Voluntary euthanasia occurs when a mentally competent person requests their own death - many moralists argue that this is permissible since it is the equivalent of assisted suicide - whereas involuntary euthanasia applies to those who are unable to make this decision for themselves. The second distinction is made between **direct** and **indirect** euthanasia, both referring to the method of inducing death. Direct euthanasia involves the use of something specific to cause it, and indirect euthanasia refers to those cases where death occurs as a side-effect of treatment (eg injecting a lethal dose of morphine to reduce pain). The third distinction, which is the subject of James Rachel's essay, is between **active** and **passive** euthanasia. Active is the same as direct euthanasia: it is the intentional act of mercy-killing; but passive euthanasia is not killing but letting die: it allows a person to die by withholding or stopping the treatment that sustains their life. Many doctors believe this is the most important distinction of all, and there is no doubt that passive euthanasia is often practised. Even the Roman Catholic Church accepts that letting patients die should sometimes be permitted. No one has the right to kill, says the Church, but equally no one is under an obligation to prolong life indefinitely. Rachels believes, however, that this much-exploited distinction is bogus and thus without moral significance. Active and passive euthanasia are one and the same thing. Therefore, if passive euthanasia is to be allowed, active euthanasia should be allowed as well.

The Right to Life and Animal Rights

The right to life is invariably held to be a right of human beings and not of everything living. If this were not assumed, weeding the garden or killing cattle would be morally equivalent to, say, infanticide. In other words, we take for granted that human life is above all other forms of life and that the life of a man, being of greater value than that of any other animal, deserves special protection. We have seen already how deep-seated this view is in our discussions of abortion and euthanasia. While we do not object to killing animals in testing foodstuffs or cosmetics, the termination of a pregnancy is surrounded by a host of moral and legal difficulties; and while it took Karen Quinlan's father many court appearances to get his daughter taken off a respirator (perhaps the most famous case of passive euthanasia) we know that there would be no such judicial qualms about slaughtering a number of monkeys to investigate drug addiction. Non-human life is thus considered inferior to human life and this allows us to use animals as we think fit, even to the point of killing them. In recent years, however, this position has been vigorously denied by a number of philosophers, who, because they do not see any morally relevant difference between human and animal life, see no reason why the life of a man should be accorded special protection. This in turn has led some activists to conduct a campaign of violence against butcher's shops, furriers, factory farms, and scientific establishments. For these people, the same arguments that forbid research on humans or eating infants forbid this being done to non-humans. Bombing the home of a vivisectionist is none the less illegal but it is not, therefore, ethically wrong: all that one is doing is intimidating a murderer.

For the philosopher Peter Singer the crucial question in this debate is: 'Is it ever right to treat one kind of thing in the way that we would not treat another kind?' His answer is that, if one entity shares an equal capacity with another to be harmed or benefited - particularly in the capacity to experience pleasure or pain - then, whatever other differences may exist between them, this equality requires us to treat them equally. This explains why we do not teach dogs to read just because we teach children to or extend to giraffes the right to vote or to stones the more general right of freedom from having pain inflicted on them: they do not share with humans an equal capacity to benefit or derive pleasure or pain from these things.

On the other hand, if we denied other human beings these rights, simply because they were black and not white, we would be accused of racial discrimination, of denying them things from which they *could* benefit purely on the grounds of racial origin. But what, asks Singer, if the comparison is between a monkey and a severely retarded infant? Drawing the line here is not so easy since the capacities of the monkey - his ability to act, to solve problems, to communicate, not to mention his capacity to feel pleasure and pain - will almost certainly equal and probably surpass those of the child. Does this mean we would select the child rather than the monkey for our experiments? We would not.

Despite its evident superiority in capacity, the monkey would still be chosen because *it is not biologically a member of our own species*. To do this, however, is morally unacceptable since it flouts the rights of the monkey to equal treatment. The monkey, indeed, is the victim of another form of discrimination - not racism but **speciesism** - which is widely practised by all those who, while protecting the right to life of senile humans or human foetuses or brain-damaged humans, see no reason to stop the wholesale and wanton slaughter of non-human animals.

1. Judith Jarvis Thomson: A Defense of Abortion[1]

I propose . . . that we grant that the foetus is a person from the moment of conception. How does the argument go from here? Something like this, I take it. Every person has a right to life. So the foetus has a right to life. No doubt the mother has a right to decide what shall happen in and to her body, everyone would grant that. But surely a person's right to life is stronger and more stringent than the mother's right to decide what happens in and to her body, and so outweighs it. So the foetus may not be killed; an abortion may not be performed.

It sounds plausible. But now let me ask you to imagine this. You wake up in the morning and find yourself back to back in bed with an unconscious violinist. A famous unconscious violinist. He has been found to have a fatal kidney ailment, and the Society of Music Lovers has canvassed all the available medical records and found that you alone have the right blood type to help. They have therefore kidnapped you, and last night the violinist's circulatory system was plugged into yours, so that your kidneys can be used to extract poisons from his blood as well as your own. The director of the hospital now tells you, 'Look, we're sorry the Society of Music Lovers did this to you - we would never have permitted it if we had known. But still, they did it, and the violinist now is plugged into you. To unplug you would be to kill him. But never mind, it's only for nine months. By then he will have recovered from his ailment, and can safely be unplugged from you.'

Is it morally incumbent on you to accede to this situation? No doubt it would be very nice of you if you did, a great kindness. But do you have to? What if it were not nine months, but nine years? Or longer still? What if the director of the hospital says, 'Tough luck, I agree, but you've now got to stay in bed, with the violinist plugged into you, for the rest of your life. Because remember this. All persons have a right to life, and violinists are persons. Granted you have a right to decide what happens in and to your body, but a person's right to life outweighs your right to decide what happens in and to your body. So you cannot ever be unplugged from him.' I imagine you would regard this as outrageous, which suggests that something really is wrong with that plausible-sounding argument I mentioned a moment ago . . .

Suppose you find yourself trapped in a tiny house with a growing child. I mean a very tiny house, and a rapidly growing child - you are already up against the wall of the house and in a few minutes you'll be crushed to death. The child on the other hand won't be crushed to death; if nothing is done to stop him from growing he'll be hurt, but in the end he'll simply burst open the house and walk out a free man. Now I could well understand it if a bystander were to say, 'There's nothing we can do for you. We cannot choose between your life and his, we cannot be the ones to decide who is to live, we cannot intervene.' But it cannot be concluded that you too can do nothing, that you cannot attack it to save your life. However innocent the child may be, you do not have to wait passively while it crushes you to death. Perhaps a pregnant woman is vaguely felt to have the status of a house, to which we don't allow the right of self-defense. But if the woman houses the child, it should be remembered that she is a person who houses it.

I should perhaps stop to say explicitly that I am not claiming that people have a right to do anything whatever to save their lives. I think, rather, that there are drastic limits to the right of self-defense. If someone threatens you with death unless you torture someone else to death, I think you have not the right, even to save your life, to do so. But the case under consideration here is very different. In our case there are only two people involved, one whose life is threatened, and one who threatens it. Both are innocent: the one who is threatened is not threatened because of any fault, the one who threatens does not threaten because of any fault. For this reason we may feel that we bystanders cannot intervene. But the person threatened can . . .

Where the mother's life is not at stake, the argument I mentioned at the outset seems to have a much stronger pull. 'Everyone has a right to life, so the unborn person has a right to life.' And isn't the child's right to life weightier than anything other than the mother's own right to life, which she might put forward as ground for an abortion.

This argument treats the right to life as if it were unproblematic. It is not, and this seems to be precisely the source of the mistake.

---

1. Judith Jarvis Thomson, 'A Defense of Abortion', *Philosophy and Public Affairs*, I, No 1 (Fall 1971). Reprinted in *Moral Problems*, ed James Rachels (New York & London: Harper & Row, 1979) pp. 130-150.

For we should now ask what it comes to, to have a right to life. In some views, having a right to life includes having a right to be given at least the bare minimum one needs for continued life. But suppose that what in fact is the bare minimum a man needs for continued life is something he has no right at all to be given? . . . To return to the story I told earlier, the fact that for continued life that violinist needs the continued use of your kidneys does not establish that he has a right to be given the continued use of your kidneys. He certainly has no right against you that you should give him continued use of your kidneys. For nobody has any right to use your kidneys unless you give him such a right; and nobody has the right against you that you shall give him this right. If you do allow him to go on using your kidneys, this a kindness on your part, and not something he can claim from you as his due. Nor has he any right against the Society of Music Lovers that they should plug him into you in the first place. And if you now start to unplug yourself, having learned that you will otherwise have to spend nine years in bed with him, there is nobody in the world who must try to prevent you, in order to see to it that he is given something he has a right to be given . . .

There is another way to bring out the difficulty. In the most ordinary sort of case, to deprive someone of what he has a right to is to treat him unjustly. Suppose a boy and his small brother are jointly given a box of chocolates for Christmas. If the older boy takes the box and refuses to give his brother any of the chocolates, he is unjust to him, for the brother has been given a right to half of them. But suppose that, having learned that otherwise it means nine years in bed with that violinist, you unplug yourself from him. You surely are not being unjust to him, for you gave him no right to use your kidneys, and no one else can have given him any such right. But we have to notice that in unplugging yourself, you are killing him; and violinists, like everybody else, have a right to life, and thus, in the view we were considering just now, the right not to be killed. So here you do what he supposedly has a right you shall not do, but you do not act unjustly to him in doing it.

The emendation which may be made at this point is this: the right to life consists not in the right not to be killed, but rather in the right not to be killed unjustly . . . But if this emendation is accepted, the gap in the argument against abortion stares us plainly in the face: it is by no means enough to show that the foetus is a person, and to remind us that all persons have a right to life - we need to be shown also that killing the foetus violates its right to life, ie, that abortion is unjust killing. And is it?

I suppose we may take it as a datum that in a case of pregnancy due to rape the mother has not given the unborn person a right to the use of her body for food and shelter. Indeed, in what pregnancy could it be supposed that the mother has given the unborn person such a right? It is not as if there were unborn persons drifting about the world, to whom a woman who wants a child says 'I invite you in.'

But it might be argued that there are other ways one can have acquired a right to the use of another person's body than by having been invited to use it by that person. Suppose a woman voluntarily indulges in intercourse, knowing of the chance it will issue in pregnancy, and then she does become pregnant; is she not in part responsible for the presence, in fact the very existence, of the unborn person inside? No doubt she did not invite it in. But doesn't her partial responsibility for its being there itself give it a right to the use of her body? If so, then her aborting it would be more like the boy's taking away the chocolates, and less like your unplugging yourself from the violinist - doing so would be depriving it of what it does have a right to, and thus would be doing it an injustice.

And then, too, it might be asked whether or not she can kill it even to save her own life: If she voluntarily called it into existence, how can she now kill it, even in self-defense?

The first thing to be said about this is that it is something new. Opponents of abortion have been so concerned to make out the independence of the foetus, to establish that it has a right to life, just as its mother does, that they have tended to overlook the possible support they might gain from making out that the foetus is dependent on the mother; in order to establish that she has a special kind of responsibility for it, a responsibility that gives it rights against her which are not possessed by any independent person.

On the other hand, this argument would give the unborn person a right to its mother's body only if her pregnancy resulted from a voluntary act, undertaken in full knowledge of the chance a pregnancy might result. It would leave out entirely the unborn person whose existence is due to rape. Pending the availability of some further argument, then, we would be left with the conclusion that unborn persons whose existence is due to rape have no right to the use of their mothers' bodies; so aborting them is not depriving them of anything they have a right to and hence is not unjust killing.

We should also notice that it is not at all plain that this argument really does go even as far as it seems to. For there are cases and cases, and the details make a difference. If the room is stuffy, and I therefore open a window to air it, and a burglar climbs in, it would be absurd to say, 'Ah, now he can stay, she's given him a right to the use of her house - for she is partially responsible for his presence there, having voluntarily done what enabled him to get in, in full knowledge that there are such things as burglars, and that burglars burgle.' It would be even more absurd to say this if I had had bars installed outside my windows, precisely to prevent burglars from getting in, and a burglar got in only because of a defect in the bars. It remains equally absurd if we imagine it is not a burglar who climbs in, but an innocent person who blunders or falls in. Again, suppose it were like this: people-seeds drift about in the air like pollen, and if you open your windows, one may drift in and take root in your carpets and upholstery. You don't want children, so you fix up your windows with fine mesh screens, the very best you can buy. As can happen, however, and on very, very rare occasions does happen, one of the screens is defective; and a seed drifts in and takes root . . . Someone may argue that you are responsible for its rooting, that it does have a right to your house, because after all you could have lived out your life with bare floors and furniture, or with sealed windows and doors. But this won't do - for by the same token, anyone can avoid a pregnancy due to rape by having a hysterectomy.

There is room for yet another argument: We must surely all grant that there may be cases in which it would be morally indecent to detach a person from your body at the cost of his life. Suppose you learn that what the violinist needs is not nine years of your life, but only one hour . . . Admittedly you were kidnapped. Admittedly you did not give anyone permission to plug him into you. Nevertheless, it seems to me plain that you ought to allow him to use your kidnesy for that one hour - it would be indecent to refuse . . .

Now some people are inclined to use the term 'right' in such a way that it follows from the fact that you ought to allow a person to use your body for the hour he needs, that he has a right to use your body for the hour he needs, even though he has not been given that right by any person or act . . . Suppose that box of chocolates I mentioned earlier had not been given to both boys jointly, but was given only to the older boy. There he sits, stolidly eating his way through the box, his small brother watching enviously. Here we are likely to say 'You ought not to be so mean. You ought to give your brother some of those chocolates.' My own view is that it just does not follow from the truth of this that the little brother has any right to any of the chocolates. If the boy refuses to give his brother any, he is greedy, stingy, callous - but not unjust. I suppose that the poeple I have in mind will say it does follow that the brother has a right to some of the chocolates, and thus that the boy does act unjustly if he refuses to give his brother any. But the effect of saying this is to obscure what we should keep distinct, namely the difference between the boy's refusal in this case and the boy's refusal in the earlier case, in which the box was given to both boys jointly, and in which the small brother thus had what was from any point of view clear title to half . . .

So my own view is that even though you ought to let the violinist use your kidneys for the one hour he needs, we should not conclude that he has a right to do so. We should say that if you refuse, you are, like the boy who owns all the chocolates and will give none away, self-centered and callous, indecent in fact, but not unjust. Similarly, that even supposing a case in which a woman pregnant due to rape ought to allow the unborn person to use her body for the hour he needs, we should not conclude that he has a right to do so; we should conclude that she is self-centered, callous, indecent, but not unjust, if she refuses. The complaints are no less grave; they are just different. However, there is no need to insist on this point. If anyone does wish to deduce 'he has a right' from 'you ought', then he must surely grant that there are cases in which it is not morally required of you that you allow that violinist to use your kidneys, and in which he does not have a right to use them, and in which you do not do him an injustice if you refuse.

And so also for mother and unborn child. Except in such cases as the unborn person has a right to demand it - and we were leaving open the possibility that there may be such cases - nobody is morally required to make large sacrifices, of health, of all other interests and concerns, of all other duties and commitments, for nine years, or even nine months, in order to keep another person alive . . .

Questions: Thomson

1. Consider this argument against Thomson: While the right of self-defence may justify killing someone who knowingly threatens my life, it does not justify killing the innocent (ie someone who neither knows that they threaten my life nor intends to do so). How would Thomson respond to this criticism?

2. Consider this argument against Thomson: While it may be true that a woman is not obliged to save X's life by giving him the use of her body (or anything else for that matter), this does not mean that she has the right to kill X for using it. In the same way I am not obliged to save X's life by letting him use my home; but that does not mean that I have the right to kill him if I find him there. How would Thomson respond to this criticism?

3. A woman in labour will die unless an operation is performed in which the head of the unborn child is crushed or dissected. If it is not performed, the child can be successfully delivered by post-mortem Caesarean section. Construct arguments for and against these alternatives.

4. How do you account for the psychological fact that many persons who agree with abortion would shudder at the thought of murdering an innocent member of their own family.

5. Consider the following case. Assume you are the physician. What justification would you have for performing or not performing the abortion? What difference would it make if the foetus was defective?

> *A 35-year-old married woman, sixteen weeks pregnant, undergoes amnio-centesis to determine the presence of foetal defects. The procedure, which takes about three weeks to complete, involves removing foetal cells from the fluid surrounding the foetus in the uterus, growing, and then analyzing the cells. The procedure carries little risk for either mother or child. Her physician reports that the foetus shows no signs of abnormality and that the woman can expect to give birth to a girl. Several days later the woman requests an abortion. The reason she gives the doctor is that she does not want to have another daughter. She has two children, 3 and 5 years old - both girls. Her husband is opposed to abortion and would prefer to have the additional child. The marriage appears to be stable and happy, and the couple are well-to-do. The physician did not know that the information regarding the sex of the foetus would lead to a request for an abortion.*[2]

2. *Ethics in Medicine* (eds) Reiser,S J, Dyck, A J & Curran, W J (Cambridge, Mass: The MIT Press, 1977) p 485.

2. *James Rachels: Active and Passive Euthanasia*[3]

The distinction between active and passive euthanasia is thought to be crucial for medical ethics. The idea is that it is permissible, at least in some cases, to withhold treatment and allow a patient to die, but it is never permissible to take any direct action designed to kill the patient. This doctrine seems to be accepted by most doctors . . . However, a strong case can be made against it. In what follows I will set out some of the relevant arguments, and urge doctors to consider this matter.

To begin with, a familiar type of situation, a patient who is dying of incurable cancer of the throat is in terrible pain, which can no longer be satisfactorily stopped. He is certain to die within a few days, even if present treatment is continued, but he does not want to go on living for those days since the pain is unbearable. So he asks the doctor for an end to it, and his family joins in the request.

Suppose the doctor agrees to withhold treatment, as the conventional doctrine says he may. The justification for his doing so is that the patient is in terrible agony, and since he is going to die anyway, it would be wrong to prolong his suffering needlessly. But now notice this. If one simply withholds treatment, it may take the patient longer to die, and so he may suffer more than he would if more direct action were taken and a lethal injection given. This fact provides strong reason for thinking that, once the initial decision not to prolong his agony has been made, active euthanasia is actually preferable to passive euthanasia. To say otherwise is to endorse the option that leads to more suffering rather than less, and is contrary to the humanitarian impulse that prompts the decision not to prolong his life in the first place . . .

One reason why so many people think that there is an important moral difference between active and passive euthanasia is that they think killing someone is morally worse than letting someone die. But is it? Is killing, in itself, worse than letting die? To investigate this issue, two cases may be considered that are exactly alike except that one involves killing whereas the other involves letting someone die. Then, it can be asked whether this difference makes any difference to the moral assessments. It is important that the cases be exactly alike, except for this one difference, since otherwise one cannot be confident that it is this difference and not some other that accounts for any variation in the assessments of the two cases. So, let us consider this pair of cases:

In the first, Smith stands to gain a large inheritance if anything should happen to his six-year old cousin. One evening while the child is taking his bath, Smith sneaks into the bathroom and drowns the child, and then arranges things so that it will look like an accident.

In the second, Jones also stands to gain if anything should happen to his six-year old cousin. Like Smith, Jones sneaks in planning to drown the child in his bath. However, just as he enters the bathroom Jones sees the child slip and hit his head, and fall face down in the water. Jones is delighted; he stands by, ready to push the child's head back under if it is necessary, but it is not necessary. With only a little thrashing about, the child drowns all by himself, as Jones watches and does nothing.

Now Smith killed the child, whereas Jones 'merely' let the child die. That is the only difference between them. Did either man behave better, from a moral point of view? If the difference between killing and letting die were in itself a morally important matter, one should say that Jones' behaviour was less reprehensible than Smith's. But does one really want to say that? I think not. In the first place, both men acted from the same motive, personal gain, and both had exactly the same end in view when they acted. It may be inferred from Smith's conduct that he is a bad man, although that judgement may be withdrawn or modified if certain further facts are learned about him - for example, that he is mentally deranged. But would not the very same thing be inferred about Jones from his conduct? And would not the same further considerations also be relevant to any modification of this judgement? Moreover, suppose Jones pleaded, in his own defense, 'After all, I didn't do anything except just stand there and watch the child drown. I didn't kill him; I only let him die.' Again, if letting die were in itself less bad than killing, this defense should have at least some weight. But it does not. Such a 'defense' can only be regarded as a grotesque perversion of moral reasoning. Morally speaking, it is no defense at all.

3. James Rachels, 'Active and Passive Euthanasia', *New England Journal of Medicine*, 292 (1975). Reprinted in *Moral Problems*, ed James Rachels (New York & London: Harper & Row, 1979) pp 490-497.

Now, it may be pointed out, quite properly, that the cases of euthanasia with which doctors are concerned are not like this at all. They do not involve personal gain or the destruction of normal healthy children. Doctors are concerned only with cases in which the patient's life is of no further use to him, or in which the patient's life has become or will soon become a terrible burden. However, the point is the same in these cases: the difference between killing and letting die does not, in itself, make a moral difference. If a doctor lets a patient die, for humane reasons, he is in the same moral position as if he had given the patient a lethal injection for humane reasons. If his decision was wrong - if, for example, the patients's illness was in fact curable - the decision would be equally regrettable no matter which method was used to carry it out. And if the doctor's decision was the right one, the method used is not in itself important . . .

Many people will find this judgement hard to accept. One reason, I think, is that it is very easy to fuse the question of whether killing is, in itself, worse than letting die, with the very different question of whether most actual cases of killing are more reprehensible than most actual cases of letting die. Most actual cases of killing are clearly terrible (think, for example, of all the murders reported in the newspapers), and one hears of such cases every day. On the other hand, one hardly ever hears of a case of letting die, except for the actions of doctors who are motivated by humanitarian reasons. So one learns to think of killing in a much worse light than of letting die. But this does not mean that there is something about killing that makes it in itself worse than letting die, for it is not the bare difference between killing and letting die that makes the difference in these cases. Rather, the other factors - the murderer's motive of personal gain, for example, contrasted with the doctor's humanitarian motivation - account for different reactions to the different cases.

I have argued that killing is not in itself any worse than letting die; if my contention is right, it follows that active euthanasia is not any worse than passive euthanasia. What arguments can be given on the other side? The most common, I believe, is the following:

> The important difference between active and passive euthanasia is that, in passive euthanasia, the doctor does not do anything to bring about the patient's death. The doctor does nothing , and the patient dies of whatever ills already afflict him. In active euthanasia, however, the doctor does something to bring about the patient's death: he kills him. The doctor who gives the patient with cancer a lethal injection has himself caused his patient's death; whereas if he merely ceases treatment, the cancer is the cause of death.

A number of points need to be made here. The first is that it is not exactly correct to say that in passive euthanasia the doctor does nothing, for he does do one thing that is very important: he lets the patient die. 'Letting someone die' is certainly different, in some respects, from other types of action - mainly in that it is a kind of action that one may perform by way of not performing certain other actions. For example, one may let a patient die by way of not giving medication, just as one may insult someone by way of not shaking his hand. But for any purpose of moral assessment, it is a type of action none the less. The decision to let a patient die is subject to moral appraisal in the same way that a decision to kill him would be subject to moral appraisal: it may be assessed as wise or unwise, compassionate or sadistic, right or wrong. If a doctor deliberately lets a patient die who was suffering from a routinely curable illness, the doctor would certainly be to blame for what he had done, just as he would be to blame if he had needlessly killed the patient. Charges against him would then be appropriate. If so, it would be no defense at all for him to insist that he didn't 'do anything'. He would have done something very serious indeed, for he let his patient die.

Fixing the cause of death may be very important from a legal point of view, for it may determine whether criminal charges are brought against the doctor. But I do not think that this notion can be used to show a moral difference between active and passive euthanasia. The reason why it is considered bad to be the cause of someone's death is that death is regarded as a great evil - and so it is. However, if it has been decided that euthanasia - even passive euthanasia - is desirable in a given case, it has also been decided that in this instance death is no greater an evil than the patient's continued existence. And if this is true, the usual reason for not wanting to be the cause of someone's death simply does not apply.

Finally, doctors may think that all of this is only of academic interest - the sort of thing that philosophers may worry about but that has no practical bearing on their own work. After all, doctors, must be concerned about the legal consequences of what they do, and active euthanasia is clearly forbidden by the law. But even so, doctors should also be concerned with the fact that the law is forcing upon them a moral doctrine that may be indefensible, and has a considerable effect on their practices .

Questions: Rachels

1. What is the difference between active and passive euthanasia. Do you think this difference is morally justified? What are its practical implications for the medical profession?

2. 'No human being should be allowed to exist in a state which we would mercifully end in any other creature.' Discuss.

3. What dangers can you foresee in the legalization of euthanasia?

4. Analyse the teleological character of Rachel's argument. How would a deontologist reply?

5. Does a person have the right to commit suicide? If they have this right, should the state provide them with the means to achieve it?

3. Peter Singer: All Animals are Equal [4]

If a being suffers, there can be no moral justification for refusing to take that suffering into consideration. No matter what the nature of the being, the principle of equality requires that its suffering be counted equally with the like suffering - in so far as rough comparisons can be made - of any other being. If a being is not capable of suffering, or of experiencing enjoyment or happiness, there is nothing to be taken into account. This is why the limit of sentience (using the term as a convenient, if not strictly accurate shorthand for the capacity to suffer or experience enjoyment or happiness) is the only defensible boundary of concern for the interests of others. To mark this boundary by some characteristic like intelligence or rationality would be to mark it in an arbitrary way. Why not choose some other characteristic, like skin colour?

The racist violates the principle of equality by giving greater weight to the interests of members of his own race, when there is a clash between their interests and the interests of those of another race. Similarly the speciesist allows the interests of his own species to override the greater interests of members of other species. The pattern is the same in each case. Most human beings are speciesists. I shall now very briefly describe some of the practices that show this.

For the great majority of human beings, especially in urban, industrialized societies, the most direct form of contact with members of other species is at mealtimes: we eat them. In doing so we treat them purely as means to our ends. We regard their life and well-being as subordinate to our taste for a particular kind of dish. I say 'taste' deliberately - this is purely a matter of pleasing our palate. There can be no defense of eating flesh in terms of satisfying nutritional needs, since it has been established beyond doubt that we could satisfy our need for protein and other essential nutrients far more efficiently with a diet that replaced animal flesh by soy beans, or products derived from soy beans, and other high protein vegetable products.

It is not merely the act of killing that indicates what we are ready to do to other species in order to gratify our tastes. The suffering we inflict on the animals while they are alive is perhaps an even clearer indication of our speciesism than the fact that we are prepared to kill them. In order to have meat on the table at a price that people can afford, our society tolerates methods of meat production that confine sentient animals in cramped, unsuitable conditions for the entire duration of their lives. Animals are treated like machines that convert fodder into flesh, and any innovation that results in a higher 'conversion ratio' is liable to be adopted . . .

Since, as I have said, none of these practices cater to anything more than our pleasure of taste, our practice of rearing and killing other animals to eat them is a clear instance of the sacrifice of the most important interests of other beings in order to satisfy trivial interests of our own. To avoid speciesism we must stop this practice, and each of us has a moral obligation to cease supporting this practice. Our custom is all the support that the meat industry needs. The decision to cease giving it that support may be difficult, but it is no more difficult than it would have been for a white Southerner to go against the traditions of his society and free his slaves; if we do not change our dietary habits, how can we censure those slaveholders who would not change their own way of living?

The same form of discrimination may be observed in the widespread practice of experimenting on other species in order to see if certain substances are safe for human beings, or to test some psychological theory about the effect of severe punishment on learning, or to try out various new compounds just in case something turns up . . .

In the past, argument about vivisection has often missed the point, because it has been put in absolutist terms: would the abolitionist be prepared to let thousands die if they could be saved by experimenting on a single animal? The way to reply to this purely hypothetical question is to pose another: would the experimenter be prepared to perform his experiment on an orphaned human infant, if that were the only way to save many lives? (I say 'orphan' to avoid the complication of parental feelings, although in doing so I am being overfair to the experimenter, since the non-human subjects of experiments are not orphans). If the experimenter is not prepared to use an orphaned human infant, then his readiness to use non-humans is

4. Peter Singer, 'All Animals are Equal', *Philosophic Exchange*, 2, No 2 (1974). Abridged reprint in *Applied Ethics*, ed Singer (Oxford: Oxford University Press, 1986) pp 222-225.

simple discrimination, since adult apes, cats, mice and other mammals are more aware of what is happening to them, more self-directing and, so far as we can tell, at least as sensitive to pain, as any human infant. There seems to be no relevant characteristic that human infants possess that adult mammals do not have to the same or a higher degree.(Someone might try to argue that what makes it wrong to experiment on a human infant is that the infant will, in time and if left alone, develop into more than the non-human, but one would then, to be consistent, have to oppose abortion, since the foetus has the same potential as the infant - indeed, even contraception and abstinence might be wrong on this ground, since the egg and sperm, considered jointly, also have the same potential. In any case, this argument still gives us no reason for selecting a non-human, rather than a human with severe and irreversible brain damage, as the subject for our experiments.)

The experimenter, then, shows a bias in favour of his own species whenever he carries out an experiment on a non-human for a purpose that he would not think justified him in using a human being at an equal or lower level of sentience, awareness, or ability to be self-directing. No one familiar with the kind of results yielded by most experiments on animals can have the slightest doubts that if this bias were eliminated, the number of experiments performed would be a minute fraction of the number performed today . . .

Questions: Singer

1. What is it that makes men superior to animals and animals superior to men? Do these differences justify speciesism?

2. What is your moral attitude towards the transplantation of animal organs into the human body?

3. 'But so far as animals are concerned, we have no direct duties. Animals . . . are there merely as a means to an end. That end is man . . . Our duties towards animals are merely indirect duties towards humanity' (Kant). Comment on this argument.

4. Are animal rights activists justified in conducting a campaign of violence against those who practise speciesism?

5. To what extent do advances in medical science justify animal experimentation?

Bibliography: The Right to Life

* denotes text referred to or extracted in main text

a) The Right to Life and Abortion

Batchelor, Edward (ed) *Abortion: The Moral Issues* (New York: The Pilgrim Press, 1982) A general anthology.
Feinberg, Joel (ed) *The Problem of Abortion* (Belmont, Calif: Wadsworth, 1973) Contains Thomson's essay and Michael Tooley's important article, 'A Defense of Abortion and Infanticide'.
Glover, Jonathan *Causing Death and Saving Lives* (Harmondsworth: 1977)
Harris, John *The Value of Life* (Routledge & Kegan Paul, 1985) Extensive discussion, with chapters on abortion and euthanasia.
Hursthouse, Rosalind *Beginning Lives* (Oxford: Basil Blackwell, in association with the Open University, 1987)
Perkins, Robert (ed) *Abortion. Pro and Con* (Cambridge, Mass: 1974) Anthology.
Reiser, S J (ed with A J Dyck and W J Curran) *Ethics in Medicine** (Cambridge, Mass: The MIT Press, 1977)
Sumner, L W *Abortion and Moral Theory* (Princeton, NJ: Princeton University Press, 1981) Argues that both the liberal and conservative views are indefensible.
Thomson, Judith Jarvis *Rights, Restitution and Risk** ed William Parent (Cambridge, Mass: Harvard University Press, 1986) A collection of Thomson's essays, the first being her famous article on abortion.
Tooley, Michael *Abortion and Infanticide* (Oxford: Clarendon Press, 1983) One of the most influential liberal discussions.

b) The Right to Life and Euthanasia

Behnke, John A and Bok, Sissela *The Dilemmas of Euthanasia* (Garden City, NY: Anchor Books, 1975) An excellent anthology.
Downing, A E (ed) *Euthanasia and the Right to Death* (London: 1969) Essays arguing for voluntary euthanasia.
Gorovitz, S, Janeton, A L et al (eds) Moral Problems in Medicine (Englewood CLiffs, NJ: Prentice-Hall, 1976) Excellent anthology.
Gould, Jonathan (ed with Lord Craigmyle) *Your Death Warrant?* (London: Chapman, 1971) Essays against euthanasia.
Horan, Dennis J (ed with David Mall). *Death, Dying and Euthanasia* (Frederick, Maryland: University Publications of America, 1980) Thorough anthology.
Kohl, Marvin (ed) *Beneficent Euthanasia* (Buffalo, NY: Prometheus Books, 1975) Wide-ranging anthology.
Kubler-Ross, Elizabeth *On Death and Dying* (New York: Macmillan, 1974) A famous psychiatrist on the attitudes of the terminally ill.
Ladd, John (ed) *Ethical Issues Relating to Life and Death* (Oxford: Oxford University Press, 1979) A collection of philosophical discussions.
Ramsey, Paul *Ethics at the Edges of Life*, Pt 2 (New Haven, Conn: Yale University Press, 1978) A stimulating, if difficult, analysis by a leading contemporary moralist.
Rachels, James 'Active and Passive Euthanasia',* *New England Journal of Medicine*, 292 (1975). Reprinted in *Moral Problems*, ed James Rachels (New York & London: Harper & Row, 1979) pp 490-497.
Supreme Court of New Jersey, *In the Matter of Karen Quinlan. An Alleged Incompetent*, decided March 31, 1976, Supreme Court of New Jersey 355A 2nd 647. Reprinted in *Killing and Letting Die*, ed Bonnie Steinbeck (Englewood NJ: Prentice-Hall, 1980) pp 23-44. The most famous recent case of involuntary euthanasia.
Williams, Robert H *To Live and To Die: When, Why, and How?* (New York: Springer-Verlag, 1973) A wide-ranging anthology.

c) The Right to Life and Animal Rights

Frey, R G *Rights, Killing and Suffering: Moral Vegetarianism and Applied Ethics* (Oxford: Basil Blackwell, 1983)
Godlovitch, R & S (ed with J Harris) *Animals, Men and Morals* (London: Victor Golancz, 1971)
Linzey, Andrew *Animal Rights* (London: SCM Press, 1976) An argument from the Christian perspective.
Miller, H B (ed with W H Williams) *Ethics and Animals* (Clifton, NJ: Humana Press, 1983)
Noske, Barbara *Humans and Other Animals* (London: Pluto Press, 1989) Examination by an anthropologist of those animal activities previously thought to be exclusively human.
Rollin, Bernard E *Animal Rights and Human Morality* (Buffalo, NY: Prometheus Books, 1981)
Singer, Peter 'All Animals are Equal',* *Philosophic Exchange*, 2, No 2 (1974) Abridged reprint in *Applied Ethics*, ed Peter Singer (Oxford: Oxford University Press, 1986) pp 215-228;
Animal Liberation (London: Jonathan Cape, 1975) The most influential contemporary discussion of the issue.
Practical Ethics (Cambridge: Cambridge University Press, 1979) Excellent introduction, concentrating on contemporary issues, particularly animal rights, euthanasia and abortion.
Singer, Peter (ed with T Regan) *Animal Rights and Human Obligations* (Englewood Cliffs, NJ: Prentice-Hall, 1976)
Singer, Peter (ed) *In Defence of Animals* (Oxford: Basil Blackwell, 1985)

Chapter 3

Utilitarianism: The Theory of Jeremy Bentham

Egoism, in as much as it calculates what we ought to do in terms of an action's consequences, is a straightforward teleological theory of moral behaviour. Its weakness, as we have seen, lies primarily in the fact that it appears to take no account of the effects of such an action on other people. This weakness, however, is easily overcome in another ethical and teleological theory which maintains that it is the *total* consequences of an action which determines its rightness or wrongness; that, in other words, it is not just my happiness or self-interest which counts but the happiness or self-interest of everyone concerned. This is the theory known as **utilitarianism.** Utilitarianism states that *an action is right if it produces the greatest good for the greatest number*.

Jeremy Bentham

The two greatest advocates of utilitarianism are Jeremy Bentham (1748-1832) and his disciple John Stuart Mill (1806-1873). While it is true that Mill gives the most famous 'proof' of utilitarianism, it is to Bentham that we must first turn as the theory's chief exponent and popularizer.

Jeremy Bentham was a man of extraordinary intellectual gifts: at three years old he began to study Latin, at five French, and, in 1763, he took his degree at Oxford at the age of sixteen. Given these abilities, and the fact that both his father and grandfather were attornies, a great legal career was predicted. However, five years later, while reading Priestley's *Essay on Government*, he came upon the expression, 'the greatest good of the greatest number', and says that he cried out, like Archimedes, 'Eureka'. Bentham decided to apply this principle, which he called the *principle of utility*, to all areas of social activity and thereby to do for human society what Newton had done for natural science.

His chief interest was 'legislation', for it is the legislator, he maintained, who alone has the power of determining the conditions under which men live. In his great work, the *Principles of Morals and Legislation* (1789) he impressed on his contemporaries the belief that existing institutions were not to be taken for granted but critically judged by their *effects* or *consequences*, and so reformed as to produce the 'greatest good of the greatest number.' This procedure extended across the whole range of social life and initiated a series of reforms for which Bentham was either directly or indirectly responsible: the reform of the representative system of Parliament and the drafting of its Acts; the reform of the criminal law, the jury system, and prisons; the abolition of transportation and imprisonment for debt; the development of saving banks, cheap postage, and the registration of births and deaths.

As if this were not enough, he was probably the first man to suggest the Suez and Panama canals and the formation of a League of Nations. Following his belief that the dead should be of some use to the living, he left his body to be dissected in the presence of friends. His skeleton was then reconstructed, clothed in Bentham's usual attire, and set upright in a glass-fronted case: it is now kept in University College, London.

1. The Principle of Utility

From this brief sketch of Bentham's life we can see the clear teleological character of the utilitarian argument. Just as we judge a law or an institution in terms of its effect on the majority of citizens, so the morality of our own actions is to be judged in terms of their effect on all concerned, ie, whether they do or do not lead to the greatest happiness for the greatest number. According to Bentham, therefore, the correct ethical standard is the **principle of utility**, the word 'utility' referring to the tendency of something to produce happiness, not to its usefulness:

> *By the principle of utility is meant that principle which approves or disapproves of every action whatsoever, according to the tendency which it appears to have to augment or diminish the happiness of the party whose interest is in question: or, what is the same thing in other words, to promote or to oppose that happiness. I say of every action whatsoever; and therefore not only of every action of a private individual, but of every measure of government.*[1]

The principle of utility states, therefore, that an action ought to be done if and only if it brings about the maximum possible happiness for those parties affected by that action. But what counts as an 'affected party'? Even though it is quite possible to treat a state of community as an affected party - after all, we can speak of crimes against the state or of serving the community - it is quite clear that Bentham is here talking of individuals. For him 'state', 'community', 'nation' are nothing more than collective terms denoting groups of individuals. One cannot, therefore, speak of the 'state' over against those persons who compose it. Accordingly, the principle of utility refers only to individual actions by individuals, its simple message being that the more happiness produced by these actions the better the world will be. These actions must of course be voluntary because the very idea of moral responsibility depends on the person concerned having a real choice of whether to perform the action or not.

But how does one choose? If an immediate action (A) produces less happiness than an action in the future (B), I should perform B rather than A. However, in deciding between A and B, I must also take account of the possible *unhappiness* resulting from them. If A produces less happiness but also less unhappiness than B, then B's greater unhappiness detracts from its greater happiness. Thus I must choose A if thereby a greater *sum total* of happiness is produced. If, on the other hand, *both* A and B produce the same amounts of happiness, but B more unhappiness, I must still choose A. By this action I produce the greatest balance of happiness over unhappiness.

This explains why, when there is a choice between **1.)** greater happiness for myself, and **2.)** less happiness for myself and greater happiness for others, I must choose the latter. My greater happiness cannot take precedence over the greatest *net* happiness, ie, the happiness of all those involved. It is of course quite possible that one action will produce both my greatest happiness *and* the greatest total happiness; but when there is a conflict of interest - when my happiness conflicts with the greater *collective* happiness - then utilitarianism advises self-sacrifice, even to the point of death. Needless to say, in such extreme circumstances, it is all the more important to be convinced that one's calculations are correct.

In making these calculations, however, another feature of Bentham's theory should be noted. Bentham was a **hedonist** and thus believed, like Epicurus before him, that pleasure was the sole good and pain the sole evil. This is clearly stated in the opening sentences of the *Principles of Morals and Legislation*:

---

1. *An Introduction to the Principles of Morals and Legislation*, ed J H Burns and H L A Hart (London & New York: Methuen, 1982) p 12.

Nature has placed mankind under the governance of two sovereign masters, pain and pleasure. It is for them alone to point out what we ought to do, as well as to determine what we shall do. On the one hand the standard of right and wrong, on the other the chain of causes and effects, are fastened to their throne. They govern us in all we do, in all we say, in all we think: every effort we can make to throw off our subjection, will serve but to demonstrate and confirm it. In words a man may pretend to abjure their empire: but in reality he will remain subject to it all the while. The principle of utility recognises this subjection, and assumes it for the foundation of that system, the object of which is to rear the fabric of felicity by the hands of reason and of law. Systems which attempt to question it, deal in sounds instead of sense, in caprice instead of reason, in darkness instead of light.[2]

More exactly, then, it is the twin experiences of pleasure and pain which govern the operation of the principle of utility: it is the *fact* of these experiences that determines what we ought and ought not to do. If we generally accept, for example, that such things as honesty, affection and mercy are characteristics of the moral life, this is not because, to use an earlier terminology, they have any **intrinsic** value (ie, that they are pleasurable in themselves), but because they have an **instrumental** value (ie, that these are qualities that lead to pleasure.)

If, on the other hand, these things did not have this effect - if they brought us misery instead - then we would not credit them with any moral value. For Bentham, an act is right only when it is instrumentally good; and its goodness consists in the pleasure produced. Thus the moral worth of one action over against another is directly proportional to the *amount* or *quality* of pleasure (or pain) that each action brings. This being the case, a more accurate account of the principle of utility would read: *For all those affected by an action, that action is right if it brings pleasure (or prevents pain), and wrong if it brings pain (or prevents pleasure.)*

---

2. *Ibid*, p 11.

how to calculate

2. The Hedonic Calculus

As soon as we state the principle of utility in this new form, another problem immediately arises. If, in our calculation of what we ought to do, we must take into account the possible pleasure or pain involved for everyone (including the agent), then how do we *assess* or *estimate* the quantity of pleasure and pain involved? How, for instance, do we gauge whether this pleasure is greater than another, or whether this particular pain outweighs that particular pleasure? It is in order to help us in these calculations that Bentham introduces his **hedonic calculus.**

Bentham's hedonic calculus turns on the idea that human pleasures and pains are *measurable*, and that accordingly actions can be judged right or wrong on the basis of a kind of 'moral arithmetic', the sums involved corresponding to the amount of pleasure or pain these actions contain. Bentham is quite ready to admit that the experience of pleasure is unusually complex, that few pleasures are completely 'pure', and that most have a fair measure of pain mixed up with them. Nor does he *minimise* the difficulty in trying to calculate the amount of pleasure found, say, in wealth as against power, or in the use of one's skill as against one's imagination; but all these factors are, he says, accounted for in the calculus and quantifiable in terms of the seven *circumstances* or *dimensions* in which pleasure occurs:

*To a person considered by **himself**, the value of a pleasure or pain considered by itself, will be greater or less, according to the four following circumstances:*

1. *Its **intensity***
2. *Its **duration***
3. *Its **certainty** or **uncertainty***
4. *Its **propinquity** or **remoteness***

*These are the circumstances which are to be considered in estimating a pleasure or a pain. But when the value of any pleasure or pain is considered for the purpose of estimating the tendency of any **act** by which it is produced, there are two other circumstances to be taken into the account:*

5. *Its **fecundity**, or the chance it has of being followed by sensations of the **same** kind: that is, pleasures, if it be a pleasure: pains, if it be a pain.*
6. *Its purity, or the chance it has of **not** being followed by sensations of the **opposite** kind: that is, pains, if it be a pleasure; pleasures, if it be a pain.*

These last two, however, are in strictness scarcely to be deemed properties of the pleasure or the pain itself; they are not, therefore, in strictness to be taken into the account of the value of that pleasure or that pain. They are in strictness to be deemed properties only of the act, or other event, by which such pleasure or pain has been produced; and accordingly are only to be taken into the account of the tendency of such act or such event.

*To a **number** of persons, with reference to each of whom the value of a pleasure or a pain is considered, it will be greater or less, according to seven circumstances: to wit, the six preceding ones . . . and one other; to wit:*

7. *Its **extent**; that is, the number of persons to whom it extends; or (in other words) who are affected by it.[3]*

---

3. *Ibid*, p 38-39. In order to popularize his hedonic calculus and to give it more general appeal, Bentham composed the following memoriter verses:
Intense, long, certain, speedy, fruitful, pure -
Such marks in *pleasures* and in *pains* endure.
Such pleasures seek if *private* be thy end:
If it be *public*, wide let them *extend*.
Such *pains* avoid, whichever be thy view:
If pains *must* come, let them *extend* to few.

To see how this calculus works, let us suppose that you are a poor man badly in need of a drink. An acquaintance of yours, whom you know to be rich, passes you in the street and accidentally drops his wallet. You pick it up and inside find £50. Should you return it to him? You decide by consulting the hedonic calculus. Various factors can be dismissed immediately: *extent*, because clearly only the two of you are involved; and *certainty* and *propinquity*, because, in this case, there is little doubt that both of you will experience some pleasure and some pain, and that these experiences will be near in time to the actual moment when you picked up the wallet. On the other hand, if you do decide to keep the money, one factor will almost certainly count against you - *purity* - because it is highly probable that your pleasure will also contain some pain (ie, a feeling of guilt at taking the money, a possible hangover from taking the drink.)

Nevertheless, even these possibilities will not detract from the *overall* balance of pleasure in your favour. It is, for example, a fair bet that your pleasure at finding the money will be more *intense* than the rich man's irritation at its loss; that your pleasure will *last longer* than his pain; and that your pleasure will produce other pleasures in a way that his initial pain will not produce other pains - indeed, being rich, he will probably quickly forget all about it.

On these calculations, it is clear that you should keep the money. You could, of course, return the money; but even then it is unlikely that the rich man's pleasure at its recovery will equal your pain at its loss.

Exercise 1

In which of the following cases would you adopt utilitarian principles? Explain your answers.

> **a.** During the Second World War, all German officers had to swear an oath of personal loyalty to Adolf Hitler. One of these, Lieutenant Colonel Claus von Stauffenberg, made an unsuccessful attempt to assassinate Hitler in July 1944. Was he right to do so? Was Hitler right to have him shot?
>
> **b.** A priest hears the confession of an undetected murderer, who may well kill again. Should the priest tell the police?
>
> **c.** Should a doctor be permitted to administer a drug that will painlessly kill a person with an incurable disease? Would it make any difference to your opinion if that patient were your rich father?
>
> **d.** Would you condemn an innocent man to death if you knew that his execution would restore law and order?
>
> **e.** Would you, like President Truman, have authorized the use of atomic bombs against Japan to end the Second World War?
>
> **f.** If you liked veal, would you eat it?
>
> **g.** If the statistics prove that wearing seatbelts reduces the number of serious car accidents, is the government right to compel you to wear one?
>
> **h.** Mother Theresa, Louis Pasteur and Joe Bloggs an ex-convict are in a boat. The boat is sinking. Who should drown to save the other two?

Questions: Bentham

1. One objection to Bentham's theory is that it can be used to justify immoral actions. Do you agree? How do you think Bentham would reply to this criticism?

2. Should Bentham's principle of utility extend to animals? What would the consequences be if it did?

3. In the following passage, the contemporary philosopher Ayn Rand objects to Bentham's formula, 'the greatest good of the greatest number'. What are the grounds of her objection? Do you agree with her?

> *'the good of others' is a magic formula that transforms anything into gold... your code hands out, as its version of the absolute, the following rule of moral conduct: if you wish it, it's evil; if others wish it, it's good; if the motive of your action is your welfare, don't do it; if the motive is the welfare of others, anything goes... For those of you who might ask questions, your code provides a consolation prize and a booby trap: it is your own happiness, it says, that you serve the happiness of others, the only way to achieve your joy is to give it up to others... and if you find no joy in this procedure, it is your own fault and the proof of your evil... a morality that teaches you to scorn a whore who gives her body indiscriminately to all men - this same morality demands that you surrender your soul to promiscuous love for all comers.*[4]

---

4. *Atlas Shrugged*, (New York: Random House, 1957), p.1030-1033.

Utilitarianism: The Theory of John Stuart Mill

For Bentham there can be no moral rules other than those ordained by the principle of utility. As we saw in the previous case of finding £50, this often means that the consequences of a so-called 'immoral' act - stealing, lying, breaking promises, killing, - are preferable to those of the alternative so-called 'moral' act. This does not mean that Bentham rejects all the rules of conventional morality, since he is quite ready to accept that, in most cases, they serve to increase human happiness; but these rules, he maintains, must never be followed blindly. When taking ethical decisions, we should be guided by the principle of utility and not by the rules of social custom or convention.

John Stuart Mill

All this seems quite straightforward. Most of us would agree that, while stealing is in general wrong, it would be right to steal a weapon from a homicidal maniac. Similarly, we say that lying is wrong but would approve, say, of someone giving false information to an enemy agent. Common sense, and an overall desire to increase the sum total of human happiness, dictate that we would be justified in doing these things.

Bentham's theory, gets into difficulties when it condones actions which, even though increasing the total amount of pleasure, are still held to be *morally inexcusable*. Suppose that a group of sadistic guards are torturing a prisoner. If the guards' pleasure outweighs the prisoner's pain, then, according to the hedonic calculus, their action is justified. Indeed, we soon see that the calculus may be used to support any number of morally repugnant acts. It will, for example, justify any majority of persons suppressing the human rights of any minority. If the majority receives happiness because a small minority are slaves, it will support slavery. This does not of course imply that Bentham would have approved of slavery, sadism or genocide; but they do lead us to reject a principle which may be used to justify such repugnant acts.

This does not mean, however, that we have found a sufficient reason for rejecting utilitarianism altogether; if only because Bentham presents only one particular version of the theory. Another is proposed by his disciple and friend, John Stuart Mill. Mill's version is an explicit attempt to meet the kind of objection just raised.

At first sight Mill's theory does not appear to be very different from Bentham's. Like his predecessor, Mill is a hedonist, believing that pleasure is the sole intrinsic good, and that it is the promotion of pleasure and the prevention of pain that determines our moral decisions. Thereafter, however, the difference between the two theories is considerable, and appears primarily when Mill rejects Bentham's purely **quantitative** assessment of pleasure and replaces it with a **qualitative** one. Mill puts far greater stress on the variety of pleasures and distinguishes between their respective *values*. He maintains that some pleasures, namely those of the mind, are higher and more estimable than others, namely, those of the body. With this new version of utilitarianism, Mill believed that he could defend the doctrine against the kind of attack earlier levelled against Bentham. It is now possible to say, for instance, that the pleasure experienced by the sadistic guards does not justify their actions because this particular *kind* of pleasure is of so low a value that it does not outweigh the acute pain experienced by the prisoner. Mill describes his position in the following extract from his essay, *Utilitarianism* (1863):

Mill: The Greatest Happiness Principle[1]

The creed which accepts as the foundation of morals Utility, or the Greatest Happiness Principle, holds that actions are right in proportion as they tend to promote happiness, wrong as they tend to produce the reverse of happiness. By 'happiness' is intended pleasure, and the absence of pain; by 'unhappiness', pain, and the privation of pleasure. To give a clear view of the moral standard set up by the theory, much more requires to be said; in particular, what things it includes in the ideas of pain and pleasure; and to what extent this is left an open question. But these supplementary explanations do not affect the theory of life on which this theory of morality is grounded - namely, that pleasure, and freedom from pain, are the only things desirable as ends; and that all desirable things (which are as numerous in the utilitarian as in any other scheme) are desirable either for the pleasure inherent in themselves, or as means to the promotion of pleasure and the prevention of pain.

Now such a theory of life excites in many minds, and among them in some of the most estimable in feeling and purpose, inveterate dislike. To suppose that life has (as they express it) no higher end than pleasure, no better and nobler object of desire and pursuit, they designate as utterly mean and grovelling; as a doctrine worthy only of swine, to whom the followers of Epicurus were, at a very early period, contemptuously likened; and modern holders of the doctrine are occasionally made the subject of equally polite comparisons by its German, French, and English assailants.

When thus attacked, the Epicureans have always answered that it is not they, but their accusers, who represent human nature in a degrading light; since the accusation supposes human beings to be capable of no pleasures except those of which swine are capable. If this supposition were true, the charge could not be gainsaid, but would then be no longer an imputation: for if the sources of pleasure were precisely the same to human beings and to swine, the rule of life which is good enough for the one would be good enough for the other. The comparison of the Epicurean life to that of beasts is felt as degrading, precisely because a beast's pleasures do not satisfy a human being's conceptions of happiness. Human beings have faculties more elevated than the animal appetites, and when once made conscious of them, do not regard anything as happiness which does not include their gratification . . . But there is no known Epicurean theory of life which does not assign to the pleasure of the intellect, of the feelings and imagination, and of the moral sentiments, a much higher value as pleasures than those of mere sensation . . . It is quite compatible with the principle of utility to recognize the fact, that some *kinds* of pleasure are more desirable and more valuable than others. It would be absurd that while, in estimating all other things, quality is considered as well as quantity, the estimation of pleasures should be supposed to depend on quantity alone.

If I am asked what I mean by difference of quality in pleasures, or what makes one pleasure more valuable than another, merely as a pleasure, except its being greater in amount, there is but one possible answer. Of two pleasures, if there be one to which all or almost all who have experience of both give a decided preference, irrespective of any feeling of moral obligation to prefer it, that is the more desirable pleasure. If one of the two is, by those who are competently acquainted with both, placed so far above the other that they prefer it, even though knowing it to be attended with a greater amount of discontent, and would not resign it for any quantity of the other pleasure which their nature is capable of, we are justified in ascribing to the preferred enjoyment a superiority in quality, so far outweighing quantity as to render it, in comparison, of small account.

Now it is an unquestionable fact that those who are equally acquainted with, and equally capable of appreciating and enjoying, both, do give a most marked preference to the manner of existence which employs their higher faculties. Few human creatures would consent to be changed into any of the lower animals, for a promise of the fullest allowance of a beast's pleasures; no intelligent human being would consent to be a fool, no instructed person would be an ignoramus, no person of feeling and conscience would be selfish and base, even though they should be persuaded that the fool, the dunce, or the rascal is better satisfied with his lot than they are with theirs. They would not resign what they possess more than he, for the most complete satisfaction of all the desires which they have in common with him. If they ever

---

1. Reprinted in *Utilitarianism, Liberty, and Representative Government*, with an introduction by A D Lindsay (London: J M Dent & Sons, 1948) pp 6-11.

fancy they would, it is only in cases of unhappiness so extreme, that to escape from it they would exchange their lot for almost any other, however undesirable in their own eyes. A being of higher faculties requires more to make him happy, is capable probably of more acute suffering, and certainly accessible to it at more points, than one of an inferior type; but in spite of these liabilities, he can never really wish to sink into what he feels to be a lower grade of existence . . . It is better to be a human being dissatisfied than a pig satisfied; better to be Socrates dissatisfied than a fool satisfied. And if the fool, or the pig, is of a different opinion, it is because they only know their own side of the question. The other party to the comparison knows both sides.

It may be objected, that many who are capable of the higher pleasures, occasionally, under the influence of temptation, postpone them to the lower. But this is quite compatible with a full appreciation of the intrinsic superiority of the higher. Men often, from infirmity of character, make their election for the nearer good, though they know it to be the less valuable; and this no less when the choice is between two bodily pleasures, than when it is between bodily and mental. They pursue sensual indulgences to the injury of health, though perfectly aware that health is the greater good. It may be further objected, that many who begin with youthful enthusiasm for everything noble, as they advance in years sink into indolence and selfishness. But I do not believe that those who undergo this very common change, voluntarily choose the lower description of pleasures in preference to the higher. I believe that before they devote themselves exclusively to the one, they have already become incapable of the other. Capacity for the nobler feelings is in most natures a very tender plant, easily killed, not only by hostile influences, but by mere want of sustenance; and in the majority of young persons it speedily dies away if the occupations to which their position in life has devoted them, and the society into which it has thrown them, are not favourable to keeping that higher capacity in exercise. Men lose their higher aspirations as they lose their intellectual tastes, because they have not time or opportunity for indulging them; and they addict themselves to inferior pleasures, not because they deliberately prefer them, but because they are either the only ones to which they have access, or the only ones which they are any longer capable of enjoying. It may be questioned whether anyone who has remained equally susceptible to both classes of pleasures, ever knowingly and calmly preferred the lower; though many, in all ages, have broken down in an ineffectual attempt to combine both.

From this verdict of the only competent judges, I apprehend there can be no appeal. On a question which is the best worth having of two pleasures, or which of two modes of existence is the most grateful to the feelings, apart from its moral attributes and from its consequences, the judgement of those who are qualified by knowledge of both, or, if they differ, that of the majority among them, must be admitted as final. And there needs be the less hesitation to accept this judgement respecting the quality of pleasures, since there is no other tribunal to be referred to even on the question of quantity. What means are there of determining which is the acutest of two pains; or the intensest of two pleasurable sensations, except the general suffrage of those who are familiar with both? Neither pains nor pleasures are homogeneous, and pain is always heterogeneous with pleasure. What is there to decide whether a particular pleasure is worth purchasing at the cost of a particular pain, except the feelings and judgement of the experienced? When, therefore, those feelings and judgement declare the pleasures derived from the higher faculties to be preferable in kind, apart from the question of intensity, to those of which the animal nature, disjoined from the higher faculties, is susceptible, they are entitled on this subject to the same regard.

I have dwelt on this point, as being a necessary part of a perfectly just conception of Utility, or Happiness, considered as the directive rule of human conduct. But it is by no means an indispensable condition to the acceptance of the utilitarian standard; for that standard is not the agent's own greatest happiness, but the greatest amount of happiness altogether; and if it may possibly be doubted whether a noble character is always the happier for its nobleness, there can be no doubt that it makes other people happier, and that the world in general is immensely a gainer by it. Utilitarianism, therefore, could only attain its end by the general cultivation of nobleness of character, even if each individual were only benefited by the nobleness of others, and his own, so far as happiness is concerned, were a sheer deduction from the benefit. But the bare enunciation of such an absurdity as this last, renders refutation superfluous.

Exercise 2

Which of the following do you consider 'higher' or 'lower' pleasures? List both sets of pleasures in an order of preference - counting +10 and -10 for maximum and minimum pleasure -and then compare your list with other people's. Have you come to a majority view? Has Mill's distinction proved useful or not?

	A		B
4 **a**	Having money	8 **a**	Forgiving your enemies
6 **b**	Having power	2 **b**	Drinking champagne
1 **c**	Having friends	1 **c**	Drinking water
10 **d**	Saying your prayers	7 **d**	Playing football
9 **e**	Eating pork	10 **e**	Playing chess
3 **f**	Giving love	4 **f**	Playing an instrument
2 **g**	Receiving love	3 **g**	Listening to Mozart
5 **h**	Making love	6 **h**	Going to a rock concert
7 **i**	Taking a walk	5 **i**	Reading poetry
8 **j**	Taking revenge	9 **j**	Writing poetry

Exercise 3

You are 16 and have the choice of leaving school or staying on to study for university. To help you decide, you outline two possible careers up to the age of 25 and award points for each stage (counting +20 and -20 for maximum pleasure and pain respectively). Would such calculations help you in your decision? What *qualitative* distinctions would you make between the two careers?

Staying		**Leaving**	
Career	**pts**	**Career**	**pts**
Working weekends in shop = £20 = run s/h bike	—	Full-time in bank = £100 per wk = run new bike	—
Wearing uniform	—	Wearing new clothes	—
Homework at night	—	Social life after school	—
Obeying rules at school	—	Obeying rules at work	—
Friends at school	—	Friends at work	—
Playing soccer for school	—	Playing soccer for firm	—
Passing into university	—	Large rise in pay	—
Being at university	—	Remaining in job	—
Dating Alice and saving for own home in 5 years	—	Dating Alice and saving for own home in 2 years	—
Getting a degree and job at £10,000 p.a.	—	Getting promotion and £12,000 p.a.	—
Job satisfaction and prospects	—	Job satisfaction and prospects	—
Satisfying parental ambitions	—	Satisfying parental ambitions	—
TOTAL	—	**TOTAL**	—

Questions: Mill

1. Do you think an intellectual's life is qualitatively superior to that of a fool?

2. What are the social implications of Mill's theory?

3. Why is there a conflict between Bentham's utilitarianism and justice? Illustrate your answer with a specific example. Does Mill overcome this conflict?

4. How successful is Mill's defence against the charge that utilitarianism is a 'swine ethic'?

5. How would you distinguish between the music of Mozart and the Beatles? Would you say that one involves a 'higher' art than the other?

Some Criticisms of Utilitarianism

In substituting quality for quantity, Mill's version of utilitarianism differs radically from Bentham's. Mill rejects a quantitative estimate of pleasure because, he argues, human beings, while experiencing 'lower' pleasures in common with the animals are capable of certain other 'higher' pleasures - those of the intellect - which are beyond the reach of all other sentient beings. This difference between the 'higher' and 'lower' pleasures is, says Mill, sufficient to establish the distinctive range and variety of human happiness, and the unique character of man's pursuit of it in his moral life.

But how do we distinguish between these two orders of pleasure? People's opinions as to what are the higher and lower pleasures differ widely, and it is difficult to see how any general agreement could ever be reached. Mill answers by appealing to what he calls the 'competent judges'. If we want to know which are the higher and lower pleasures, then we must appeal to those who have experienced *both* kinds of pleasure. If these judges consistently opt for one pleasure over another, no matter how much pain or discomfort may accompany it, then this pleasure must be qualitatively superior. An opinion poll amongst these judges would reveal that they consistently choose the pleasures of the intellect in preference to the so-called 'higher' pleasures. As Mill remarked, ' . . . it is an unquestionable fact that those who are equally capable of appreciating and enjoying (both kinds of pleasure), do give a marked preference to the manner of existence which employs their higher faculties.'

This is all very well; but is it really an unquestionable fact that these so-called competent judges would always decide in favour of the higher pleasures? Certainly there is no *logical* reason why they should. Doubtless Mill would think it inconceivable for an intelligent Victorian gentleman to prefer the lower pleasures; but inconceivable though it may be to Mill, it is not for that reason impossible. Cases abound in which a man has thought an action pleasureable even though his society has regarded it with distaste; but this alone does not make it *wrong*. Majority opinion, even among the most educated, cannot, in other words, make a particular action *morally right* any more than it can make a scientific theory *empirically true*. The fact that the majority of citizens in ancient Rome approved of slavery does not justify their having slaves.

There are, however, other objections to utilitarianism, to which both Mill's version and Bentham's are equally exposed. Three in particular should be mentioned:

1. The Problem of Consequences. If the rightness of an action depends on it producing the greatest balance of happiness over unhappiness, of pleasure over pain, then making a moral decision involves calculating that action's effects. But how is it possible to calculate all the possible consequences of an action? How can we ever be sure that any action will produce the greatest net happiness? We might be able to say, with some certainty, that this action (A) will have this consequence (B) in five minutes time; but B will inevitably have other consequences, and these consequences will in turn have other effects, and so on, until the end of time. At what point, therefore, do we make our calculations and determine that our original action was right or wrong?

2. The Problem of Special Responsibilities. Most of us accept that we have special responsibilities to particular people; we further accept that the rightness of these responsibilities does *not* necessarily derive from the fact that they increase the sum total of human happiness. This, however, is precisely what the utilitarian does not appear to admit. If, to use an earlier example, two men are drowning, and one is your father and the other a famous scientist on the verge of curing cancer, the utilitarian would urge you to save the scientist. Many of us would disagree and find such a suggestion repugnant. We would reply that we have a special duty towards our parents that outweighs any claim that a stranger, however illustrious, may have upon us. Other examples can be given. A teacher has a special obligation to his pupils; and despite what his pupils may think, this does not necessarily involve giving maximum marks in order to maximize the overall happiness of the class concerned. Indeed, in these cases, it is not unknown that an increase in quality is effected by an increase in pain. Thus it is that a teacher may discharge his duty without regard to the principle of utility.

3. The Problem of Justice. It may seem strange that justice should be a problem for utilitarianism. After all, the theory does correct the apparent 'selfishness' of ethical egoism, and it does insist that, when we calculate the effects of an action, no one person can claim special privileges and set aside the happiness of others in the pursuit of their own. Utilitarianism does seek to be *impartial*, and this we might think is necessary to any meaningful idea of justice - as indeed it is. But in another sense utilitarianism is *not* specifically egalitarian. For while we are told to aim for the greatest possible amount of happiness, and to count everybody's happiness equally, we are not told how this happiness is to be *distributed*. What happens, for instance, in those cases where the greatest amount of happiness is achieved but through an *unequal* distribution; in which, say, one person is deprived of happiness altogether? One such case involves the punishment of an innocent person. If we assume, as Bentham did, that the main aim of punishment is deterrence (making people obey the law through fear of what will happen to them if they don't), then a utilitarian judge would be right to condemn someone to death, knowing that they were innocent, if he believed that a greater good would result - such as restoring law and order, preventing an increase in crime, and so on. The problem is, that while this action may well maximize the sum total of happiness, it may yet be regarded as unjust in the way this sum is distributed. For justice also demands *dealing with individuals according to their deserts or merits*. On this reasoning, people are not punished because of what they may do or because of the effects of their punishment on others, but solely because of what they themselves have or have not done. If it is shown that no offence was committed, then their innocence is *alone* sufficient to justify their acquittal.

This conclusion is extremely significant. If justice is not necessarily served by the principle of utility, if the production of the greatest happiness does not imply that justice has been done, then we must conclude that deciding what is right and wrong requires more than a mere analysis of effects. We must move, that is, away from teleological theories and towards those which consider the extent to which the morality of an act depends on the nature of the act itself. In a word, we must begin to think **deontologically**.

Exercise 4

> The following extracts are taken from the writings of Niccolo Machiavelli (1469-1527), Fyodor Dostoyevsky (1821-1881) and Aldous Huxley (1894-1963). Read them carefully and then consider the questions which follow each passage.

1. *Machiavelli: The Prince* [2]

I say that whenever men are discussed (and especially princes, who are more exposed to view), they are noted for various qualities which earn them either praise or condemnation. Some, for example, are held to be generous, and others miserly . . . Some are held to be benefactors, others are called grasping; some cruel, some compassionate; one man faithless, another faithful . . . and so forth. I know everyone will agree that it would be most laudable if a prince possessed all the qualities deemed to be good among those I have enumerated. But, human nature being what it is, princes cannot possess those qualities, or rather cannot always exhibit them. So a prince should be so prudent that he knows how to escape the evil reputation attached to those vices which could lose him his state, and how to avoid those vices which are not so dangerous, if he possibly can; but, if he cannot, he need not worry so much about the latter. And then, he must not flinch from being blamed for vices which are necessary for safeguarding the state. This is because, taking everything into account, he will find that some of the things that appear to be virtues will, if he practises them, ruin him, and some of the things that appear to be wicked will bring him security and prosperity . . .

I say that a prince should want to have a reputation for compassion rather than for cruelty: none the less, he should be careful that he does not make bad use of compassion . . . So a prince should not worry if he incurs reproach for his cruelty so long as he keeps his subjects united and loyal. By making an example or two he will prove more compassionate than those who, being too compassionate, allow disorders which lead to murder and rapine. These nearly always harm the whole community, whereas executions ordered by a prince only affect individuals.

From this arises the following question: whether it is better to be loved than feared, or the reverse. The answer is that one would like to be both the one and the other; but because it is difficult to combine them, it is far better to be feared than loved if you cannot be both . . . The bond of love is one which men, wretched creatures that they are, break when it is to their advantage to do so; but fear is strengthened by a dread of punishment which is always effective . . .

However, when a prince is campaigning with his soldiers and is in command of a large army then he need not worry about having a reputation for cruelty; because, without such a reputation, he can never keep his army united and disciplined. Among the admirable achievements of Hannibal is included this: that although he led a huge army, made up of countless different races, on foreign campaigns, there was never any dissension, either among the troops themselves or against their leader, whether things were going well or badly. For this, his inhuman cruelty was wholly responsible. It was this, along with his countless other qualities, which made him feared and respected by his soldiers. If it had not been for his cruelty, his other qualities would not have been enough. The historians, having given little thought to this, on the one hand admire what Hannibal achieved, and on the other condemn what made his achievements possible . . .

Everyone realizes how praiseworthy it is for a prince to honour his word and to be straightforward rather than crafty in his dealings; none the less contemporary experience shows that princes who have achieved great things have been those who have given their word lightly, who have known how to trick men with their cunning, and who, in the end, have overcome those abiding by honest principles . . . So it follows that a prudent ruler cannot, and should not, honour his word when it places him at a disadvantage and when the reasons for which he made his promise no longer exist. If all men were good, this precept would not be good; but because men are wretched creatures who would not keep their word to you, you need not keep your word to them. And a prince will never lack good excuses to colour his bad faith . . .

A prince, therefore, need not necessarily have all the good qualities I mentioned above, but he should certainly appear to have them. I would even go so far as to say that if he has these qualities and always behaves accordingly he will find them ruinous; if he only appears to have them they will render him service. He should appear to be compassionate, faithful to his word, guileless, and devout. And indeed he should be so. But his disposition should be such that, if he needs to be the opposite, he knows how. You must realize this: that a prince, and especailly a new prince, cannot observe all those things which give men a reputation for virtue, because in order to maintain his state he is often forced to act in defiance of good faith, of charity, of kindness, of religion. And so he should have a flexible disposition, varying as fortune and circumstances dictate. As I said above, he should not deviate from what is good, if that is possible, but he should know how to do evil, if that is necessary.

---

2. *The Prince*, translated and with an introduction by George Bull (Penguin Books, 1961) pp 90-2, 95-101.

Questions: Machiavelli

1. To what extent does Machiavelli in this passage adopt utilitarian principles?

2. When, if ever, is a ruler justified in acting immorally for the good of the state? Give examples.

2. *Dostoyevsky: Crime and Punishment* [3]

In my opinion (said Raskolnikov), if for some reason or another the discoveries of the Keplers and Newtons could not be made known to people except by sacrificing the lives of one, or a dozen, or a hundred, or even more men who made these discoveries impossible or in any way prevented them from being made, then Newton would have had the right, and indeed would have been in duty bound, to *eliminate* the dozen or the hundred people so as to make his discoveries known to all mankind. That, however, does not at all mean that Newton would have had the right to murder anyone he liked indiscriminately or steal every day in the street market. Then, as far as I can remember, I go on to argue in my article that all - shall we say? - lawgivers and arbiters of mankind, beginning from ancient times and continuing with the Lycurguses, Solons, Mahomets, Napoleons, and so on, were without exception criminals because of the very fact that they had transgressed the ancient laws handed down by their ancestors and venerated by the people. Nor, of course, did they stop short of bloodshed, if bloodshed - sometimes of innocent people fighting gallantly in defence of the ancient law - were of any assistance to them. It is indeed a remarkable fact that the majority of these benefactors and arbiters of mankind all shed rivers of blood. In short, I maintain that all men who are not only great but a little out of the common, that is, even those who are capable of saying something that is to a certain extent new, must by their very nature be criminals - more or less, of course. Otherwise they would find it difficult to get out of the rut, and to remain in the rut they could by their very nature never agree, and to my mind they ought never to agree to it. In short, as you see, there is nothing particularly new in all that. Indeed, it has been printed and read thousands of times. As for my division of men into ordinary and extraordinary, I admit it is somewhat arbitrary, but after all I don't insist that it can be fixed exactly. I only believe in my principal idea. And all this idea claims is that men are *in general* divided by a law of nature into two categories: an inferior one (ordinary), that is to say, the material whose only purpose is to reproduce its kind, and the people proper, that is to say, those who possess the gift or talent to say a *new word* in their particular environment. There are, of course, innumerable subdivisions, but the distinguishing features of both categories are well marked: the first category, that is to say, the masses, comprises all the people who, generally speaking, are by nature conservative, respectable, and docile, or love to be docile. In my opinion it is their duty to be docile, for that is their vocation in life, and there is nothing at all humiliating in it for them. The men belonging to the second category all transgress the law and are all destroyers, or are inclined to be destroyers, according to their different capacities. The crimes of these people are, of course, relative and various; mostly, however, they demand, in proclamations of one kind or another, the destruction of the present in the name of a better future. But if for the sake of his idea such a man has to step over a corpse or wade through blood, he is, in my opinion, absolutely entitled, in accordance with the dictates of his conscience, to permit himself to wade through blood, all depending of course on the nature and the scale of his idea - note that, please. It is only in this sense alone that I declare in my article that they have a right to commit a crime . . . Still, there is really nothing to be afraid of: the mob hardly ever acknowledges their right to do this, but goes on beheading or hanging them (more or less) and, in doing so, quite honestly fulfils its own conservative vocation in life, with the proviso, however, that in the subsequent generations this same mob places the executed men on a pedestal and worships them (more or less). The first category is always the master of the present; the second category the master of the future. The first preserves the world and increases its numbers; the second moves the world and leads it to its goal. Both have an absolutely equal right to exist. In short, with me all have the same rights and - *vive la guerre éternelle* - till the New Jerusalem, of course.

---

3. *Crime and Punishment*, translated with an introduction by David Magarshack (Penguin Books, 1951) pp 276-278.

Questions: Dostoyevsky

1. To what extent does Dostoyevsky in this passage adopt utilitarian principles?

2. Does genius justify any means to an end?

3. *Huxley: Brave New World* [4]

'My dear young friend,' said Mustapha Mond, 'civilization has absolutely no need of nobility or heroism. These things are symptoms of political inefficiency. In a properly organized society like ours, nobody has any opportunities for being noble or heroic. Conditions have got to be thoroughly unstable before the occasion can arise. Where there are wars, where there are divided allegiances, where there are temptations to be resisted, objects of love to be fought for or defended - there, obviously, nobility and heroism have some sense. But there aren't any wars nowadays. The greatest care is taken to prevent you from loving anyone too much. There's no such thing as a divided allegiance; you're so conditioned that you can't help doing what you ought to do. And what you ought to do is on the whole so pleasant, so many of the natural impulses are allowed free play, that there really aren't any temptations to resist. And if ever, by some unlucky chance, anything unpleasant should somehow happen, why, there's always *soma* to give you a holiday from the facts. And there's *soma* to calm your anger, to reconcile you to your enemies, to make you patient and long-suffering. In the past you could only accomplish these things by making a great effort and after years of hard moral training. Now, you swallow two or three half-gramme tablets, and there you are. Anybody can be virtuous now. You can carry at least half your morality about in a bottle. Christianity without tears - that's what *soma* is.'

'But the tears are necessary (said the Savage). Don't you remember what Othello said? "If after every tempest come such calms, may the winds blow till they have wakened death." There's a story one of the old Indians used to tell us, about the Girl of Mátsaki. The young men who wanted to marry her had to do a morning's hoeing in her garden. It seemed easy; but there were flies and mosquitoes, magic ones. Most of the young men simply couldn't stand the biting and stinging. But the one that could - he got the girl.'

'Charming! But in civilized countries,' said the Controller, 'you can have the girls without hoeing for them; and there aren't any flies or mosquitoes to sting you. We got rid of them all centuries ago.'

The Savage nodded, frowning. 'You got rid of them. Yes, that's just like you. Getting rid of everything unpleasant instead of learning to put up with it. Whether 'tis nobler in the mind to suffer the slings and arrows of outrageous fortune, or to take arms against a sea of troubles and by opposing end them . . . But you don't do either. Neither suffer nor oppose. You just abolish the slings and arrows. It's too easy . . . Isn't there something in living dangerously?'

'There's a great deal in it,' the Controller replied. 'Men and women must have their adrenals stimulated from time to time.'

'What?' questioned the Savage, uncomprehending.

'It's one of the conditions of perfect health. That's why we've made the VPS treatment compulsory.'

'VPS?'

'Violent Passion Surrogate. Regularly once a month. We flood the whole system with adrenin. It's the complete physiological equivalent of fear and rage. All the tonic effects of murdering Desdemona and being murdered by Othello, without any of the inconveniences.'

'But I like the inconveniences.'

'We don't,' said the Controller. 'We prefer to do things comfortably.'

'But I don't want comfort. I want God, I want poetry, I want real danger, I want freedom, I want goodness. I want sin.'

'In fact,' said Mustapha Mond, 'you're claiming the right to be unhappy.'

'All right, then,' said the Savage defiantly, 'I'm claiming the right to be unhappy.'

'Not to mention the right to grow old and ugly and impotent; the right to have syphilis and cancer; the right to have too little to eat; the right to be lousy; the right to live in constant apprehension of what may happen tommorow; the right to catch typhoid; the right to be tortured by unspeakable pains of every kind.'

There was a long silence.

'I claim them all,' said the Savage at last.

Mustapha Mond shrugged his shoulders. 'You're welcome,' he said.

---

4. *Brave New World* (Penguin Books, 1977) pp 190-192.

Questions: Huxley

1. To what extent does Huxley in this passage adopt utilitarian principles?

2. When, if ever, would a government be justified in secretly administering drugs to its citizens? Give examples.

Questions: Utilitarianism

1. In the Roald Dahl story, *Genesis and Catastrophe*[5], a doctor saves both mother and child in a difficult birth. His concluding words are, 'You'll be alright now, Mrs Hitler.' To what extent is this story a justified criticism of utilitarianism?

2. Give examples of what you consider to be the higher and lower pleasures. What problems does the difference between them present for deciding between right and wrong actions?

3. Justify the use of drugs to a) alleviate physical pain; b) to reduce stress; c) to induce a state of well-being.

4. Consider the following case. Does it represent a justified criticism of utilitarianism? How would a utilitarian reply?

> *Jim finds himself in the central square of a small South American town. Tied up against the wall are a row of twenty Indians, most terrified, a few defiant, in front of them several armed men in uniform. A heavy man in a sweat-stained khaki shirt turns out to be the captain in charge and, after a good deal of questioning of Jim which establishes that he got there by accident while on a botanical expedition, explains that the Indians are a random group of the inhabitants who, after recent acts of protest against the government, are just about to be killed to remind other possible protestors of the advantages of not protesting. However, since Jim is an honoured visitor from another land, the captain is happy to offer him a guest's privilege of killing one of the Indians himself. If Jim accepts, then as a special mark of the occasion, the other Indians will be let off. Of course, if Jim refuses, then there is no special occasion, and Pedro here will do what he was about to do when Jim arrived, and kill them all. Jim, with some desperate recollection of schoolboy fiction, wonders whether if he got hold of a gun, he could hold the captain, and the rest of the soldiers to threat, but it is quite clear from the set-up that nothing of that kind is going to work: any attempt at that sort of thing will mean that all the Indians will be killed, and himself. The men against the wall, and the other villagers, understand the situation, and are obviously begging him to accept. What should he do?[6]*

5. *Kiss Kiss* (Harmondsworth: Penguin Books, 1962) pp.156-163.
6. Bernard Williams, *Utilitarianism: For and Against* (Cambridge: Cambridge University Press, 1973) pp 98-99.

Bibliography: Utilitarianism

* denotes text referred to or extracted in main text

Bayles, Michael D (ed), *Contemporary Utilitarianism* (Garden City, NY: Doubleday, 1968) Collection of essays by contemporary philosophers.

Bentham, Jeremy *An Introduction to the Principles of Morals and Legislation*,* ed J H Burns and H L A Hart (London & New York: Methuen, 1982)

Dostoyevsky, Fyodor *Crime and Punishment*,* translated with an Introduction by David Magarshack (Harmondsworth: Penguin Books, 1951)

Gorovitz, Samuel (ed) *John Stuart Mill: Utilitarianism with Critical Essays* (Indianapolis: Bobbs-Merrill, 1971)

Huxley, Aldous *Brave New World*,* (Harmondsworth: Penguin Books, 1977)

Machiavelli, Niccolo *The Prince*,* translated and with an Introduction by George Bull (Harmondsworth: Penguin Books, 1961)

Mill, John Stuart 'Utilitarianism'* *Utilitarianism, Liberty, and Representative Government*, with an Introduction by A D Lindsay (London: J M Dent & Sons, 1948)

Plamenatz, J *The English Utilitarians* (Oxford: Basil Blackwell, 1966) Ch 4 on Bentham, Ch 6 on Mill.

Quinton, Anthony *Utilitarian Ethics* (London: Gerald Duckworth, 1989) Excellent short introduction, with chapters on Bentham, Mill, and their critics.

Smart, J J C (with Bernard Williams) *Utilitarianism: For and Against** (Cambridge: Cambridge University Press, 1973) A defence and criticism of utilitarianism by two contemporary philosophers.

Sen, Amartya (ed with Bernard Williams) *Utilitarianism and Beyond* (Cambridge: Cambridge University Press, 1982) A wide range of argument for and against.

Sprigge, T L S *The Rational Foundation of Ethics* (London & New York: Routledge & Kegan Paul, 1988) Especially Ch 1, Ch 2 contains an equally useful account of Moore and Ross.

Discussion: Punishment

When lawbreakers are caught they are punished. Punishment may involve the loss of money, liberty, and even, in the most extreme cases, the loss of life. We have become so accustomed to these practices, and so ancient are they, that most of us accept them without question. And yet punishment does require justification, if only because it involves the calculated infliction of pain upon an individual. So why is the state allowed to proceed in this way, to do deliberate injury to certain of its citizens? What is the justification of punishment? Traditionally two answers have been given to this question: the utilitarian and the retributivist.

As we might expect, the **utilitarian theory of punishment** concerns itself with the consequences of punishment and judges whether these consequences are good or bad according to the principle of utility, that is, whether they do or do not increase the sum total of human happiness. As Bentham makes clear, punishment involves pain and is therefore an evil; but it is a justifiable evil if the increase in pain for the criminal leads to the prevention of crime and thus to a corresponding increase in society's general security and happiness. Punishment in this sense is an instrumental good. Crime is prevented by the *deterrent* effect of punishment: the infliction of pain on criminals provides them with a motive not to repeat their offence (the fear of future pain), and provides potential lawbreakers with an illustration of what will happen to them if they commit similar acts. If it should happen, however, that punishment deters neither the actual nor the potential criminal, then it has what Bentham calls the final 'incapacitative' power of removing such people from society altogether by imprisonment or death. In the last resort, then, punishment protects society by making it physically impossible for wrongdoers to repeat their actions.

The **retributive theory of punishment** is commonly expressed in the Old Testament command: 'An eye for an eye and a tooth for a tooth.' Punishment is justified because it is what the criminal deserves; the lawbreaker must repay society for the damage he or she has done to it; because a positive injustice would be done if people could inflict pain on others without the others being able to inflict pain on them in return. Unlike the utilitarian theory, the theory of retribution is backward-looking rather than forward-looking: it advocates punishment because of what has been done but not to prevent what might be done. Indeed, even if no good consequences follow, punishment should still be administered. Suppose, for example, we discover the whereabouts of a notorious Nazi war criminal: he is living in South America, has taken a new identity, and is now a respected and useful member of the community. Suppose further that we possess the means of bringing him to justice. In these circumstances, his arrest and punishment may well have little positive utilitarian value: it may even have a negative value; but many of us may still regard his punishment as necessary, as a thing good in itself. For the retributivist, then, this man's guilt is alone sufficient to justify his punishment.

Neither of these theories has gone unchallenged. Utilitarianism, we have noted before, allows for the punishment of the innocent on grounds of social utility and to that extent does not adequately protect the citizen's right to be tried only for the crimes *he* has committed. Retributivism, on the other hand, while protecting that right, proceeds to punish criminals simply because they deserve it and without regard to whether punishment in fact does any good at all either for the law-breaker or the community. Injury, it would appear, is thus inflicted for no compensating greater benefit but to satisfy a primitive and barbarous desire for revenge.

It is largely for these reasons that the traditional utilitarian and retributive theories have been increasingly rejected and replaced by a third theory, known as the **theory of rehabilitation**. This theory, which has found a good deal of support among psychologists, sociologists, administrators and lawyers alike, argues that we should be less concerned with punishing criminals and more concerned with reforming them. Our response to offenders should not be directed to paying them back or deterring them, but to controlling or suppressing their criminal tendencies by a process of re-education or psychological treatment while in custody. Prison, therefore, provides a unique opportunity to equip the offender with a socially desirable set of skills and attitudes. This may be achieved in a variety of ways: it may require psychotherapy (talk-therapy) and vocational training, or behavioural conditioning (eg aversion therapy), or even the application of certain surgical, chemical and electrical methods of control. The underlying assumption is that the criminal is sick rather than wicked, and needs help rather than punishment.

Yet the rehabilitation theory is not without its faults. First of all, it overlooks the social advantages of deterrence. So concerned is it with the *habitual* offender that it tends to ignore those who never commit a crime because of their fear of punishment. But how many more people would the rehabilitationist have to 'treat' if this fear were removed? It could, of course, be argued that a form of deterrence *is* involved in rehabilitation: after all, criminals are still confined and compelled to undergo treatment. This in itself may deter them. But then another problem arises: for how long should they be detained? The answer is, as long as it takes to cure them. The theory states that lawbreakers should be confined until they are reformed, which means until there is no chance they will repeat the offence. Their cure, therefore, effects their release. But this is not as simple as it sounds. In many instances, it is the *less* serious crimes that are the most difficult to treat. For example, a murderer or an embezzler is, in the great majority of cases, unlikely to do it again; a petty thief, on the other hand, may be an habitual offender of an extreme kind, whose activities indicate severe social maladjustment. Is he, then, to get a *longer* sentence than the murderer? And what of the incurables? Are they all to receive life-sentences?

There is, however, a still more serious objection to the theory. Many argue that rehabilitation is not reforming criminals but brainwashing them. By using surgery and mind-altering drugs, the lawbreaker is coerced into a more socially acceptable pattern of behaviour, and society is protected; but whether society, in protecting itself, should have the right to act in this way against *any* of its members is another question. The criminal, it is argued, should also be protected *from* society and must be allowed that most basic of all rights: *the right to remain himself* and to retain his own distinctive, if 'anti-social', personality. We must, that is, have the right to refuse treatment, to remain bad, and to accept traditional punishment and even death. If these rights are not safeguarded, a much more sinister situation could arise. What would happen, for instance, in a society where the definition of 'crime' had been extended beyond the usual offences, like theft and murder, to include all political opposition to the state? Under these circumstances, the government, following the rehabilitation theory and believing that such opposition threatened society, would be justified in treating its opponents until 'cured' of their former opinions. This already happens in some countries. Today so-called 'dissidents' do not always go to prison for fixed terms but are often placed in hospitals and asylums for indefinite periods of therapy and re-education.

In the following three extracts, the rehabilitation theory is presented by the psychiatrist, Karl Menninger. Menninger, believing that retribution is both immoral and ineffective, advocates controlled therapeutic treatment as the only justifiable and efficient means of preventing crime. By contrast, C S Lewis, speaking from the retributivist viewpoint, argues against rehabilitation, calling it, somewhat sarcastically, the 'humanitarian' theory of punishment.

Rehabilitationists, Lewis argues, defend the individual against the public demand for retaliation, but do so by depriving the criminal of his or her basic rights as a human being. For the utilitarian position, we turn again to John Stuart Mill and to his famous speech in the House of Commons in favour of capital punishment. Mill presents some familiar arguments regarding the deterrent effects of judicial execution, but also, and more interestingly, advances arguments that are quite out of the ordinary and to which he attaches the greatest significance.

1. Karl Menninger: the Crime of Punishment [1]

Our system for controlling crime is ineffective, unjust, expensive. Prisons seem to operate with revolving doors - the same poeple going in and out and in and out. *Who cares*?

Our city jails and inhuman reformatories and wretched prisons are jammed. They are known to be unhealthy, dangerous, immoral, indecent, crime-breeding dens of iniquity. Not everyone has smelled them, as some of us have. Not many have heard the groans and curses. Not everyone has seen the hate and despair in a thousand blank, hollow faces. But, in a way, we all know how miserable prisons are. *We want them to be that way.* And they are. *Who cares*?

Professional and big-time criminals prosper as never before. Gambling syndicates flourish. White-collar crime may even exceed all others, but goes undetected in the majority of cases. We are all being robbed and we know who the robbers are. They live nearby. *Who cares*?

The public filches millions of dollars worth of food and clothing from stores, towels and sheets from hotels, jewelry and knick-knacks from shops. The public steals, and the same public pays it back in higher prices. *Who cares*? . . .

The inescapable conclusion is that society *wants* crime, *needs* crime, and gains definite satisfactions from the present mishandling of it! We condemn crime; we punish offenders for it; but we need it. The crime and punishment ritual is part of our lives . . .

I assume it to be a matter of common and general agreement that our object in all this is to protect the community from a repetition of the offense by the most economical method consonant with our other purposes. Our 'other purposes' include the desire to prevent these offenses from occurring, to reclaim offenders for social usefulness, if possible, and to detain them in protective custody, if reclamation is *not* possible. But how? . . .

Let me answer this carefully, for much misunderstanding accumulates here. I would say that according to the prevalent understanding of the words, crime is *not* a disease. Neither is it an illness, although I think it *should* be! It *should* be treated, and it could be; but it mostly isn't.

These enigmatic statements are simply explained. Diseases are undesired states of being which have been described and defined by doctors, usually given Greek and Latin appellations, and treated by long-established physical and pharmacological formulae. Illness, on the other hand, is best defined as a state of impaired functioning of such a nature that the public expects the sufferer to repair to the physician for help. The illness may prove to be a disease; more often it is only vague and nameless misery, but something which doctors, not lawyers, teachers, or preachers, are supposed to be able and willing to help.

When the community begins to look upon the expression of aggressive violence as the symptom of an illness or as indicative of illness, it will be because it believes doctors can do something to correct such a condition. At present, some better-informed individuals do believe and expect this. However angry at or sorry for the offender, they want him 'treated' in an effective way so that he will cease to be a danger to them. And they know that traditional punishment, 'treatment-punishment', will not effect this . . .

The present penal system and the existing legal philosophy do not stimulate or even expect such a change to take place in the criminal. Yet change is what medical science always aims for. The prisoner, like the doctor's other patients, should emerge from his treatment experience a different person, differently equipped, differently functioning, and headed in a different direction than when he began the treatment.

It is natural for the public to doubt that this can be accomplished with criminals. But remember that the public *used* to doubt that change could be effected in the mentally ill. No one a hundred years ago believed mental illness to be curable. Today *all* people know (or should know) that *mental illness is curable* in the great majority of instances and that the prospects and rapidity of cure are directly related to the availability and intensity of proper treatment . . .

---

1. Karl Menninger, 'The Crime of Punishment', *Saturday Review* (1968). Extract taken from *Philosophy: The Basic Issues*, ed E D Klemke, A D Kline & R Hollinger (New York; St Martin's Press, 1982) pp 143-149.

All of the participants in this effort to bring about a favourable change in the patient - ie in his vital balance and life program - are imbued with what we may call a *therapeutic attitude*. This is one in direct antithesis to attitudes of avoidance, ridicule, scorn, or punitiveness. Hostile feelings toward the subject, however justified by his unpleasant and even destructive behaviour, are not in the curriculum of therapy or in the therapist. This does not mean that therapists approve of the offensive and obnoxious behaviour of the patient; they distinctly disapprove of it. But they recognize it as symptomatic of continued inbalance and disorganization, which is what they are seeking to change. They distinguish between disapproval, penalty, price, and punishment . . .

The average citizen finds it difficult to see how any research would in any way change his mind about a man who brutally murders his children. But just such inconceivably awful acts most dramatically point up the need for research. Why should - how can - a man become so dreadful as that in our culture? How is such a man made? Is it comprehensible that he can be born to become so depraved?

The public has a fascination for violence, and clings tenaciously to its yen for vengeance, blind and dead to the expense, futility, and dangerousness of the resulting penal system. But we are bound to hope that this will yield in time to the persistent, penetrating light of intelligence and accumulating scientific knowledge. The public will grow increasingly ashamed of its cry for retaliation, its persistent demand to punish. This is its crime, *our* crime against criminals - and, incidentally, our crime against ourselves. For before we can diminish our sufferings from the ill-controlled aggressive assaults of fellow citizens, we must renounce the philosophy of punishment, the obsolete, vengeful penal attitude. In its place we would seek a comprehensive constructive social attitude - therapeutic in some instances, restraining in some instances, but preventive in its total social impact.

Questions: Menninger

1. How convinced are you of Menninger's connection between criminal behaviour and illness? Construct a case-study illustrating this connection.

2. Would it ever be right to imprison someone before they had committed a crime?

3. What improvements, if any, would you make to the present penal system?

4. A man has been charged with a serious crime. As his attorney, construct a defence adopting Menninger's theories.

2. C S Lewis: The Humanitarian Theory of Punishment [2]

According to the Humanitarian theory, to punish a man because he deserves it, and as much as he deserves, is mere revenge and, therefore, barbarous and immoral. The only legitimate motives for punishing are the desire to deter others by example, or to mend the criminal. When this theory is combined, as frequently happens,with the belief that all crime is more or less pathological, the idea of mending tails off into that of healing or curing, and punishment becomes therapeutic. Thus it appears at first sight that we have passed from the harsh and self-righteous notion of giving the wicked their deserts to the charitable and enlightened one of tending the psychologically sick. What could be more amiable? . . .

My contention is that this doctrine, merciful though it appears, really means that each one of us, from the moment he breaks the law, is deprived of the rights of a human being.

The reason is this. The Humanitarian Theory removes from Punishment the concept of Desert. But the concept of Desert is the only connecting link between punishment and justice. It is only as deserved or undeserved that a sentence can be just or unjust. I do not here contend that the question 'Is it deserved?' is the only one we can reasonably ask about a punishment. We may very properly ask whether it is likely to deter others and to reform the criminal. But neither of these two last questions is a question about justice. There is no sense in talking about a 'just deterrent' or a 'just cure.'

We demand of a deterrent not whether it is just but whether it will deter. We demand of a cure not whether it is just but whether it succeeds. Thus when we cease to consider what the criminal deserves and consider only what will cure him or deter others, we have tacitly removed him from the sphere of justice altogether; instead of a person, a subject of rights, we now have a mere object, a patient, a 'case.'

The distinction will become clearer if we ask who will be qualified to determine sentences when sentences are no longer held to derive their propriety from the criminal's deservings. On the old view the problem of fixing the right sentence was a moral problem. Accordingly, the judge who did it was a person trained in jurisprudence; trained, that is, in a science which deals with rights and duties, and which, in origin at least, was consciously accepting guidance from the Law of Nature and from Scripture . . . And when (say, in eighteenth-century England) actual punishments conflicted too violently with the moral sense of the community, juries refused to convict and reform was finally brought about . . . But all this is changed when we drop the concept of Desert. The only two questions we may now ask about a punishment are whether it deters and whether it cures. But these are not questions on which anyone is entitled to have an opinion simply because he is a man. We is not entitled to an opinion even if, in addition to being a man, he should happen also to be a jurist, a Christian, and a moral theologian . . . Only the expert 'penologist' (let barbarous things have barbarous names), in the light of previous experiment, can tell us what is likely to deter: Only the psychotherapist can tell us what is likely to cure. It will be in vain for the rest of us, speaking simply as men, to say, 'But this punishment is hideously unjust, hideously disproportionate to the criminal's deserts.' The experts with perfect logic will reply, 'But nobody was talking about deserts. No one was talking about *punishment* in your archaic, vindictive sense of the word. Here are the statistics proving that this treatment deters. Here are the statistics proving that this other treatment cures. What is your trouble?'

On (this) remedial view of punishment the offender should, of course, be detained until he was cured. And of course the official straighteners are the only people who can say when that is. The first result of the Humanitarian theory is, therefore, to substitute for a definite sentence (reflecting to some extent the community's moral judgement on the degree of ill-desert involved) an indefinite sentence terminable only by the word of those experts - and they are not experts in moral theology nor even in the Law of Nature - who inflict it. Which of us, if he stood in the dock, would not prefer to be tried by the old system? . . .

2. C S Lewis, 'The Humanitarian Theory of Punishment', *The Twentieth Century: An Australian Quarterly Review*, III, No. 3 (1953). Reprinted in *God in the Dock*, ed Walter Hooper (Grand Rapids: William B Eerdmans, 1970) pp 287-294.

If we turn from the curative to the deterrent justification of punishment we shall find the new theory even more alarming. When you punish a man . . . make of him an 'example' to others, you are admittedly using him as a means to an end; someone else's end. This, in itself, would be a very wicked thing to do. On the classical theory of Punishment it was of course justified on the ground that the man deserved it. That was assumed to be established before any question of 'making him an example' arose. You then, as they saying is, killed two birds with one stone; in the process of giving him what he deserved you set an example to others. But take away desert and the whole morality of the punishment disappears. Why, in heaven's name, am I to be sacrificed to the good of society in this way? - unless, of course, I deserve it.

But that is not the worst. If the justification of exemplary punishment is not to be based on desert but solely on its efficacy as a deterrent, it is not absolutely necessary that the man we punish should even have committed the crime . . . The punishment of a man actually guilty whom the public think innocent will not have the desired effect; the punishment of a man actually innocent will, provided the public think him guilty. But every modern State has powers which make it easy to fake a trial. When a victim is urgently needed for exemplary purposes and a guilty victim cannot be found, all the purposes of deterrence will be equally served by the punishment (call it 'cure' if you prefer) of an innocent victim, provided that the public can be cheated into thinking him guilty. It is no use to ask me why I assume that our rulers will be so wicked. The punishment of an innocent, that is, an undeserving, man is wicked only if we grant the traditional view that righteous punishment means deserved punishment . . .

It is, indeed, important to notice that my argument so far supposes no evil intentions on the part of the Humanitarian and considers only what is involved in the logic of his position. My contention is that good men (not bad men) consistently acting upon that position would act as cruelly and unjustly as the greatest tyrants. They might in some respects act even worse. Of all tyrannies a tyranny sincerely exercised for the good of its victims may be the most oppressive. It may be better to live under robber barons than under omnipotent moral busybodies. The robber baron's cruelty may sometimes sleep, his cupidity may at some point be satiated; but those who torment us for our own good will torment us without end, for they do so with the approval of their own conscience. They may be more likely to go to Heaven yet at the same time likelier to make a Hell of earth. Their very kindness stings with intolerable insult. To be 'cured' against one's will and cured of states which we may not regard as disease is to be put on a level with those who have not yet reached the age of reason or those who never will; to be classed with infants, imbeciles, and domestic animals. But to be punished, however severely, because we have deserved it, because we 'ought to have known better,' is to be treated as a human person made in God's image.

Questions: Lewis

1. What are Lewis' principal objections to the remedial view of punishment? Do you agree with him?

2. Should criminals have the right to refuse treatment and request punisment instead - including death?

3. 'Two wrongs don't make a right'. Is this a justified criticism of retributivism?

4. Who are the 'official straighteners'? Is Lewis right to be wary of them?

3.*John Stuart Mill: In Favour of Capital Punishment* [3]

When there has been brought home to any one, by conclusive evidence, the greatest crime known to the law; and when the attendant circumstances suggest no palliation of the guilt, no hope that the culprit may even yet not be unworthy to live among mankind, nothing to make it probable that the crime was an exception to his general character rather than a consequence of it, then I confess it appears to me that to deprive the criminal of the life of which he has proved himself to be unworthy - solemnly to blot him out from the fellowship of mankind and from the catalogue of the living - is the most appropriate, as it is certainly the most impressive, mode in which society can attach to so great a crime the penal consequences which for the security of life it is indispensable to annex to it. I defend this penalty, when confined to atrocious cases, on the very ground on which it is commonly attacked - on that of humanity to the criminal; as beyond comparison the least cruel mode in which it is possible adequately to deter from the crime. If, in our horror of inflicting death, we endeavour to devise some punishment for the living criminal which shall act on the human mind with a deterrent force at all comparable to that of death, we are driven to inflictions less severe indeed in appearance, and therefore less efficacious, but far more cruel in reality . . . What comparison can there really be, in point of severity, between consigning a man to the short pang of a rapid death, and immuring him in a living tomb, there to linger out what may be a long life in the hardest and most monotonous toil, without any of its alleviations or rewards - debarred from all pleasant sights and sounds, and cut off from all earthly hope . . . Yet even such a lot as this, because there is no one moment at which the suffering is of terrifying intensity, and, above all, because it does not contain the element, so imposing to the imagination, of the unknown, is universally reputed a milder punishment than death . . .

There is not, I should think, any human infliction which makes an impression on the imagination so entirely out of proportion to its real severity as the punishment of death . . . As my hon. Friend the Member for Northampton (Mr Gilpin) has himself remarked, the most that human laws can do to anyone in the matter of death is to hasten it; the man would have died at any rate; not so very much later, and on the average, I fear, with a considerably greater amount of bodily suffering. Society is asked, then, to denude itself of an instrument of punishment which, in the grave cases to which alone it is suitable, effects its purposes at a less cost of human suffering than any other; which, while it inspires more terror, is less cruel in actual fact than any punishment that we should think of substituting for it. My hon. Friend says that it does not inspire terror, and that experience proves it to be a failure. But the influence of a punishment is not to be estimated by its effect on hardened criminals. Those whose habitual way of life keeps them, so to speak, at all times within sight of the gallows, do grow to care less about it; as, to compare good things with bad, an old soldier is not much affected by the chance of dying in battle. I can afford to admit all that is often said about the indifference of professional criminals to the gallows. Though of that indifference one-third is probably bravado and another third confidence that they shall have the luck to escape, it is quite probable that the remaining third is real. But the efficacy of a punishment which acts principally through the imagination, is chiefly to be measured by the impression it makes on those who are still innocent; by the horror with which it surrounds the first prompting of guilt; the restraining influence it exercises over the beginning of the thought which, if indulged, would become a temptation . . . As for what is called the failure of death punishment, who is able to judge of that? We partly know who those are whom it has not deterred; but who is there who knows whom it has deterred, or how many human beings it has saved who would have lived to be murderers if that awful association had not been thrown round the idea of murder from their earliest infancy? . . .

Much has been said of the sanctity of human life, and the absurdity of supposing that we can teach respect for life by ourselves destroying it. But I am surprised at the employment of this argument, for it is one which might be brought against any punishment whatever. It is not human life only, not human life as such, that ought to be sacred to us, but human feelings. The human capacity of suffering is what we should cause

3. John Stuart Mill, 'Parliamentary debate on Capital Punishment Within Prisons Bill', *Hansard Parliamentary Debates*, 3rd Series, April 21, 1868 (London: Hansard, 1868). Reprinted in *Applied Ethics*, ed Peter Singer (Oxford: Oxford University Press, 1986) pp 98-103.

to be respected, not the mere capacity of existing. And we may imagine somebody asking how we can teach people not to inflict suffering by ourselves inflicting it? But to this I should answer - all of us would answer - that to deter by suffering from inflicting suffering is not only possible, but the very purpose of penal justice. Does fining a criminal show want of respect for property, or imprisoning him, for personal freedom? Just as unreasonable is it to think that to take the life of a man who has taken that of another is to show want of regard for human life. We show, on the contrary, most emphatically our regard for it, by the adoption of a rule that he who violates that right in another forfeits it for himself, and that while no other crime that he can commit deprives him of his right to live, this shall.

There is one argument against capital punishment, even in extreme cases, which I cannot deny to have weight . . . It is this, that if by an error of justice an innocent person is put to death, the mistake can never be corrected; all compensation, all reparation for the wrong is impossible. This would be indeed a serious objection if these miserable mistakes, among the most tragic occurrences in the whole round of human affairs, could not be made extremely rare. The argument is invincible where the mode of criminal procedure is dangerous to the innocent, or where the Courts of Justice are not trusted . . . But we all know that the defects of our procedure are the very opposite. Our rules of evidence are even too favourable to the prisoner; and juries and Judges carry out the maxim, 'It is better that ten guilty should escape than that one innocent person should suffer,' not only to the letter, but beyond the letter. Judges are most anxious to point out, and juries to allow for, the barest possibility of the prisoner's innocence. No human judgement is infallible . . . ; but in so grave a case as that of murder, the accused, in our system, has always the benefit of the merest shadow of a doubt. And this suggests another consideration very germane to the question. The very fact that death punishment is more shocking than any other to the imagination, necessarily renders the Court of Justice more scrupulous in requiring the fullest evidence of guilt. Even that which is the greatest objection to capital punishment, the impossibility of correcting an error once committed, must make, and does make, juries and Judges more careful in forming their opinion, and more jealous in their scrutiny of the evidence.

Questions: Mill

1. Identify Mill's arguments in favour of the death penalty. To what extent do you agree with them?

2. Present a utilitarian case against capital punishment.

3. Is the possibility that an innocent man may be put to death an insuperable objection to capital punishment? How does Mill tackle this question?

4. Are there categories of murder for which the death penalty alone is appropriate? Carefully define these categories.

Questions: Punishment

1. 'Criminal law proceeds upon the principle that it is morally right to hate criminals' (James Stephen.) Discuss.

2. In 1960 Israel captured and tried Adolf Eichmann for his role in the extermination of Jews in the Second World War. He was subsequently hanged. How do you think a retributivist, a utilitarian, and a rehabilitationist would view his punishment?

3. Punishments are usually more severe for completed rather than attempted crimes. How would a utilitarian and a retributivist justify this difference?

4. At his trial in Frankfurt in 1965, Bruno Schlage, a former prison bunker guard at Auschwitz and described as a 'willing and brutal recipient of orders', made the following statement before sentence. How would a retributivist, a utilitarian and a rehabilitationist view his remarks? How do you view them?

> *If I were the kind of man depicted here, I would always have been like that. A murderer isn't made in four or five years, especially not if he comes of a decent family. A murderer is born. I have no criminal record. When I became a soldier, they immediately began to lie to me. I was told I would become a member of a police unit, but instead I was assigned to the 22nd SS Standarte. I never had the chance to get myself transferred. I had the misfortune of coming to Auschwitz. When I found out that it was an extermination camp I applied for a transfer. I was told: 'You're not serious, are you?' The application was torn up and tossed into the wastebasket. When I made a second application, Sergeant Nebbe told me that I had to do my duty wherever I was sent. If I filed a third application, he said, I could think about it behind barbed wire.*
>
> *Now I ask you, Your Honour, and all those who were soldiers, what I should have done if I did not want to endanger the life of my family and my own. My answer is that I had to follow the orders of my superiors whether I wanted to or not. Your Honour, even today, in normal times, it is not simple to refuse to serve. And how much more rigorously would we have been punished had we refused to carry out orders in a time of total war? My answer is, all of us would have been shot if we had refused to obey. The oath I swore to the supreme commander (Hitler) was binding on me . . . We were not able to weigh and reject our orders. We were told these orders had to be carried out on the spot. What was the purpose of the training and lectures at Auschwitz? They only contributed to the extermination of people.[4]*

4. Quoted from Bernard Naumann, *Auschwitz*, trans Jean Steinberg, with an introduction by Hannah Arendt (London: Pall Mall Press, 1966) pp 406-407.

Bibliography: Punishment

* denotes text referred to or extracted in main text

Gerber, R J (ed with P D McAnany), *Contemporary Punishment* (Notre Dame & London: University of Notre Dame Press, 1972) Anthology of the major theories.

Grupp, Stanley E (ed) *Theories of Punishment* (Bloomington & London: Indiana University Press, 1971) Useful collection of essays on Deterrence, Retribution and Rehabilitation.

Hart, H L A *Punishment and Responsibility* (London: Oxford University Press, 1968) Essays on punishment, criminal responsibility and rehabilitation by an influential legal philosopher.

Honderich, T *Punishment: The Supposed Justifications* (London: Hutchinson, 1969) Provocative assessment of traditional theories.

Lewis, C S 'The Humanitarian Theory of Punishment'* *The Twentieth Century: An Australian Quarterly Review*, III, No. 3 (1953) Reprinted in *God in the Dock*, ed Walter Hooper (Grand Rapids: William B Eardmans, 1970) pp 287-294.

Menninger, Karl, 'The Crime of Punishment'* *Saturday Review* (1968) Extract reprinted in *Philosophy: The Basic Issues*, ed E D Klemke, A O Kline & R Hollinger (New York: St Martin's Press, 1992) pp 143-149;
     The Crime of Punishment (New York: Viking, 1968) A major defence of rehabilitation.

Mill, John Stuart, 'Parliamentary Debate on Capital Punishment Within Prisons Bill'* *Hansard Parliamentary Debates*, 3rd Series, April 21, 1868 (London: Hansard, 1868) Reprinted in *Applied Ethics*, ed Peter Singer (Oxford: Oxford University Press, 1986)

Murphy, Jeffrie G (ed) *Punishment and Rehabilitation* (Encino, Calif: Wadsworth, 1973) Excellent general anthology.

Naumann, Bernard *Auschwitz*,* trans Jean Steinberg, with an introduction by Hannah Arendt (London: Pall Mall Press, 1966)

Szasz, Thomas S *Law, Liberty and Psychiatry* (New York: Macmillan, 1963) Powerful and influential attack on theory of rehabilitation.

Chapter 4

The Theory of Immanuel Kant

Of the three theories we have looked at so far, utilitarianism, egoism, and the moral view of Socrates, it is utilitarianism and egoism that have had most in common. Each maintains, that there is a highest good - something which is good in itself - and that this alone must be the goal of the moral life. This intrinsic good they call pleasure or happiness. Each further maintains that an action is right or wrong according to whether it produces this highest good. In other words, both utilitarianism and egoism are **teleological** in character because each judges the morality of an action in terms of its consequences or effects. Where they differ is in their view of *whose* happiness should be taken into account. For the egoist, priority is given to the happiness of the individual. For the utilitarian, it is given to the greater collective happiness of everyone.

Immanuel Kant

Neither of these theories, however, has much in common with the position adopted by Socrates. Socrates, in conversation with his friend Crito, denies that any action is right because of its consequences: it is right, he says, only because it conforms to certain independently valid principles or rules - rules like 'Never harm anyone' or 'Never break your promises'. This position, is the hallmark of **deontological** ethics. These rules are not held because they promote the good but because they are good, because they provide the standard of what is right and wrong. It is true that keeping these rules may sometimes have disastrous results as Socrates' own death makes clear, but that alone can never justify the breaking of them.

It is now time to look more closely at deontological ethics, and in particular at one major problem it has left unresolved. If I am being told that certain rules have independent moral worth - independent, that is, of their possible consequences - and that I should adhere to them, then how do I know that the moral rule I think I ought to obey *has* moral worth? How do I know that it is a rule that I, and everybody else, ought to obey? After all, if your view of the world is different from mine, it seems likely that your good rule will not necessarily be my good rule. So how do I establish what *the* good rule is, the rule which is good for all and which demands absolute obligation from everyone? What we want, then, is some *method* of assessing the moral worth of rules, so that we can say of them that these, and not those, are to hold for others as well as for myself. What we require, is some sort of *test* which will enable us to pinpoint the laws to be obeyed. For this we must turn to the most influential of all theories of deontological ethics: **the theory of Immanuel Kant**.

Immanuel Kant (1724-1804) is generally regarded as one of the greatest thinkers of all time, being one of the last philosophers to construct a complete philosophical 'system', comprehensive in scope and covering most of the major issues of philosophy. This achievement is all the more remarkable because Kant, on the face of it, was a man of very limited experience. He spent his entire life in the provincial town of Königsberg in East Prussia, first as a student, than as a private tutor, and finally as Professor of Logic and Metaphysics. He never married, he never travelled, and his life followed a rigid routine which rarely altered. The German poet, Heinrich Heine, has given us an amusing description of the impression Kant made upon his neighbours:

The life of Immanuel Kant is hard to describe; he has indeed neither life nor history in the proper sense of the words. He lived an abstract, mechanical, old-bachelor existence, in a quiet remote street in Königsberg, an old city at the north-eastern boundary of Germany. I do not believe that the great cathedral clock of that city accomplished its day's work in a less passionate and more regular way than its countryman, Immanuel Kant. Rising from bed, coffee-drinking, writing, lecturing, eating, walking, everything had its fixed time; and the neighbours knew that it must be exactly half-past four when they saw Professor Kant, in his grey coat, with his cane in his hand, step out of his house door, and move towards the little limetree avenue, which is named, after him, the Philosopher's Walk. Eight times he walked up and down that walk at every season of the year; and when the weather was bad, his servant, old Lampe, was seen anxiously following him with a large umbrella under his arm, like an image of Providence. Strange contrast between the outward life of the man and his world- destroying thought. Of a truth, if the citizens of Königsberg had had any inkling of the meaning of that thought, they would have shuddered before him as before an executioner. But the good people saw nothing in him but a professor of philosophy; and when he passed at the appointed hour, they gave him friendly greetings - and set their watches.[1]

Although Kant's philosophy is sufficiently complicated to defy easy classification, one aspect of his thought should be emphasized at the beginning of our discussion. This is the importance that Kant, in common with other philosophers of the Enlightenment, attaches to man's ability to **reason**. Two of his greatest works, the *Critique of Pure Reason* (1781) and the *Critique of Practical Reason* (1788) testify to his belief that it is man's rational faculty, his ability to think objectively and apart from his own circumstances or preferences, that distinguishes him from all other creatures. A human being is essentially a rational being, and it is this that constitutes his intrinsic dignity. More than that, reason binds man to man. Since reason, Kant argues, is an innate intellectual power existing more or less equally in all men, it enables the individual to resolve his problems in a way more or less acceptable to everyone. For example, if one person, reasoning logically, concludes that a particular argument is self-contradictory, then another person, going through the same argument and also reasoning logically, will arrive at the same conclusion. *Here, reason dictates that their answers are the same.* Now, significantly enough, Kant holds that this is also true when we apply our reason to moral problems. If, for instance, I conclude, using my reason, that a particular action is right, then this, says Kant, is the conclusion that would be reached by anyone in my position. What is right for me, using my reason, is right for everyone, using their reason.

We can now see the direction Kant takes in his search for the test that will decide which moral laws should be unconditionally obeyed. *This test will be found in the operation of reason.* This is so because, if reason is universal, the moral commands generated by reason will be universal and applicable to all men. All that remains to be seen is how reason creates these rules and what these rules are. For this we must turn to Kant's famous book, *Groundwork of the Metaphysic of Morals* (1783).

---

1. Quoted by E W F Tomlin, *The Western Philosophers* (London: Hutchinson & Co, 1968) p 202.

1. The Good Will

In the *Groundwork* Kant says that, if a moral law is to be unconditionally and universally binding, it must contain something that is unconditionally and universally *good*, something that is *good in itself*, and the *highest good*. But what can this good be? Kant reviews various possibilities. There are the 'talents of the mind', like intelligence and judgement; there are qualities of character, like courage, resolution and perseverance; there are the so-called 'gifts of fortune', like power, wealth and honour; and lastly, there is the utilitarian suggestion, happiness. However, Kant rejects all these for the same reason: all are capable of making a situation *morally worse*. For example, if a criminal is intelligent or powerful or rich, his crimes are generally more serious. Similarly, if a torturer gains pleasure from his deeds, or a murderer honour from his crime, we think his actions more reprehensible, not less. All these qualities, therefore, whatever their individual merits, can on occasion create something thoroughly bad; and for this reason alone they cannot be called intrinsically good or, what Kant terms, 'good without qualification'. For what is good without qualification must be incapable of reducing the moral worth of any situation.

This being the case, what does Kant himself propose as the greatest good? He writes:

> *It is impossible to conceive anything at all in the world, or even out of it, which can be taken as good without qualification, except a* **good will**.[2]

Being a good man means, therefore, having a good will: without it, one cannot be good. But what exactly is a 'good will'? The first thing to note is that the good will 'is not good because of what it effects or accomplishes - because of its fitness for attaining some proposed end.'[3] In other words, the goodness of a good will is not derived from the goodness of its *results* - a point which underlines the deontological character of Kant's thought. After all, a murderer, willing evil, may inadvertently do good; but this unexpected turn of events would not transform his original evil desires into good ones: they remain evil, even though the consequence is good. Moreover, says Kant, if the moral value of the good will were to depend on its effects, it could no longer be considered of unconditional value. For in that case we would have to judge it merely as a means to an end, as an *instrumental* good, as a good dependent on the achievement of a result: it would not however be the *intrinsic* good, the good 'without qualification'.

In determining the moral worth of an action, whether it is or is not governed by a good will, the consequences of that action are therefore irrelevant. For Kant, it is not what an act accomplishes that is decisive, but the motive behind the act: *it is having the right intention that makes the good will good*. But what kind of intention might this be? Kant's famous reply is that a good will's only motive is *to act for the sake of duty*. In other words, a person is good when their only motive for doing something is that it is their duty to do it.

This is by no means easy to understand; and, in order to help us at this point, Kant introduces the following examples:

> *. . . it certainly accords with duty that a grocer should not overcharge his inexperienced customer; and where there is much competition a sensible shopkeeper refrains from so doing and keeps to a fixed and general price for everybody so that a child can buy from him just as well as anyone else. Thus people are served honestly; but this is not nearly enough to justify us in believing that the shopkeeper has acted in this way from duty or from principles of fair dealing; his interest required him to do so. We cannot assume him to have in addition an immediate inclination towards his customers, leading him, as it were out of love, to give no man preference over another in the matter of price. Thus the action was done neither from duty nor from immediate inclination, but solely from purposes of self-interest.*[4]

2. *Groundwork of the Metaphysic of Morals*, translated, with analysis and notes, by H J Paton in The Moral Law (London: Hutchinson & Co, 1972) p 59.
3. *Ibid*, p 60 .
4. *Ibid*, p 63 .

Kant is here telling us what doing one's duty does not involve: it does not involve serving one's own interests. This grocer is honest because being honest is good for business, not because he believes it is his duty to be honest. If he does not cheat his customers, his profits will increase. He does not therefore do what he does because it is his duty to do it, but because it serves his own ends. This, then, is not the good will at work. Of course, it may be the case that this particular grocer is also *by inclination* honest and trustworthy; that acting in this way comes naturally to him, and that he derives pleasure from it. But even this, Kant adds, does not indicate the presence of a good will. No special merit can be attached to someone who does what is natural to them, even though what they do coincides with what their duty demands. An ulterior motive still exists, to do what they *enjoy* rather than what their duty prescribes, and the possibility always remains that, if they no longer enjoyed doing it, they would do otherwise: they will be honest as long as it pleases them to be so. Thus, Kant concludes, their will fails to be the good will, just as if they had acted from self-interest.

In describing the man of good will, Kant is therefore describing the kind of motive or intention a man must have for his actions to be good. This motive, to repeat, must be entirely free from the person's self-interest or calculation of what the consequences will be of his actions. Nor is it distinguished by certain kinds of pleasurable emotion - by feelings of kindliness, generosity or love - because these have to do with a person's inclinations and not with the selfless will to do one's duty, regardless of personal desires. By contrast, the man of good will acts solely in accordance with duty and for the sake of duty; and his only motive for doing what is right is his awareness that it is the right thing to do. He does what is right because it is right, and for no other reason.

Exercise 1

Which of the following duties would Kant eliminate as examples of the good will at work? Give reasons for your answers.

> It is my duty . . .
>
> **a**   to preserve my life, even though I find life unbearable
> **b**   to commit suicide when I find life unbearable
> **c**   to keep my promise, even though my friend will suffer as a result
> **d**   to steal that bread because my children are starving
> **e**   to punish my child
> **f**   to take care of my old parents because they took care of me
> **g**   to take care of my old parents, even though they didn't take care of me
> **h**   to refuse my son the blood transfusions that will save his life because of my religious convictions
> **i**   as a parent to send my son to a good school
> **j**   as a doctor to cure this patient, even though it is Adolf Hitler
> **k**   as a motorist to obey traffic lights
> **l**   as a Nazi to kill Jews

2. The Categorical Imperative

We have learnt that, according to Kant, the morally good man is the man of good will, and that the man of good will is the man who does his duty. An action, therefore, only has moral worth if it is done from duty. We have also learnt what doing one's duty does *not* involve: it has nothing to do with obeying one's inclinations, serving one's own interests, and is not estimated in terms of consequences. So far so good. We can at least say that we know what doing one's duty *isn't*; but we have still to discover what it *is*. Kant has still to tell us where our duty *lies*.

However, we do already know two things about this, as yet unnamed, duty. The first is that, since Kant has rejected the idea that the moral worth of an action lies in its results - the teleological position - he must subscribe to the only other alternative - the deontological position, and say that the moral worth of an action lies in its obedience to a particular rule or principle regardless of inclinations, self-interest or consequences. Thus, whatever this principle or law is, it is in obeying it that we do our duty.

The second thing we know about this duty is that it must be of universal application, applicable to *everyone* irrespective of their situation. Accordingly, it must appeal to that aspect of man's nature which already binds man to man, namely, to his *reason*. This duty, in other words, must be of such a kind that to obey it is to exercise the rational faculty and not to obey it is to fall into irrational confusion. In obeying this law, then, the man of good will is exercising his reason in a moral matter, and what he does is what every reasonable man would do in similar circumstance. Conversely, making an irrational decision is contrary to acting in obedience to one's duty. For Kant, what is contradictory is immoral.

What, then, is this supreme principle of morality? What is this rule or law that the man of good will consciously or unconsciously recognizes when he obeys his duty? Kant calls it the **categorical imperative**. An imperative tells me which of my possible actions would be good, and it does this in the form of a command, expressed by the words 'I ought'. Kant gives three versions of the categorical imperative, the first and most important of which runs as follows: *I ought never to act except in such a way that I can also will that my maxim should become a universal law.*[5]

Let us first note that this imperative or command is categorical, not hypothetical. A **hypothetical imperative** tells us what actions would be good solely as a means to something else, for example, 'If I want to lose weight, I must eat less'. The point here is that the imperative (to eat less) is dependent on the desire to achieve a certain result (to lose weight); but if I didn't want to lose weight, the command would lose its force. Eating less, therefore, is not considered good in itself but only as a means to an end: it is an instrumental good.

The categorical imperative, on the other hand, is obeyed precisely because what it commands is accepted as being good in itself, as being an intrinsic good. The action is undertaken because of the very nature of the action itself and not because it is the means of achieving something else. Nor is consideration given to the possible consequences of the action. 'If you want to be respected, tell the truth' is a hypothetical imperative. The categorical equivalent, however, would read simply 'Tell the truth'. It is a command that must be obeyed for its own sake and not for any ulterior motive. All moral commands, says Kant, are of this type. The categorical imperative is the *imperative of morality*.

However, the most important feature of the categorical imperative is its emphasis on **universalizability** - the willing 'that my maxim should become a universal law' - for it is this, Kant tells us, that provides us with the method of pinpointing those laws which have universal moral worth. In other words, the test we have been looking for, the test that will tell us what rules *all of us* should obey, is whether or not the rule in question can be universalized or, as Kant puts it in another

---

5. *Ibid* p 67. Kant's third formulation is very similar: *So act that your will can regard itself at the same time as making universal law through its maxim* (p 96).

formulation, whether I can will that it become a 'law of nature'. What I must discover is whether this rule can be consistently acted upon by all those in similar circumstances; and here it is the *consistency* of the rule that is decisive.

For inconsistency, we remember, is the essence of immorality because it strikes at the very basis of our nature as rational human beings. Thus any rule which, when universalized, becomes contradictory must be dismissed as immoral. So, for example, the command 'Always accept help and never give it' lacks moral worth. It would, of course, be quite possible for *you* to obey it, but it would be quite impossible for *everybody* to obey it. It could not be universalized because, if everybody refused to help, there would be no help to receive. Thus this imperative, when extended to everybody, is contradictory and cannot therefore be accepted as a genuine moral command. Here the inability to universalize entails the lack of moral worth.

To clarify his argument at this stage, Kant gives the following four examples:

1. A man feels sick of life as the result of a series of misfortunes that have mounted to the point of despair, but he is still so far in possession of his reason as to ask himself whether taking his own life may not be contrary to his duty to himself. He now applies the test 'Can the maxim of my action really become a universal law of nature?' His maxim is 'From self-love I make it my principle to shorten my life if its continuance threatens more evil than it promises pleasure'. The only further question to ask is whether this principle of self-love can become a universal law of nature. It is then seen at once that a system of nature by whose law the very same feeling whose function is to stimulate the furtherance of life should actually destroy life would contradict itself and consequently could not subsist as a system of nature and is therefore entirely opposed to the supreme principle of all duty.

2. Another finds himself driven to borrowing money because of need. He well knows that he will not be able to pay it back; but he sees too that he will get no loan unless he gives a firm promise to pay it back within a fixed time. He is inclined to make such a promise; but he has still enough conscience to ask 'Is it not unlawful and contrary to duty to get out of difficulties in this way?' Supposing, however, he did resolve to do so, the maxim of his action would be: 'Whenever I believe myself short of money, I will borrow money and promise to pay it back, though I know that this will never be done.' Now this principle of self-love or personal advantage is perhaps quite compatible with my own entire future welfare; only there remains the question 'Is it right?' I therefore transform the demand of self-love into a universal law and frame my question thus: 'How would things stand if my maxim became a universal law?' I then see straight away that this maxim can never rank as a universal law of nature and be self-consistent, but must necessarily contradict itself. For the universality of a law that everyone believing himself to be in need can make any promise he pleases with the intention not to keep it would make promising, and the very purpose of promising, itself impossible, since no one would believe he was being promised anything, but would laugh at utterances of this kind as empty shams.

3. A third finds in himself a talent whose cultivation would make him a useful man for all sorts of purposes. But he sees himself in comfortable circumstances, and he prefers to give himself up to pleasure rather than to bother about increasing and improving his fortunate natural aptitudes. Yet he asks himself further 'Does my maxim of neglecting my natural gifts, besides agreeing in itself with my tendency to indulgence, agree also with what is called duty?' He then sees that a system of nature could indeed always subsist under such a universal law, although (like the South Sea Islanders) every man should let his talents rust and should be bent on devoting his life solely to idleness, indulgence, procreation, and, in a word, to enjoyment. Only he cannot possibly will that this should become a universal law of nature or should be implanted in us as such a law by a natural instinct. For as a rational being he necessarily wills that all his powers should be developed, since they serve him, and are given him, for all sorts of possible ends.

4. Yet a fourth is himself flourishing, but he sees others who have to struggle with great hardships (and whom he could easily help); and he thinks 'What does it matter to me? Let every one be as happy as Heaven wills or as he can make himself; I won't deprive him of anything; I won't even envy him; only I have no wish to contribute anything to his well-being or to his support in distress!' Now admittedly if such an attitude were a universal law of nature, mankind could get on perfectly well - better no doubt than if everybody prates about sympathy and goodwill, and even takes pains, on occasion, to practise them, but on the other hand cheats where he can, traffics in human rights, or violates them in other ways. But although it is possible that a universal law of nature could subsist in harmony with this maxim, yet it is impossible to will that such a principle should hold everywhere as a law of nature. For a will which decided in this way would be in conflict with itself, since many a situation might arise in which the man needed love and sympathy from others, and in which, by such a law of nature sprung from his own will, he would rob himself of all hope of the help he wants for himself.[6]

These examples tell us more about the inherent contradictory nature of all immoral actions. In the first two examples we find what Kant calls **contradictions in the law of nature**. These involve rules that cannot even be conceived as universal because they are straightforwardly self-contradictory. Such a rule would be 'Do this but don't'. There are, however, other rules, just as impossible, which do not appear so at first. Take Kant's example of keeping promises. It would be quite possible for you or I to adopt the rule. 'Only keep your promises when it is in your interest to do so'; but what would happen if this rule were universalized? A contradiction results. For if everyone could, when convenient, make a false promise, no one would trust the promises of others; and if this happened, the very practice of promise-keeping, which this rule presupposes, would be destroyed.

In examples **3.** and **4.**, we find what Kant calls **contradictions in the will**. It is quite possible to have rules which, unlike those just mentioned, are not contradictory in themselves but which the person involved could not possibly wish to see universalized. This is because the resulting situation *must* be totally unacceptable to him. Thus people who have no concern for others cannot wish that everybody should act like them because the situation might arise when they also need help. Even selfish people, pursuing their own interests, could not possibly want to live in a world in which no one helps them because pursuing their own interests may require this help. Here, then, the contradiction lies in the universalization of a rule that might later be used against them.

---

6. *Ibid*, pp 85-86.

Exercise 2

Are the following imperatives universalizable? If they are not, is this because they are contradictions in the *law of nature* or in *the will*?

---

a Come first in examinations
b Never speak until you are spoken to
c Do not give money to the poor
d Sell all you have and give to the poor
e Jump the queue
f Lie when it is convenient to do so
g Shoot first and argue later
h Be different: dye your hair blue
i Keep the population down: abstain from sexual relations
j Take what you want
k Be polite: let the other person enter first
l Defend yourself but never start the fight

In concluding this account of Kant's moral theory, it is worth repeating that at its heart stands the belief that rational beings should always treat all other rational beings equally and in the same way that they would treat themselves. This view is best expressed in Kant's second formulation of the categorical imperative, which is one of the great humanistic doctrines of the Enlightenment : *Act in such a way that you always treat humanity, whether in your own person or in the person of any other, never simply as a means, but always at the same time as an end.*[7]

Because human beings are rational beings, they have an inherent value: they are ends in themselves, counting equally one with another. Their value does not therefore consist in how they can be used by others, as means to ends: their value is intrinsic, not instrumental. The principle of universalization underlines this view of the intrinsic worth of individual men and women. Suicide is wrong because it involves a person's use of himself or herself as a means to escape an intolerable situation. Similarly, making false promises is wrong because it involves making use of someone else as a means to greater gain. As with the first formulation of the categorical imperative, the second requires that no rule of conduct which is applicable universally to all rational beings can either sanction action favouring one over another or prescribe conduct by which one being treats another as a means to an end. To do so is to demean oneself and thereby humanity at large.

---

7. *Ibid*, p 91.

Exercise 3

Analyse the following as examples of universalization:

> **a.** Being a diabetic I have to have an insulin injection every day. Since it is right for me to do this, it is right for everybody to do this. Therefore everybody should have an insulin injection every day.
>
> **b.** If I prefer pork to lamb, everybody should prefer pork to lamb.
>
> **c.** Jesus was wrong to say 'Love your enemies' because, if everyone loved their enemies, there would be no enemies left to love.

Exercise 4

According to Kant, where would your duty lie in the following examples? Where do you think your duty lies?

> **a.** In his book *Les Miserables*, Victor Hugo tells the story of an escaped convict, Jean Valjean, who, living under an assumed name, becomes a town's major benefactor, employer, and mayor. Later he discovers that an old tramp has been arrested as Jean Valjean and sentenced to the galleys. The real Valjean considers it his duty to reveal his true identity and so save the tramp from unjust punishment.
>
> **b.** A plane crashes in the Andes. Many passengers survive. However, no rescue comes and their food rapidly runs out. In this extreme situation, facing death by starvation, they consider it their duty to eat the flesh of those who did not survive the crash.
>
> **c.** Mr and Mrs Smith are Jehovah's Witnesses. Their son, David, is involved in a serious accident and requires immediate surgery. His parents are not against the operation but will not allow a blood transfusion. This, they say, is against their religious beliefs. The doctors reply that, without the transfusion, David will die.

Exercise 5

According to Kant suicide is wrong. As he argues:

to use the power of a free will for its own destruction is self-contradictory. If freedom is the condition of life it cannot be employed to abolish life and so to destroy and abolish itself. To use life for its own destruction, to use life for producing lifelessness, is self-contradictory. These preliminary remarks are sufficient to show that man cannot rightly have any power of disposal in regard to himself and his life, but only in regard to his circumstances.[8]

> This viewpoint is challenged by the Roman Stoic philosopher and poet, Lucius Annaeus Seneca (c 4 BC - AD 65.) How far do you agree or disagree with Seneca's alternative?
>
> *. . . life has carried some men with the greatest rapidity to the harbour, the harbour they were bound to reach even if they tarried on the way, while others it has fretted and harassed. To such a life, as you are aware, one should not always cling. For mere living is not a good, but living well. Accordingly, the wise man will live as long as he ought, not as long as he can. He will mark in what place, with whom, and how he is to conduct his existence, and what he is about to do. He always reflects concerning the quality, and not the quantity, of his life. As soon as there are many events in his life that give him trouble and disturb his peace of mind, he sets himself free. And this privilege is his, not only when the crisis is upon him, but as soon as Fortune seems to be playing him false; then he looks about carefully and sees whether he ought, or ought not, to end his life on that account. He holds that it makes no difference to him whether his taking-off be natural or self-inflicted, whether it comes later or earlier. He does not regard it with fear, as if it were a great loss; for no man can lose very much when but a driblet remains. It is not a question of dying earlier or later, but of dying well or ill. And dying well means escape from the danger of living ill .*[9]

---

8. *Lectures on Ethics*, trans Louis Infield (New York: Harper & Row, 1963) pp 147-148.
9. *Epistula Morales*. 'On Suicide', Leob edition, Vol. 2, trans Richard M Gummere (London: William Heinemann, 1970) pp 57-59.

Some Criticisms and Amendments of Kant

The power of Kant's argument is undeniable and its importance has increased rather than diminished with the years. Various features of his theory remain particularly attractive.

The first is that it takes account of *justice*. More specifically, it corrects the utilitarian presumption that the punishment of the innocent can be justified in terms of majority benefit. This, Kant does not allow. The morality of an action does not derive from the benefit produced or from the number of those who obtain that benefit, but from the intrinsic rightness of the action performed. Justice towards the individual is thus safeguarded by the universal, and impartial, character of the categorical imperative, which imposes duties upon us all, equally and alike. An action taken against the individual, if contrary to duty, is therefore wrong, no matter how many may think otherwise.

Kant reaches the same conclusion from a different direction, namely, in his account of man as a being of intrinsic worth. Here it is each man's dignity as a *rational creature*, as the highpoint of creation, that resists all use of him as a mere means to an end, as something to be exploited for the greater happiness of others. This point of view is well illustrated by a remark Kant made just before his death. Although very sick and weak, Kant nevertheless struggled to his feet when his doctor entered the room and refused to sit down until his visitor had taken a chair. 'The feeling for humanity,' he explained, 'has not yet left me.' This gesture is made, in other words, not because his guest is a doctor but because he is a human being. Here good manners is an expression of the respect to be accorded each man or woman as a rational being. This 'feeling for humanity' dominates Kant's entire philosophy.

Kant is also to be applauded for the sharp distinction he makes between duty and inclination. It prevents individuals from assuming that what is good for them, what brings them pleasure or benefit, is morally good, something that will be good for everyone. All of us are prone to make unjustifiable exceptions in our moral judgements - exceptions notably in favour of ourselves and our friends and to the detriment of those we dislike - but after Kant this becomes less excusable and, as a matter of logic, less consistent with the moral life. People of good will obey a law which is the same for all, and only thus do they subordinate their own natural inclinations, however generous these may be, become less self-centered and more appreciative of the rights of others. This indeed is the great strength of universalizability. For me to assert that you ought to do X in situation Y commits me, as a matter of moral necessity, to the general rule that everyone should do things like X in situations like Y. In this way, I perceive that my duties to others are no different from my duties to myself and that my rights are identical to theirs. As has been pointed out many times before, this is Kant's equivalent of the Golden Rule of Christian ethics: 'Do unto others as you would have them do unto you.'

Yet many find fault with Kant's position, in particular with his claim that moral people are those who must conduct their lives solely in obedience to the rules generated by the categorical imperative. For if this is the case, they argue, then doing one's duty must also include obeying rules towards which we feel no moral obligation whatsoever, or obeying rules which allow for the very exceptions that Kant sought to eliminate in his distinction between duty and inclination. Consider the following maxims:

1. Whenever anybody buys a new book, the purchaser should write his or her name on the fly-leaf.
2. Whenever anyone is over six feet tall, bald, without his right ear and little finger of his left hand, and working in Manchester as a nuclear physicist, he may be excused paying income tax.

The important thing to notice about these maxims is that neither is self-contradictory and that both are universalizable according to Kant's criteria (Whenever anyone is X, they are to do Y.) Yet, in the first example, we have a rule which is neither good nor bad but morally neutral, and which few would hold to be obligatory; and, in the second, a rule so precisely defined that it benefits no one but a particular individual. This being so, it cannot be correct to say, as Kant does, that the moral person is one who acts in accordance with the categorical imperative. For while there are many actions which the process of universalization rightly condemns, it is also quite possible, by the same procedure, to arrive at rules that the majority of us would consider either preferential or without moral significance. What these examples tell us, then, is that the ability of a rule to be universalized does not of itself guarantee that the rule will be morally good or even moral at all.

How, therefore, is the person of good will to decide whether a suggested rule is a good one? In his discussion of the so-called **contradictions in the will**, Kant suggests a way out of this difficulty, and indeed offers us a kind of practical test. We can reject those rules which, if universalized, would produce a state of affairs utterly objectionable to all rational people. Thus no individuals can rationally will that the helpless should never be helped because, as rational beings, they necessarily desire their own happiness, and to achieve this they will sometimes require the help of others. They must reject what is contrary to the objectives that all rational people must have.

But this is not very helpful. What Kant appears to overlook is that, while all people may be rational, we do not all have the same temperaments or desires, and that consequently *we do not all find the same situations intolerable.* Who is to say, for instance, that sadists would not wish to see sadism universalized? They might well prefer to have sadism universally practised, with themselves as both practitioners and victims, rather than to have no such practices at all. Similarly, thieves might well prefer stealing universalized, believing that they still stand to gain financially, even though their own property is at greater risk. Or consider Kant's own example of 'Never help the helpless'. Now it may well be true and rational beings, neither liking nor wanting to see their interests frustrated, will dislike this rule applying to themselves; but that is very different from saying that they will consider the universalization of this rule morally unjustified, that they will think this rule immoral when it applies to everybody, including themselves. Again, this depends on the temperament of the person concerned. A ruthless landlord, evicting his tenants, may well concede that he would not like the same thing happening to him; but that doesn't mean that he considers their eviction wrong, or that he wouldn't consider his own eviction right, if he were in their place. Indeed, one suspects that there are many people who think like this, who accept that, just as they neglect others, others may neglect them. This, after all, is the capitalistic doctrine of self-help, according to which the individual realizes that life is cut-throat and competitive and accepts the chance of failure in the pursuit of success. But there is nothing *irrational* in this. What would be irrational is if such an individual positively wanted his interests neglected or liked it when they were. There is nothing irrational in a *man of this type* accepting that others may treat him as ruthlessly as he treats others.

An equally damaging criticism can be made of Kant's so-called **contradictions in nature.** Telling lies or breaking promises is always wrong, he says, because neither can be consistently universalized. If we attempted to do so, we should quickly find the very business of telling the truth and keeping promises collapsing. For this reason the prohibition against lying and breaking promises is absolute and as such applies to everyone without exception.

But again, the problem lies in Kant's exclusion of exceptions. Must telling the truth *always* be right, irrespective of the circumstances in which I find myself? Can there be *no* situations in which, say, telling a lie is morally justified? There are, of course, many people who would agree with Kant about the absoluteness of certain rules. Conscientious objectors, who refuse to fight whatever the circumstances because 'life is sacred', are adopting his position, as indeed are those who oppose capital punishment for the same reason. But many others would disagree and say that there are times when making an exception is morally permissable: that fighting Hitler was one such exception and that hanging terrorists is another. Indeed, if exceptions are always disallowed, it is quite easy to imagine situations in which either no decision is possible or in which the decision made is morally reprehensible.

Take, for example, a situation where our *duties conflict*. If it is always wrong to break a promise and always wrong to tell a lie, what happens when I have to tell a lie to keep a promise? Suppose I promise a friend that I will hide him from a murderer, and that the murderer later asks me where my friend is. How am I to reply? If I tell the truth, I break a promise; and if I keep the promise, I must tell a lie. It is a major weakness of Kant's theory that it provides no answer to this dilemma. Most of us, however, would resolve it quite easily: we would introduce an exception to the rule about truth-telling, which would avoid the evil consequences of our friend's death (eg, 'tell the truth, except when it leads to the death of an innocent person'). Making exceptions of this kind also helps us to resolve another problem. What would happen if I had made no promise to hide my friend? In that case, there is no conflict of duty and I am duty bound to tell the murderer the truth. In other words, if I do not here make an exception, my duty obliges me to do something which, in all probability, I regard as morally reprehensible. Thus, in these examples, Kant's theory leads either to a kind of moral stalemate, in which no moral decision can be made, or to a situation in which I may well regard doing my duty as being equivalent to doing wrong.

1. The Theory of W D Ross

It is because of problems like these that an important amendment has been made to Kant's ethics by the modern philosopher W D Ross (1877-1971.) Kantian duties, Ross argues, should not be taken as absolute duties but as duties *which allow exceptions*. These duties Ross calls ***prima facie* duties** (*prima facie* meaning 'at first sight'). A *prime facie* duty is a non-absolute or conditional duty, a duty which can always be overridden by a more compelling duty. So 'Never take a human life' is a *prima facie* duty: it is not something I must always do but something I must do only when it is not outweighed by another and more compelling obligation or rule of *prima facie* duty (eg 'Never take a human life except in self-defence'). Such obligations arise from the situations in which I find myself, and may, says Ross, be classified into six groups, of which the first two are past-looking and the rest future-looking:

*1. **Duties of fidelity** in which I act in accordance with a former promise of mine; and **duties of reparation** in which I act to make amends for my previous wrongful act.*
*2. **Duties of gratitude** in which I act to repay a debt (ie services done by other men to me).*
*3. **Duties of justice** in which I act to obtain an equal distribution of pleasure and happiness.*
*4. **Duties of beneficence** in which I act to better the lot of others in respect of virtue or of intelligence or of pleasure.*
*5. **Duties of self-improvement** in which I act to improve myself in respect of virtue or of intelligence.*
*6. **Duties of nonmalificence** in which I refrain from doing people harm.*[1]

To see how this works, let us take the duty of gratitude. If I see my father and a famous doctor drowning, whom should I save? The utilitarian, we remember, will urge me to save the doctor because of the greater good accruing to mankind. Yet many of us would find this advice repugnant because we have a special duty of gratitude to our parents, who have cared for us and supported us, which outweighs any duty I might have to a stranger, no matter how much happiness his life will bring to the greater number. This, then, says Ross, is an entirely personal duty owed to a particular person on the basis of who they are and what they have done for us: it is also entirely past-looking and not future-looking.

As we shall see in a moment. Ross's list, which he admits is incomplete, presents its own problems. More immediately, his theory has the great merit of extending the range of our duties beyond that prescribed by Kant. Indeed, once we realize what is required of a duty to be absolute and exceptionless, we soon see that few, if any, duties can be regarded in this way. Invariably, there is some situation in which an absolute Kantian duty can be overridden. Thus, it is not enough to say with Kant that, for a duty to be a moral duty, it must be capable of consistent universalization. For as Ross indicates, there is no such thing as a rule without possible exceptions. In making these exceptions much will depend on the circumstance in which my duty is done, on the probable consequences of doing my duty, and on the personal relation that may exist between myself and those to whom I believe a duty is owed.

---

1. W D Ross. *The Right and the Good* (Oxford University Press, 1930) p 21.

Exercise 6

Apart from saying that the duty of nonmaleficence is in general more binding than the duty of beneficence, Ross does not place his *prima facie* duties in any order of importance. One order has been suggested by Richard Purtill.[2] Do you agree with his ranking? If not, how would you alter or add to it?

> **a.** Not to harm others
> **b.** To make reparations for harm done by us
> **c.** To keep our commitments
> **d.** To repay our benefactors
> **e.** To treat people as well as they deserve to be treated
> **f.** To do some good to some people, deserving or not
> **g.** To improve ourselves in some ways

There are two outstanding objections to Ross's theory:
1. How do we know what a *prima facie* duty actually is?
2. How do we know which *prima facie* duty to obey when there is a conflict between them?
Ross's reply to both questions is the same. Both the utilitarian and Kantian theories make the mistake of assuming that an absolute criterion of what is right and wrong can be found, the one using the criterion of pleasure, the other of duty. Given the infinite variety and range of our pleasures and duties, not to mention the infinite range of their effects, it was inevitable, says Ross, that no such criterion, whether teleological or deontological, could be achieved. This is not to say, however, that our ethical decisions are without cognitive value. We simply *know* that acts like fulfilling a promise, or effecting a just distribution of good, or promoting the good of others are *prima facie* right; and we know that they are simply by consulting our deepest moral convictions. That these things are right is 'self-evident' to us, not in the sense that we have always known that they are, nor in the sense that we can prove that they are, but in the sense that 'we have reached sufficient mental maturity' just to know that they are. They have become, like the axioms of geometry or arithmetic, instances of knowledge and part of the fundamental nature of the universe:

> *It would be a mistake to found a natural science on 'what we really think', ie on what reasonably thoughtful and well-educated people think about the subjects of the science before they have studied them scientifically. For such opinions are interpretations, and often misinterpretations, of sense-experience; and the man of science must appeal from these to sense-experience itself, which furnishes his real data. In ethics no such appeal is possible. We have no more direct way of access to the facts about rightness and goodness and about what things are right or good, than by thinking about them; the moral convictions of thoughtful and well-educated people are the data of ethics just as sense-perceptions are the data of a natural science. Just as some of the latter have to be rejected as illusory, so have some of the former; but as the latter are rejected only when they are in conflict with other more accurate sense-perceptions, the former are rejected only when they are in conflict with other convictions which stand better the test of reflection. The existing body of moral convictions of the best people is the cumulative product of the moral reflection of many generations, which has developed an extremely delicate power of appreciation of moral distinctions; and this the theorist cannot afford to treat with anything other than the greatest respect. The verdicts of the moral consciousness of the best people are the foundation on which he must build; though he must first compare them with one another and eliminate any contradictions they may contain.[3]*

2. *Thinking about Ethics* (Englewood Cliffs, NJ: Prentice-Hall, 1976) p 44.
3. *Op cit*, pp 40-41.

Many find this answer unsatisfactory. What would happen, for example, if a person decided that returning services rendered was *not* a *prima facie* duty or that the duty of retribution (not included in Ross's list) was? Presumably Ross would then claim that this person did not possess 'sufficient mental maturity' to make a proper judgement or had somehow misread his own mind, in which case this person's inner moral convictions cannot be considered, as Ross supposes, knowledge of self-evident truths. What we require here, and what Ross does not give us, is some method for determining when a person is morally mature and when he has read his moral convictions correctly. Moreover, to rely upon the moral convictions of other people as the data of ethics, albeit those who are thoughtful and well-educated, is to assume that these are the 'best people' precisely because they know what a *prima facie* duty is: that indeed they possess what Ross denied they could possess, namely, a criterion for deciding between a right and wrong action.

Exercise 7

How do you think Kant and Ross would resolve the following dilemmas? How would you resolve them?

> **a.** A friend of yours, who once saved your life, has committed murder and asks you to hide him. Should you?
>
> **b.** You are a trade union leader involved in a lengthy strike. Many of your members are already impoverished. Are you justified in relieving their distress by accepting funds from a universally despised foreign power?
>
> **c.** Your child will die unless he undergoes an expensive operation. You are a poor man. Would you be justified in obtaining this money illegally?
>
> **d.** A wife suspects that her husband, with whom she has been happily married for many years, is a spy. He is due to retire in a year. Should she inform the authorities immediately?
>
> **e.** Would you be justified in blackmailing a landlord into reducing his rents in a seriously deprived area?
>
> **f.** Would you, as a doctor, consider it your duty to inform the parents of a fourteen year old girl that she is using contraceptives?
>
> **g.** You have information about a Mafia shipment of heroin into this country. If the shipment is seized by the police, the Mafia will know you were the informer and will seek to kill you. Should you tell the police?
>
> **h.** Your cellmate, who is old and dying, helps you escape and tells you where a large amount of money is hidden. His only condition is that you promise to support his family. You agree, find the treasure, but then discover that the business that your own family depends on is going bankrupt. Should you invest your cellmate's money?

2. Rule-Utilitarianism

In as much as it contains both deontological and teleological elements, Ross's theory is a hybrid. He accepts with Kant that there are certain rules of duty that we are obliged to fulfil (notably the past-looking duties of fidelity and gratitude); and at the same time he accepts with the utilitarians that we are not obliged to obey these rules if the consequences of so doing should prove disastrous. The fact that we have made a promise is always a strong moral reason for keeping it; but this promise may not hold in all circumstances and may be outweighed by more urgent obligations (notably by the future-looking duties of beneficence, self-improvement and nonmalificence.)

Ross's theory has much in common with a further amendment of Kantian ethics: **rule-utilitarianism**. This, the last theory of normative ethics we shall examine, is also a hybrid: it agrees with Ross about the centrality of rules and also accepts that sometimes the consequences of obeying them require the breaking of them; but these conclusions are reached for very different reasons. Rule-utilitarianism has no concept of *prima facie* duty, it denies that there are any past-looking duties, and, above all, it provides an absolute criterion of judgement for making moral decisions. Accordingly many believe it overcomes the objections levelled against Ross.

It will be remembered that, following Bentham, the ultimate criterion of ethical judgment is the *principle of utility*: an action is right if it brings pleasure (or prevents pain) and wrong if it brings pain (and prevents pleasure.) But the principle of utility, here applying to actions - hence the more specific description of Bentham's theory as 'act-utilitarianism' - can equally well apply to rules. All we have to do is evaluate the rule in terms of whether anyone obeying it will maximize overall happiness or unhappiness. What we have to do, in other words, is determine whether, *if everyone obeyed this rule*, it would promote the greatest good or not. If it does, then any action which conforms to that rule will be deemed right and any that does not will be deemed wrong.

For example, consider the question, 'Should I drive on the left or the right?' If the reply to this is, 'Well, it depends on my needs at the time: it might be on the left one day and on the right the next', the results would be clearly disastrous for motorists and pedestrians alike. For this reason one consults the law of the land, knowing that in this instance safety is best served by everybody doing the same thing. In other words, the principle of utility here dictates that everyone should act, and always act, in accordance with a specific rule. This avoids the hazards of individual choice. If the law states 'Always drive on the right', then the action of doing so is right because it conforms to the law.

In act-utilitarianism, therefore, right action is determined solely by that action's consequences. In rule-utilitarianism right action is determined not by the action's consequences but by the consequences of the rule under which that action is performed. More precisely, what distinguishes the two forms of utilitarianism is the extent to which rule-utilitarianism *incorporates Kant's notion of universalizability*: it is the consequences of a rule's universalization which determine whether it is a good or bad rule. Where rule-utilitarianism parts company from Kant is in evaluating the rule in terms of its consequences and in therefore retaining the principle of utility as the ultimate criterion of all moral decision.

We can make this distinction clearer with another example. Suppose a teacher sees an able and otherwise reliable student cheating in an examination. Nobody else has seen him cheating and the examination is crucial for the student's career and for his young family. What should the teacher do? As an act-utilitarian he could argue that, given the disastrous consequences for the student, he should turn a blind eye particularly since his action, being performed in secret, cannot set a bad example to others. The rule-utilitarian, however, would argue differently. While the teacher in this particular case may do more good for this particular student by saying nothing, and while it may be true that saying nothing can have no consequences for future cases because nobody will ever find out, it is still a bad thing to do because if *everybody* did this the whole business of taking examinations would be undermined. The fact indeed that it was done in secret - which for the act-utilitarian was an important consideration in limiting the possible evil consequences of his action - only makes it worse because nobody would then know who was keeping silent and nobody would then know whether the results of *any* examination were accurate. Here, then, it is the disastrous consequences of universalizability which decide the issue. The belief that the teacher did wrong comes not from our conviction that cheating doesn't produce happiness - in the case of the student it probably did - but from our conviction that even greater unhappiness would result if we universalized the rule under which the teacher operated. The teacher's action is condemned, therefore, not because of what *he* did, but because, to put the matter in Kantian terms, the maxim of his action - 'Allow cheating if it produces happiness' - would, if universalized, have evil results. Here again utility determines which rule applies.

Exercise 8

How would a rule-utilitarian deal with the following commands?

a. Since everybody smokes in the cinema anyway, ignore the signs telling you not to

b. Always help your own children more than other people's

c. Try to escape from prison if the law has convicted you of a crime you didn't commit

d. Steal from the rich to give to the poor

e. If you disapprove of the war, escape the draft

f. Never give a pupil extra marks in public but in secret only

g. Don't become a vegetarian: too many people eat meat for your action to make any difference

h. Catholic priests don't marry, so neither should you

i. If a tax includes payment for nuclear weapons, don't pay it

Rule-utilitarians maintain that their position resolves two outstanding issues: The problem of conflicting duties, which faced both Kant and Ross, and the problem of justice, which faced the act-utilitarians.

1. The Problem of Conflicting Duties. Ross, like Kant before him, provides no criterion by which to decide which duty to obey when duties conflict; all he claims is that the person concerned, through a process of introspection, will somehow know which to choose. Rule-utilitarianism, however, does appeal to an absolute criterion - the principle of utility - and it does so in such a way that the specific circumstances in which the conflict occurs are taken into account. For instance, consider again the Kantian dilemma: If 'Never break a promise' and 'Never tell a lie' are both categorical imperatives, what do I tell the murderer who wants to kill the friend I have promised to protect? If I tell him where my friend is, I break a promise; if I keep the promise, I must tell a lie.[4] What rule-utilitarianism asks here is: Which rule will maximize happiness in this particular case? Clearly telling a lie. In other words, the imperative 'Never break a promise' is rejected following the application of the principle of utility to the specific circumstances in which I find myself.

This procedure has two important implications for rule-making. The first is that, in tying the rule to the situation, it inevitably makes the rule more complicated. We are no longer faced with the simplicity of Kantian absolutes like 'Never kill' - a command given irrespective of consequences - but with a whole host of separate commands which may deal with killing in self-defence, killing in war, killing as a legal deterrent, killing as an act of mercy, and so on. But any of these rules, although more complicated, is still better than the Kantian rule because they address themselves to the actual rather than the general case and because any possible conflict of duty can be resolved through the empirical test of utility. This test, rule-utilitarians insist, is entirely future-looking, and applies even to such duties as making restitution for harm done or the obligation of gratitude to our parents. Once again these are upheld not because, as Ross maintained, they involve special *prima facie* duties to special people but because a society in which these rules are generally held will be better - that is, will be capable of maximizing happiness more effectively - than one in which they are not. Their assessment remains teleological.

The second implication for rule-making is as follows. For Kant and Ross the obligation to obey certain rules stands irrespective of the conditions existing in any particular society: their universality requires obedience no matter what the time or place. In rule-utilitarianism, however, the principle of utility generates rules that may be applicable to one society but not to another. For example, a rule to preserve the water supply will be beneficial in the Sahara but not in Scotland. A rule requiring rigorous birth control will be applicable in China but not in a seriously depopulated area. Not all rules, however, are of this character. There will be some rules that are so basic to the welfare of any society and the preservation of its citizens - eg the rules against wantonly killing people - that they have universal application. The point to remember, however, is that the fact that people and societies disagree in their ethical judgements does not upset the normative ethical principle espoused by rule-utilitarianism. Despite the historical or cultural differences that may exist between societies, it is still the rules generated by the principle of utility which will determine whether an action is right or wrong in any given case.

2. The Problem of Justice. It will be remembered that one of the criticisms levelled against act-utilitarianism was that it does not adequately take account of justice; does not secure an *equal distribution* of happiness and need not, therefore, deal with the individual according to his or her deserts or merits. Thus a utilitarian judge would be justified in condemning an innocent man to

---

4. See above p 107.

death if he or she believed that a greater good would result, such as restoring law and order.[5] Can the same criticism be levelled against rule-utilitarianism?

Needless to say, Rule-Utilitarians argue that it cannot. In the example just given, the question to ask is: 'What would be the consequences of having a rule which sanctioned the punishment of the innocent?' The effects would clearly be disastrous. The institution of such a rule - the general acceptance that punishment could be administered without regard to desert - would destroy our trust in the law, which is necessary for the maintenance of society, and induce in us a constant fear of arrest. It is, therefore, because rule-utilitarianism integrates the Kantian principle of universalizability with the principle of utility that it can see that justice is done to the individual; that indeed it can safeguard the rights of the citizen under the law by maintaining that, if the action of condemning an innocent person is wrong for me to do, it is wrong for everybody to do.

But here we hit a snag. In the argument just presented, justice is taken to be a part of utility, one of those conditions that goes towards maximizing happiness. But is it an *essential* condition? It would appear not. The rule-utilitarian is saying that justice is assured *only as long as* the general practice of being just actually does maximize happiness; but this implies also that, if justice doesn't do this, it can be jettisoned in favour of something else, something perhaps that we would now regard as blatantly unjust, something that does not secure an equal distribution of justice. Rule-utilitarianism has already allowed that different rules will be appropriate for different societies. In that case, it could be argued that slavery is justified in a country facing economic ruin through a labour shortage. But do we really want to say that slavery is just? It may in this instance achieve a greater balance of happiness over unhappiness but the slave is still a slave and forced to be so: he has become a slave not as a punishment for things he did but for the benefits he will bring to others (and in which he may not share.) A rule, therefore, that maximizes happiness may yet be unjust in the way it distributes happiness. Thus, although rule-utilitarianism can accommodate justice in a way that act-utilitarianism cannot, it still provides no guarantee that it will. The principle of utility is, accordingly, double-edged - it may justify either justice or injustice; and, since everything depends on the situation at hand, there is no guarantee that utility will not be best served by injustice.

It is because of this objection that a final amendment is made to rule-utilitarianism, sometimes known as **extended rule-utilitarianism**. This involves making the principle of justice - or, more precisely, the principle of just distribution - not subordinate to but equal to the principle of utility. Justice is now no longer derivative but fundamental, an essential condition of moral action. Actions are, therefore, *deemed right or wrong according to the rules generated by the twin principles of utility and justice*. The principle of utility is upheld because the teleological (and utilitarian) proposition that people do have a moral obligation to secure a balance of happiness over unhappiness is accepted: but how this balance will be distributed can only be decided by the principle of justice. This principle is upheld, therefore, because the deontological (and Kantian) proposition that people have an intrinsic right to equal treatment is also accepted. This is not to say, however, that these two principles must always operate conjointly. Each can generate separate obligations. Thus, for example, we derive the obligation not to do injury primarily from the principle of utility, and the obligation to secure equality before the law primarily from the principle of justice; other obligations, like telling the truth or helping the underpriviledged, may be properly construed from either. But however we may apportion rule to principle, it is on the basis of these two principles that rules can be constructed which will lead to a state in which a maximum balance of good over evil is as equally and extensively distributed as possible.

Those who adopt this amended form of rule-utilitarianism concede that sometimes the principles of utility and justice will conflict. It is, they say, difficult to accept that a small injustice can never win a greater justice or that unequal treatment can never produce a greater good. Is killing *never* right or truth-telling *never* wrong? The problem of conflict therefore remains; but if it does perhaps it should now be seen as an irreducible tension in the act of moral decision. All

---

5. See above p 76.

we can reasonably hope for is that, when these conflicts occur, the decisions we make will increase the sum total of human happiness while yet safeguarding the individual's right to be treated 'always as an end and never as a means only'.

Questions: The Theories of Kant and Ross

1. How does Kant base his ethics on the concept of reason?

2. How does the categorical imperative help decide between right and wrong action? Give examples when you think it does not help.

3. 'Don't do unto others as you would have them do unto you: their tastes may be different!'(George Bernard Shaw.) Discuss.

4. Is George, who resisted the temptation to kill you, morally superior to Jack, who never thought of killing you at all? In what way does this question pose a problem for Kant's distinction between duty and inclination? How do you think Kant would resolve it?

5. Kant tells us to treat individuals 'always as an end and never as a means only'. Give examples in modern society of people being used as mere 'means'. What alternative treatments would you propose?

6. What problem is Ross's notion of *prima facie* duty trying to solve? Does it succeed?

7. Do you agree with Ross that we have a 'moral sense' which tells us what is right and wrong? What difficulties are there in thinking this?

8. 'Rule-utilitarianism is no more than a disguised form of act-utilitarianism, with all the same old problems'. Discuss.

9. Is it wrong to deceive a man engaged in criminal activity?

10. Read the following extract. What are the problems involved? How would Kant, Ross and the rule-utilitarians deal with them?

> *When I was a fourth-year student, William Sidney Thayer - the great professor of medicine at Hopkins, that wonderful understanding warm human being - came to Harvard and gave a Care of the Patient lecture. He described malignant disease and told how you handled it and how you always had to tell the patient the truth. This was a vivid experience for me. He described a patient who had come to him in Baltimore because he had been put off by physicians elsewhere. He knew he wasn't getting the answer, and so it was easy, I suppose, for Dr Thayer to know that the thing to do was to tell him. The patient wanted it; that was why he came to Baltimore. So he told him. The fellow, of course, was upset; and his wife was angry with Dr Thayer. He said she berated him; 'What right did you have to tell him?' Then, two hours later, he got a telephone call. They had gone back to their hotel, and called Dr Thayer to thank him for having told, because for the first time in several months, the two of them could sit down and talk.*

That was a vivid model, and now I think of my mistakes. A woman had obvious cancer of the thyroid, and knew it. She knew it because of the way her physicians dodged telling her; everybody was alarmed. Any fool could see that her doctors were alarmed; so she made me promise the night before the operation, religiously promise, that I would tell her the truth. She suspected the truth; she outlined to me the number of reasons she needed to know. She was a widow; her children were not quite launched and so on; and I had to tell her for very practical reasons. So it was. It was a rapidly growing, undifferentiated carcinoma, the type with a wretched prognosis, perhaps nine months or a year, and it would have to be treated by radiation.

So I waited until she was over the anaesthetic, and the next morning I came in, pulled up a chair next to her, sat down by her bedside, and said: 'I will now do what you asked me to do. You have a serious condition: we are going to give you X-ray treatment. There is no doubt that these treatments will help you. It is possible we will manage to eliminate the trouble completely, but just the same you had better do what you said about rearranging your estate and taking care of your children and so on.' She thanked me very much, and I went out with great relief, thinking that I had carried it off. In the next two or three days, I was congratulating myself because she had taken it so well; I must have done a good job. On the fourth postoperative day, the nurse stopped me before I entered the room. 'You know, Mrs B is waiting. She wants to know when you are going to fulfill your promise and tell her what you found.' I was younger then than I am now; I failed to take advantage of the broad hint offered me by the patient, namely, that she had shut out the bad news. So I went in and I said, 'I hear from your nurse that I haven't told you. Don't you recall that the very day after the operation I told you?' 'Told me what?' So I went over it again. She, of course, went into a serious depression; and it was terrible. It ruined her life and, what is more, mistakes seem to be contagious. To make a long story short, the pathologist and I thought this was an undifferentiated carcinoma. It wasn't; it was one of those very peculiar tumors. The same type of tumor was found in the wall of her stomach four years later. She lived for 12 years after that to die of a coronary.[6]

6. Oliver M Cope, *Man, Mind, and Machine* (Philadelphia: J B Lippincott, 1968) pp 28-29.

Bibliography: The Theory of Immanuel Kant

* denotes text referred to or extracted in main text

Acton, H B *Kant's Moral Philosophy* (London: Macmillan, 1970)

Aune, Bruce *Kant's Theory of Morals* (Princeton, NJ: Princeton University Press, 1979)

Cope, Oliver M *Man, Mind, and Machine** (Philadelphia: J B Lippincott, 1968)

Glickman, Jack (ed) *Moral Philosophy: An Introduction* (New York: St Martin's Press, 1976) An anthology of articles on Kantian ethics.

Kant, I *Groundword of the Metaphysic of Morals*,* translated, with analysis and notes, by J J Paton in *The Moral Law* (London: Hutchinson & Co., 1972);

   Kant on the Foundation of Morality (Bloomington & London: Indiana University Press, 1970) A modern version of the *Groundwork*, trans with a commentary by B E A Liddell;

   Lectures on Ethics,* trans Louis Infield (New York: Harper & Row, 1963)

Kemp, John *The Philosophy of Kant* (Oxford: Oxford University Press, 1979) Ch 3.

Korner, S *Kant* (Harmondsworth: Penguin Books, 1955)

Paton, H J *The Categorical Imperative* (London: Hutchinson's University Library, 1946) A detailed account of Kant's moral philosophy.

Ross, W D *Kant's Ethical Theory* (Oxford: Oxford University Press, 1954)

Seneca, Lucius Annaeus *Epistulae Morales*,* Vol 2, trans Richard M Gummere (London: William Heinemann, 1970) pp 57-59.

Tomlin, E W F *The Western Philosophers** (London: Hutchinson & Co, 1968) pp 197-214.

Walker, Ralph C S *Kant* (London: Routledge & Kegal Paul, 1978) Ch 11.

Ward, Keith *The Development of Kant's View of Ethics* (Oxford: Basil Blackwell, 1972) Ch 7 contains a clear exposition of the *Groundwork.*

Williams, Bernard *Ethics and the Limits of Philosophy* (London: Collins, 1985) Especially Ch 4.

Williams, T C *The Concept of the Categorical Imperative* (Oxford: Clarendon Press, 1968) An account of various interpretations of Kant's moral theory.

Some Criticisms and Amendments of Kant

Ewing, A C Ethics (London: The English Universities Press, 1969) Excellent chapters on Kant and Ross (and Moore).

Lyons, David *Forms and Limits of Utilitarianism* (Oxford: Clarendon Press, 1964) A difficult book, questioning the validity of the distinction between act- and rule-utilitarianism.

Narveson, J *Morality and Utility* (Baltimore, Maryland: The Johns Hopkins Press, 1967) Ch 4 on rule-utilitarianism.

Nowell-Smith, Patrick *Ethics* (Baltimore: Pelican Books, 1954) Especially Ch 16.

Ross, W D *The Right and the Good* *(Oxford: Oxford University Press, 1930)

Singer, Marcus *Generalization in Ethics* (New York: Random House, 1961) An influential book, arguing that universalization (or generalization) is the fundamental, but not the only, principle required by morality.

Smart, J J C *Outlines of a Utilitarian System of Ethics* (London: Cambridge University Press, 1961) A powerful defence of rule-utilitarianism.

Discussion The Morality of War

When is war morally permissible? For the **Kantian**, the decisive objection to war is that it involves the death of the innocent. Kant himself was a retributivist and so maintained the principle that punishment must be linked to desert; but in the killing of those who have committed no crime we see this principle denied. To that extent, war punishes without justification. Additionally, killing the innocent is contrary to two major elements in Kant's ethical teaching: first, in treating human life as an expendable commodity, it reduces human beings to the level of an object or thing and so denies them their unique status as rational human beings; and second, it contradicts the principle of universalization: it condones a course of action which, if applied to everyone including myself, would create a world which I myself must condemn (namely, a world without justice, in which I am no longer protected by my own innocence.) For these reasons, it is no less wrong and no more justifiable to kill innocent people in time of war than at any other time. Just as Kantians react with moral abhorrence to the judicial murder of an innocent man to quell a rebellion, so they react with equal outrage to the sacrifice of innocent men, women and children for military or political goals. Of course, in an age of thermonuclear weapons, when possible noncombatant casualties are numbered in millions, this is tantamount to condemning modern warfare as such. Suppose country A is attacked by country B, and that this attack is unprovoked and inititated for evil reasons. Suppose further that, in this situation, there is nothing wrong in A defending itself and even killing its attackers. If it should happen that, in retaliation, innocent lives are lost, then the defender has acted immorally. Since, therefore, it is inevitable that innocent people will be killed in any modern war, any war fought today must be condemned as unjustified.

The **utilitarian** approaches this situation very differently. Here the justification of military action is not based on whether war contravenes certain fundamental moral principles, like 'never kill the innocent', but on whether it produces certain results. If an act of war obtains a greater overall balance of happiness over unhappiness, then, as the principle of utility stipulates, that act is morally permissible. Thus, in estimating the morality of a defensive or offensive war against country B, everything depends on whether the benefit to be gained by country A will outweigh the pain of those who are killed, injured or bereaved in the process. However this benefit may be construed, the sacrifice of the innocent to obtain it is justified if it contributes to the greater collective happiness. In a nuclear situation, of course, this conclusion becomes less clear-cut. For while the possession of nuclear weapons may have the laudable utilitarian effect of deterring the enemy, the power of that threat depends on the real possibility of their use. Their use, however, destroys the utilitarian benefit, because there can be no gain obtained in a war of mutual destruction. The utilitarian can therefore be just as vehement in the condemnation of nuclear warfare as the Kantian. It is not the death of innocent people that is objected to - though regrettable, this can be excused in terms of 'military necessity' - but rather the use of a weapon which inflicts pain out of all proportion to the military or political advantages gained by its use.

A third and no less influential position, somewhere between the Kantian and the utilitarian,is adopted by the great medieval philosopher and theologian, **St Thomas Aquinas** (1224/5-1274). While accepting (with Kant) that warfare is essentially wrong in its shedding of blood, Aquinas believed that at least three conditions have to be met for a war to be 'just', the second and third of which are distinctly utilitarian in tone. These are: **1.** right authority (*autoritas principia*, ie the war must be declared and waged by the legitimate government of the nation concerned);**2.** sufficient cause (*justa causa*, ie the war must be waged to prevent or rectify a real injury); and **3.** right intention (*recta intentio*, ie the methods employed must be sufficient for victory and not disproportionately savage).

Aquinas clarifies his position as follows:

Three things are required for any war to be just. The first is the authority of the sovereign on whose command war is waged. Now a private person has no business declaring war; he can seek redress by appealing to the judgement of his superiors. Nor can he summon together whole people, which has to be done to fight a war. Since the care of the commonweal is committed to those in authority they are the ones to watch over the public affairs of the city, kingdom or province in their jurisdiction. And just as they use the sword in lawful defence against domestic disturbance when they punish criminals, as Paul says, **"He beareth not the sword in vain for he is God's minister, an avenger to execute wrath upon him that doth evil"**, *so they lawfully use the sword of war to protect the commonweal from foreign attacks. Thus it is said to those in authority,* **"Rescue the weak and the needy, save them from the clutches of the wicked"**. *Hence Augustine writes,* **"The natural order conducive to human peace demands that the power to counsel and declare war belongs to those who hold the supreme authority"**.

Secondly, a just cause is required, namely that those who are attacked are attacked because they deserve it on account of some wrong they have done. So Augustine, **"We usually describe a just war as one that avenges wrongs, that is, when a nation or state has to be punished either for refusing to make amends for outrages done by its subjects, or to restore what it has seized injuriously"**.

Thirdly, the right intention of those waging war is required, that is, they must intend to promote the good and to avoid evil. Hence Augustine writes, **"Among true worshippers of God those wars are looked on as peace-making which are waged neither from aggrandisement nor cruelty, but with the object of securing peace, or repressing the evil and supporting the good"**. *Now it can happen that even given a legitimate authority and a just cause for declaring war, it may yet be wrong because of a perverse intention. So again Augustine says,* **"The craving to hurt people, the cruel thirst for revenge, the unappeased and unrelenting spirit, the savageness of fighting on, the lust to dominate, and suchlike - all these are rightly condemned in wars"**.[1]

What sets Aquinas' argument apart from those of the Kantians and the utilitarians is his concept of political authority, revealed in his quotation from St Paul's *Epistle to the Romans*(13:4). Because the state, he maintains, has a divine authorization to rule, its political decisions possess a unique moral authority. This authority, derived from God, entitles it to resist by force those who attack it by force, and to punish those whom it considers wrong-doers. Thus Aquinas justifies both defensive and offensive warfare.

Aquinas' argument has been much discussed and criticized. A common complaint against him is that, even if all three conditions for a just war were satisfied, this would not automatically justify military activity, particularly if the aims of such action could be achieved by other means, eg through diplomacy. For our present purposes, however, what is of particular interest is the distinction Aquinas makes here between the justice of war (*jus ad bellum*) and justice in wars (*jus in bello*). The former refers to the morality of the war being waged, the latter to the morality of the methods adopted in waging it. As Aquinas makes clear, the excessive use of force in the conduct of a war - to inflict more suffering than is necessary to gain the military advantage - will undermine the justice of the war itself. This distinction has far-reaching implications. It raises questions about the treatment of prisoners, the taking of hostages, guerilla warfare, saturation bombing, and, above all else, the use of nuclear weapons. How one resolves these questions depends very much on the general philosophical position one adopts.

---

1. *Summa Theologiae*, XXXV, 2a2ae. 40 (London: Eyre and Spottiswoode, 1972) pp 81-82.

In the following three extracts the pacifist tradition is represented by Mohandas K Gandhi (1869-1948). Influenced primarily by the Hindu *Bhagavad-Gita* and by Tolstoy's interpretation of the *Sermon on the Mount*, Gandhi adopted the principle of 'passive resistance' and organized the *satyagraha* (literally, truth- or love-force) campaigns of non-violence which led to Indian independence in 1947. Gandhi's repudiation of war is absolute; and the practice of non-violence is, he maintains, the only practical and effective way of eliminating war altogether from human experience.

An entirely different approach is taken by the British philosopher, Elizabeth Anscombe. For her the pacifist belief that it is necessarily wrong to fight in wars is both mistaken and dangerous. It is mistaken because it denies people the right to defend themselves; and it is dangerous because, in encouraging them to believe that *all* killing is wrong, it overlooks the important distinction between legitimate and illegitimate killing in war and so makes warfare even more murderous than it should be. Anscombe believes that there can be a justifiable war in which the sovereign authority, for the purposes of self-protection or in order to maintain the law of the land, does have the moral right to kill its enemies. What it cannot do is kill those who are innocent and not in any active sense party to the dispute. To do this is murder and cannot be justified.

This last point is taken up by Douglas Lackey and used to great effect in his rejection of present-day nuclear strategy and the policy of 'deterrence'. This policy, in so far as it involves the *threat* to slaughter many millions of innocent people and thus increases the chances of their actually being killed, is morally abhorrent and should be abandoned. It is therefore the moral duty of the United States to reverse its present nuclear stance and to dismantle its nuclear arsenal forthwith, even if no other nuclear power should follow suit. Disarmament increases the risk of conquest but continued armament increases the risk of war. Of these two, Lackey argues, the latter risk is the more serious: it involves the welfare of the entire world and not the national interests of any one country.

1. Mohandas K Gandhi: Non-violence ²

I am not a visionary. I claim to be a practical idealist. The religion of non-violence is not meant merely for the *rishis* and saints. It is meant for the common people as well. Non-violence is the law of our species as violence is the law of the brute. The spirit lies dormant in the brute, and he knows no law but that of physical might. The dignity of man requires obedience to a higher law - to the strength of the spirit.

I have therefore ventured to place before India the ancient law of self-sacrifice. For *satyagraha* and its offshoots, non-cooperation and civil resistance, are nothing but new names for the law of suffering. The *rishis*, who discovered the law of non-violence in the midst of violence, were greater geniuses than Newton. They were themselves greater warriors than Wellington. Having themselves known the use of arms, they realized their uselessness, and taught a weary world that its salvation lay not through violence but through non-violence.

Non-violence in its dynamic condition means conscious suffering. It does not mean meek submission to the will of the evil-doer, but it means putting of one's whole soul against the will of the tyrant. Working under this law of our being, it is possible for a single individual to defy the whole might of an unjust empire to save his honour, his religion, his soul, and lay the foundation for that empire's fall or its regeneration . . .

Mohandas K Gandhi

I do justify entire non-violence, and consider it possible in relation between man and man and nations and nations; but it is not 'a resignation from all real fighting against wickedness'. On the contrary, the non-violence of my conception is a more active and more real fighting against wickedness than retaliation whose very nature is to increase wickedness. I contemplate a mental, and therefore a moral, opposition to immoralities. I seek entirely to blunt the edge of the tyrant's sword, not by putting up against it a sharper-edged weapon, but by disappointing his expectation that I would be offering physical resistance. The resistance of the soul that I should offer instead would elude him. It would at first dazzle him, and at last compel recognition from him, which recognition would not humiliate him but would uplift him. It may be urged that this is an ideal state. And so it is. The propositions from which I have drawn my arguments are as true as Euclid's definitions, which are none the less true, because in practice we are unable even to draw Euclid's line on a blackboard. But even a geometrician finds it impossible to get on without bearing in mind Euclid's definitions. Nor may we . . . dispense with the fundamental propositions on which the doctrine of *satyagraha* is based . . .

Q How could a disarmed neutral country allow other nations to be destroyed? But for our army which was waiting ready at our frontier during the last war we should have been ruined.

A At the risk of being considered a visionary or a fool I must answer this question in the only manner I know. It would be cowardly of a neutral country to allow an army to devastate a neighbouring country. But there are two ways in common between soldiers of war and soldiers of non-violence, and if I had been a citizen of Switzerland and a President of the Federal State, what I would have done would be to refuse passage to the invading army by refusing all supplies. Secondly, by re-enacting a Thermopylae in Switzerland, you would have presented a living wall of men and women and children, and invited the invaders to walk over your corpses. You may say that such a thing is beyond human experience and endurance. I say that it is not so. It was quite possible. Last year in Gujarat women stood *lathi* charges unflinchingly, and in Peshawar thousands stood hails of bullets without resorting to violence. Imagine these men and women staying in front

2. M K Gandhi, *Non-violence in Peace and War,* Vol 1 (Ahmedabad: Navajivan Publishing House, 1942) pp 2, 44, 109-110, 335-336.

of an army requiring a safe passage to another country. The army would be brutal enough to walk over them, you might say. I would then say, you will still have done your duty by allowing yourself to be annihilated. An army that dares to pass over the corpses of innocent men and women would not be able to repeat that experiment. You may, if you wish, refuse to believe in such courage on the part of the masses of men and women, but then you would have to admit that non-violence is made of sterner stuff. It was never conceived as a weapon of the weak, but of the stoutest hearts.

Q Is it open to a soldier to fire in the air and avoid violence?

A A soldier, who having enlisted himself flattered himself that he was avoiding violence by shooting in the air, did no credit to his courage or to his creed of non-violence. In my scheme of things such a man would be held to be guilty of untruth and cowardice both - cowardice in that in order to escape punishment he enlisted, and untruth in that he enlisted to serve as soldier and did not fire as expected. Such a thing discredits the cause of waging war against war. The war-resisters have to be like Caesar's wife - above suspicion. Their strength lies in absolute adherence to the morality of the question . . .

This non-violence cannot be learnt by staying at home. It needs enterprise. In order to test ourselves we should learn to dare danger and death, mortify the flesh, and acquire the capacity to endure all manner of hardships. He who trembles or takes to his heels the moment he sees two people fighting is not non-violent, but a coward. A non-violent person will lay down his life in preventing such quarrels. The bravery of the non-violent is vastly superior to that of the violent. The badge of the violent is his weapon - spear, or sword, or rifle. God is the shield of the non-violent.

This is not a course of training for one intending to learn non-violence. But it is easy to evolve one from the principles I have laid down.

It will be evident from the foregoing that there is no comparison between the two types of bravery. The one is limited, the other limitless. There is no such thing as out-caring or out-fighting non-violence. Non-violence is invincible. There need be no doubt that this non-violence can be achieved. The history of the past twenty years should be enough to reassure us.

Questions: Gandhi

1. Is Gandhi justiified in calling himself a practical idealist and not a visionary?

2. Gandhi's non-violence may have worked against the British in India; but can you construct another scenario in which it would probably have failed?

3. Will non-cooperation and civil resistance always defeat an enemy?

2. G E M Anscombe: *War and Murder* [3]

Since there are always thieves and frauds and men who commit violent attacks on their neighbours and murderers, and since without law backed by adequate force there are usually gangs of bandits; and since there are in most places laws administered by people who command violence to enforce the laws against lawbreakers; the question arises: what is a just attitude to this exercise of violent coercive power on the part of rulers and their subordinate officers?

Two attitudes are possible: one, that the world is an absolute jungle and that the exercise of coercive power by rulers is only a manifestation of this; and the other, that it is both necessary and right that there should be this exercise of power, that through it the world is much less of a jungle than it could possibly be without it, so that one should in principle be glad of the existence of such power, and only take exception to its unjust exercise.

It is so clear that the world is less of a jungle because of rulers and laws, and that the exercise of coercive power is essential to these institutions as they are now - all this is so obvious, that probably only Tennysonian conceptions of progress enable people who do not wish to separate themselves from the world to think that nevertheless such violence is objectionable, that some day, in this present dispensation, we shall do without it, and that the pacifist is the man who sees and tries to follow the ideal course, which future civilization must one day pursue. It is an illusion, which would be fantastic if it were not so familiar.

In a peaceful and law-abiding country such as England, it may not be immediately obvious that the rulers need to command violence to the point of fighting to the death those that would oppose it; but brief reflection shows that this is so. For those who oppose the force that backs law will not always stop short of fighting to the death and cannot always be put down short of fighting to the death . . .

The same authority which puts down internal dissension, which promulgates laws and restrains those who break them if it can, must equally oppose external enemies. These do not merely comprise those who attack the borders of the people ruled by the authority, but also, for example, pirates and desert bandits, and, generally, those beyond the confines of the country ruled whose activities are viciously harmful to it . . . The present-day conception of 'aggression', like so many strongly influential conceptions, is a bad one. Why *must* it be wrong to strike the first blow in a struggle? The only question is, who is in the right.

Here, however, human pride, malice and cruelty are so usual that it is true to say that wars have mostly been mere wickedness on both sides. Just as an individual will constantly think himself in the right, whatever he does, and yet there is still such a thing as being in the right, so nations will constantly wrongly think themselves to be in the right - and yet there is still such a thing as their being in the right. Palmerston doubtless had no doubts in prosecuting the opium war against China, which was diabolical; just as he exulted in putting down the slavers. But there is no question but that he was a monster in the one thing, and a just man in the other.

The probability is that warfare is injustice, that a life of military service is a bad life 'militia or rather malitia', as St Anselm called it. This probability is greater than the probability (which also exists) that membership of a police force will involve malice, because of the character of warfare: the extraordinary occasions it offers of viciously unjust proceedings on the part of military commanders and warring governments, which at the time attract praise and not blame from their people. It is equally the case that the life of a ruler is usually a vicious life: but that does not show that ruling is as such a vicious activity.

The principal wickedness which is a temptation to those engaged in warfare is the killing of the innocent, which may often be done with impunity and even to the glory of those who do it. In many places and times it has been taken for granted as a natural part of waging war: the commander, and especially the conqueror, massacres people by the thousand, either because this is part of his glory, or as a terrorizing measure, or as part of his tactics . . .

---

3. G E M Anscombe, 'War and Murder', *Nuclear Weapons: A Catholic Response,* ed Walter Stein (New York: Sheed & Ward, 1961) pp 45-46, 48-49, 56-57.

What is required, for the people attacked to be non-innocent in the relevant sense, is that they should themselves be engaged in an objectively unjust proceeding which the attacker has the right to make his concern; or, the commonest case, should be unjustly attacking him. Then he can attack them with a view to stopping them; and also their supply lines and armament factories. But people whose mere existence and activity supporting existence by growing crops or making cloths, constitute an impediment to him - such people are innocent and it is murderous to attack them, or make them a target for an attack which he judges will help him towards victory. For murder is the deliberate killing of the innocent whether for its own sake or as a means to some further end.

The right to attack with a view to killing is something that belongs only to rulers and those whom they command to do it. I have argued that it does belong to rulers precisely because of that threat of violent coercion exercised by those in authority which is essential to the existence of human societies . . .

Now pacifism teaches people to make no distinction between the shedding of innocent blood and the shedding of any human blood. And in this way pacifism has corrupted enormous numbers of people who will not act according to its tenets. They become convinced that a number of things are wicked which are not; hence, seeing no way of avoiding 'wickedness', they set no limits to it. How endlessly pacifists argue that all war must be *à outrance* that those who wage war must go as far as technological advance permits in the destruction of the enemy's people. As if the Napoleonic wars were perforce fuller of massacres than the French wars of Henry V of England. It is not true: the reverse took place. Nor is technological advance particularly relevant; it is mere squeamishness that deters people who would consent to area bombing from the enormous massacres *by hand* that used once to be committed.

The policy of obliterating cities was adopted by the Allies in the last war; they need not have taken that step, and it was taken largely out of a villainous hatred, and as corollary to the policy, now universally denigrated, of seeking 'unconditional surrender'. (That policy itself was visibly wicked, and could be and was judged so at the time; it is not surprising that it led to disastrous consequences, even if no one was clever and detached enough to foresee that at the time.)

Pacifism and the respect for pacifism is not the only thing that led to universal forgetfulness of the law against killing the innocent; but its has had a great share in it . . .

Questions: Anscombe

1. What are Anscombe's arguments against pacifism as a justified moral viewpoint? What do you think of them?

2. Are there any circumstances which justify the killing of innocent people in time of war?

3. How do you think Gandhi would reply to Anscombe?

3. Douglas Lackey: Ethics and Nuclear Deterrence [4]

Suppose that for some reason or lack of reason the Soviet Union launches a nuclear first strike against the United States. Even under these conditions it would be clearly immoral for the United States to retaliate in kind against the Soviet Union, since retaliation by the United States would result in the death of millions of innocent people, for no higher purpose than useless revenge. The present policy of deterrence requires preparations for such retaliation and threats and assurances by us that it will be forthcoming if the United States is attacked. Indeed, if our deterrent is to remain credible, the response of the United States to attack should be semi-automatic. Defenders of armaments justify all the preparations on the grounds that they will prevent an attack *on us*; if retaliation is ever needed, they say, the system has already failed. Now, a Russian attack against the United States would be at least as immoral as our retaliation against the Russians. So one aspect of the moral problem of deterrence is this: Is one justified in *threatening* to do something which is immoral, if the reasoned intention behind one's threat is to prevent something immoral from occurring?

Let us consider some analogous situations:

1. It would be immoral to kill a man to prevent default on a debt, even if one had no intention of killing the man at all, so long as he paid the debt. Indeed, it is immoral to threaten to kill a man in order to pay a debt, even if one has no intention of killing him under any circumstances, including nonpayment of the debt. In this case at least, threatening evil is not justified by good results or an increased chance of good results. Perhaps this lack of justification derives from the inherent wrongfulness of such threats of violence or from the bad results that would follow if everyone regulary made threats of this sort - whatever the cause. The good results that *actually* follow from the threat do not justify it; even, I would say, in a state of nature containing no judicial system.

2. It might be objected that this example is unfair because the stakes in question are not high enough. Would it be equally immoral to threaten to kill Jones if the intention of the threat is to prevent Jones from doing murder himself, and if the threat will *be* carried out only when Jones actually does murder? This, perhaps, is the way deterrence theorists view strategic *détente*. It must be admitted that in this situation the threat to kill is not immoral. Indeed, anyone who recommends capital punishment for convicted murderers is allowing that such threats, if tempered by due process of law, are *not* immoral.

The difficulty with this example is that it does not truly reflect the structure of our present nuclear policy. Our policy is not to threaten a potential *murderer* with death in order to prevent him from murdering, and to execute *him* when he actually does murder, but rather to threaten *someone else* with death to prevent a potential murderer from attacking and to execute *someone else* when the murderer actually strikes. An American counterattack would be directed against the Russian people, and it is not the Russian people who would be ordering an attack on the American people. Similarly, if leaders in the United States ordered an attack on the Soviet Union, the Russian counterattack would fall on the American people and not on the leaders who ordered the attack . . . In the present *détente*, the leaders of each side hold the population of the other hostage, and threaten to execute the hostages if the opposing *leaders* do not meet certain conditions. The proper moral examples, then, with which to analyze the *détente* should be the examples of hostage-taking.

3. Suppose that the Hatfields and the McCoys live in an area sufficiently rural that disputes cannot be settled by appeal to a higher authority. For various reasons, the two families take a dislike to each other. Each family, let us assume, possesses hand grenades that could destroy the other family completely; and against these hand grenades there is no adequate defense. Each family, in what it considers to be a defensive move, kidnaps a child from the family of the other and holds it hostage. Each side wires its hostage to a device which will explode and kill the hostage if there is any loud noise nearby - such as the noise of a grenade attack or, what is not likely, but still *possible*, the accidental explosion of the captors' own grenades or the sounding of a nearby clap of thunder. This example, I believe, fairly represents the present policies of deterrence.

4. Douglas Lackey, 'Ethics and Nuclear Deterrence', *Moral Problems*, ed James Rachels (New York: Harper & Row, 1979) pp 437-442.

A defender of Hatfield foreign policy might justify himself as follows: 'We have no intention of killing the McCoy child, unless, of course, we are attacked. If we are attacked, we must kill him automatically (or else lose the credibility of this deterrent); but we feel that it is very unlikely that, under these conditions, any attack will occur. True, there is some small chance that the child will die by accident, but this is only a *small* chance, and so we have good reason to believe that this will not happen. At the same time, the presence of the hostage reduces the chance that the McCoys will attack, relative to the chances of attack if we had taken no hostage. If the child dies, we cannot be blamed, since we had good reason to believe that he would not, and if he lives, we are to be commended for adopting a policy which has in fact prevented an attack.'

The moral reply here is obvious: the Hatfields have no *right* to seize the McCoy child, whatever dubious advantages they gain by seizing him. True they only *threaten* to kill him, but threatening to kill him increases the chance of his being killed, and they have no right to increase these chances. The moral repulsiveness of the Hatfield policy derives from its abuse of the innocent for dubious ends. Deterring the McCoys in this manner is like deterring one's neighbours from running into you on the road by seizing their children and tying them to the front bumper of your car . . . If everyone did this, accidents might decrease and, on balance, more lives saved than lost. Perhaps it could be predicted that the chances of a single child dying on a car bumper are slight; perhaps, by a miracle, no child would die . . . Whatever the chances and whatever the gains, no one could claim the right to use a single child in this way. Yet it seems that the present American policy continues to use the entire Russian population in just this manner . . .

4. The key step in the preceding criticism is that the Hatfields have no right to increase the chances of the McCoy child dying, and analogously the United States has no right to increase the chances of the Russian population dying. The threat is illicit if the threat is real. This leads to the interesting possibility that the threat is licit if it is fraudulent. Suppose that the United States *says* that it will counterattack if the Soviet Union attacks and gives every indication that it will counterattack (missile silos are constructed, submarines cruise the oceans, etc); but, in fact, unknown to anyone except the highest officials in the government, all the American warheads are disarmed and simply cannot go off. In this case the United States does not threaten, but merely *seems* to threaten to counterattack. If the chance of Russian attack is decreased, such a plan would have good results without the intrinsic repulsiveness of the present policy.

But this plan has practical and moral flaws. The practical flaw is that the bogus threat will not serve as a deterrent unless the Soviet Union *does* discover that, according to the usual analysis, the chances of war will be greatly increased. So, it is not obvious that this plan gives good results, since one must balance the decreased chance of war (if the Soviet Union respects the deterrent) against the increased chance of war (if the Soviet Union discovers that the deterrent is bogus). Furthermore, if this plan is successfully put into effect and the Soviet Union does not have a similar plan of its own, the bogus-warhead plan will result in high and wasteful Soviet expenditures and in an increased chance of accidental or deliberate attack from the Soviet side.

The chances of nuclear war have diminished considerably since the early 1960s; . . . our policies now are safer than they were then. But these improvements should not blind us to the inherent abhorrence of the present policies and the dangers that they pose. Mutual deterrence is neither rational, nor prudent, nor moral, compared to other policies that are not beyond the power of rational men . . .

Questions: Lackey

1. Consider the following argument: While our enemies have nuclear weapons, and will not disarm, we cannot disarm and place ourselves at a disadvantage. On the other hand, if our enemies choose to disarm, we cannot disarm and thereby lose the advantage. Thus whatever our enemies do, we should not disarm. How would Lackey respond to this argument? How do you respond?

2. Is Lackey correct in arguing that anyone who justifies nuclear weapons is justifying tying a child to a bumper to prevent accidents?

3. In a speech made in the House of Commons on 10 November, 1932, Stanley Baldwin said: 'The only defence is offence which means that you have to kill more women and children more quickly than the enemy (can) if you want to save yourselves.' In an age of nuclear weapons, does such a strategy make sense?

Questions: The Morality of War

1. Aquinas argues that a 'just' war involves the use of proper means (*debito modo*) to achieve victory. What do you consider 'proper means' to be? Should a distinction be made between moral and immoral weapons?

2. 'A nation's right to wage war is justified on the same grounds as the individual's right to kill in self-defence.' Discuss.

3. What moral distinctions should be made between the arguments for unilateral and multilateral disarmament?

4. Do you agree with Sir Hartley Shawcross when he said, at the Nuremburg trials, that 'there comes a point where a man must refuse to answer to his leader, if he is also to answer to his conscience.' When would that 'point' be reached for you?

5. Comment on President Truman's justification of the atomic bomb against Japan. What kind of argument is Truman employing? How far do you agree with him?

The world will note that the first atomic bomb was dropped on Hiroshima, a military base. That was because we wished in this first attack to avoid, in so far as possible, the killing of civilians. But that attack is only a warning of things to come. If Japan does not surrender, bombs will have to be dropped on her war industries and, unfortunately, thousands of civilian lives will be lost. I urge Japanese civilians to leave industrial cities immediately, and save themselves from destruction.

I realize the tragic significance of the atomic bomb.

Its production and its use were not lightly undertaken by this Government. But we knew that our enemies were on the search for it. We know now how close they were to finding it. And we knew the disaster which would come to this Nation, and to all peace-loving nations, to all civilization, if they had found it first.

That is why we felt compelled to undertake the long and uncertain and costly labor of discovery and production.

We won the race of discovery against the Germans.

Having found the bomb we have used it. We have used it against those who attacked us without warning at Pearl Harbor, against those who have starved and beaten and executed American prisoners of war, against those who have abandoned all pretence of obeying international laws of warfare. We have used it in order to shorten the agony of war, in order to save the lives of thousands and thousands of young Americans.

We shall continue to use it until we completely destroy Japan's power to make war. Only a Japanese surrender will stop us.

The atomic bomb is too dangerous to be let loose in a lawless world. That is why Great Britain, Canada, and the United States, who have the secret of its production, do not intend to reveal that secret until means have been found to control the bomb so as to protect ourselves and the rest of the world from the danger of total destruction.[5]

5. *Public Papers of the Presidents of the United States*, 9 August, 1945 (Washington: United States Government Printing Office, 1961) pp 212-213.

Bibliography: The Morality of War

* denotes text referred to or extracted in main text

Anscombe, G E M 'War and Murder',* *Nuclear Weapons: A Catholic Response*, ed Walter Stein (New York: Sheed and Ward, 1961)

Aquinas, Thomas *Summa Theologiae*,* XXXV (London: Eyre & Spottiswoode, 1972)

Bailey, Sydney D *War and Conscience in the Nuclear Age* (London: Macmillan, 1987) Ch 1 & 2 on 'Just War'.

Blake, Nigel (ed with Kay Pole) *Objections to Nuclear Defence: Philosophers on Deterrence* (London: Routledge & Kegan Paul, 1984) Includes essays by Anthony Kenny, Michael Dummett and Bernard Williams.

Cohen, Marshall (ed with Thomas Nagel and Thomas Scanlon) *War and Moral Responsibility* (Princeton, NJ: Princeton University Press, 1974)

Davis, Howard (ed) *Ethics and Defence: Power and Responsibility in the Nuclear Age* (Oxford: Basil Blackwell, 1986)

Gandhi, M K *Non-violence in Peace and War** (Ahmedabad: Navajivan Publishing House, 1942)

Ginsberg, Robert (ed) *The Critique of War* (Chicago: Henry Regnery, 1969)

Horsburgh, H J N *Non-violence and Aggression: A Study of Gandhi's Moral Equivalent of War* (London: Oxford University Press, 1968)

Lackey, Douglas 'Ethics and Nuclear Deterrence',* *Moral Problems*, ed James Rachels (New York: Harper & Row, 1979)

Mayer, Peter (ed) *The Pacifist Conscience* (London: Rupert Hart-Davis, 1966) An important anthology, including essays by Thoreau and Gandhi.

Paskins, Barrie (ed with Michael Dockrill) *The Ethics of War* (London: Duckworth, 1979) A comprehenisve survey of the moral issues involved.

Phillips, Robert L *War and Justice* (Oklahoma: University of Oklahoma Press, 1984) Chs 1 & 2 analyse the distinction between *Jus ad Bellum* and *Jus in Bello*.

Public Papers of the Presidents of the United States (Harry S Truman), 9 August, 1945 (Washington: United States Government Printing Office, 1961)*

Wasserstrom, Richard A (ed) *War and Morality* (Belmont, Calif: Wadsworth, 1970) Excellent short anthology, with essays by William James, Elizabeth Anscombe and Jan Narveson.

Chapter 5

Determinism and Free Will

The last theory we shall deal with is the theory of **determinism**. This states that *every event has a cause*. Strictly speaking, determinism is not a theory of normative ethics but the doctrine of universal causation. Its implications for ethics are so important, however, that it has been a constant focus of debate since the beginning of philosophy. The question it raises is whether human beings possess **free will**. If they do not, then they cannot be held morally responsible for their actions; and if they cannot be held morally responsible for their actions, then the business of morality becomes meaningless.

When do we consider a man morally responsible? In our earlier discussion of psychological egoism, it was suggested that, if someone is to be held morally responsible for his actions, he must at the very least be capable of performing them. We do not blame Smith for what he could not do but for what he was capable of doing but didn't. This, we remember, was the meaning of the expression 'Ought implies can'.[1] A moral situation is one in which the individual can choose a particular course of action. Conversely, a non-moral situation is one in which he or she either has no choice, or more frequently has that choice dictated to them by something (or someone) over which they have no control. I am not to blame if I cannot breathe under water, it being physically impossible; nor am I to blame if I cannot draw a round square, it being logically impossible. Nor am I held morally responsible if forced at gunpoint to commit a crime or if, suffering from a neurosis called pyromania, I cannot help setting fire to buildings. In these last two cases the courts recognize that I am, in a special sense, less free than the normal citizen and sentences are adjusted accordingly.

But what if it could be shown that *all* human actions are caused by factors outside our control? It is this question which raises the philosophical problem of determinism and free will. People certainly behave as if they are free, as if they have a series of real choices open to them, and nowhere is this more apparent than when they make moral decisions. But suppose this is not the case? Suppose that behind these choices lies a whole range of antecedent circumstances, environment, heredity, and so on, which compels us, like the pyromaniac, to act in the way we do. In that case we should have to conclude that none of us is free, that none of us is responsible for our actions, and that moral decision is an illusion. In all matters of human choice, so the argument runs, a man cannot choose to do what he ought to do but rather does what he must.

Philosophers have reacted to this problem in a variety of ways. First there are the so-called **hard determinists**, who accept determinism and therefore reject freedom and moral responsibility. Then there are the so-called **libertarians**, who accept freedom and moral responsibility and therefore reject determinism. Common to both groups is the assumption that free will and determinism are incompatible. This assumption is, however, rejected by a third group, the so-called **soft determinists** or **compatibilists**, who argue that determinism is essential to the notion of free action. Let us now examine each of these three positions.

---

1. See above, p 37.

1. Hard Determinism

Hard determinists maintain that everything in the universe, including all human actions and choices, has a cause which precedes it; and that this is the same as saying that once the cause has occurred the thing itself (the effect) will occur. This argument, known as the theory of universal causation, carries with it the further proposition that all events are in principle predictable. If we know the causal law according to which events of the type A are followed by events of the type B - ie, that whenever friction occurs, heat occurs - then we can safely predict that, provided certain conditions remain constant, whenever a particular A-type event occurs (rubbing my hands) it will be followed by a particular B-type event (my hands get warm). The undoubted popularity of this argument stems from the fact that it is both a fundamental presupposition of science and a matter of common sense. Thus we light the fuse in the confident expectation that a particular event (the explosion) will occur: if it doesn't we look for an alternative explanation. We assume that something has gone wrong in the causal chain of events. Was the fuse dry? Has the bomb been tampered with? Admittedly there are many things whose causes we do not know; but even in these cases we rarely, if ever, consider these things to be uncaused. Instead we seek to discover the cause which we assume exists. So doctors will admit that there are diseases with unknown causes; but they are less likely to accept that there are diseases without causes.

The determinist case has gained in strength with the modern development of such disciplines as psychology, sociology, and anthropology. With their increasing ability to account for human feelings and emotions, the belief has grown that man himself, like everything else in the animate and inanimate world, acts in accordance with causal laws. Human beings are seen less as free agents and more as complicated bits of machinery, the workings of which are fully governed by environmental and genetic factors, and the performances of which are theoretically predictable once these factors are known. This, of course, is not to say that anyone *knows* the causal explanation for any given human choice or action: all that is being claimed is that such an explanation is theoretically possible. Our ignorance of what the particular causal law may be does not invalidate the determinist proposition that this law exists and is in principle knowable.

It follows from this, says the hard determinist, that, when a man appears to have a moral choice, this appearance is an illusion. Indeed, he argues, it is precisely because we are invariably ignorant of what causes these choices that we believe that they are uncaused in the first place. A classic case of this is suggested by the philosopher John Locke (1632-1704). Suppose that a sleeping man is placed in a locked room. On awakening he decides to stay where he is, not knowing that the room is already locked. This is a real decision taken by him, it is freely made and he might have decided to leave; but in reality he has no choice and it is only his ignorance of his true condition which made him think otherwise. So it is with our moral choices. We think we are free when we decide to do X and not Y; but in fact we are not. For these decisions are causally determined: they are the effects of previous causes, and these causes of still earlier causes, back and back. This is the reason why we cannot be held responsible for our actions.

These conclusions have important consequences for our earlier discussion of punishment. Punishment, to be just, must presuppose moral blame; and no person can be held morally blameworthy if deprived of their freedom of choice. What, therefore, prevents an attorney from entering a plea of 'diminished responsibility' - diminished, that is, on account of the causal laws governing his client's actions - for *all* his clients, irrespective of offence? Why, for example, do we distinguish between the kleptomaniac and the thief? Surely it is because we believe that the kleptomaniac, unlike the thief, is possessed by such powerful compulsions to steal that he cannot help doing what he does. The hard determinist argues that this is unfair to the thief: we are judging him to be morally responsible through an ignorance of what motivates him to steal. But look closely enough at his antecedents, his environment and heredity, and a different picture emerges, in which the thief, like the kleptomaniac, is also the unfortunate victim of circumstance. This is the view held by the contemporary determinist, John Hospers:

Let us suppose it were established that a man commits murder only if, sometime during the previous week, he has eaten a certain combination of foods - say tuna fish salad at a meal also including peas, mushroom soup, and blueberry pie. What if we were to track down the factors common to all murders committed in this country during the last twenty years and found this factor present in all of them, and only in them? The example is, of course, empirically absurd; but may it not be that there is some combination of factors that regularly lead to homocide? . . . When such specific factors are discovered, won't they make it clear that it is foolish and pointless, as well as immoral, to hold human beings responsible for crimes? Or, if one prefers biological to psychological factors, suppose a neurologist is called in to testify at a murder trial and produces X-ray pictures of the brain of the criminal; anyone can see, he argues, that the cella turcica *was already calcified at the age of nineteen; it should be a flexible bone, enabling the gland to grow. All the defendant's disorders might have resulted from this early calcification. Now, this particular explanation may be empirically false; but who can say that no such factors, far more complex, to be sure, exist?*[2]

Clarence Darrow

Perhaps the most famous case in which similar determinist arguments were employed by the defence occurred in 1924. Two youths, Nathan Leopold and Richard Loeb, kidnapped and murdered a 14-year-old boy, called Bobby Franks. The two killers were wealthy and highly intelligent, being the youngest graduates of the universities of Chicago and Michigan. In order to demonstrate their contempt for society and its conventional morality, the two planned the perfect crime. Their plan went wrong, they were quickly caught, and confessed. At their trial, the death penalty was demanded. For over twelve hours in his summation to the jury, Clarence Darrow, the most celebrated American attorney of his day, pleaded for mercy:

Nature is strong and she is pitiless. She works in her own mysterious way, and we are victims. We have not much to do with it ourselves. Nature takes this job in hand, and we play our parts...

What had this boy to do with it? He was not his own father; he was not his own mother; he was not his own grandparents. All this was handed to him. He did not surround himself with governesses and wealth. He did not make himself. And yet he is compelled to pay . . .

To believe that any boy is responsible for himself or his early training is an absurdity . . . If his failing came from his heredity, I do not know where or how. None of us are bred perfect and pure; and the colour of our hair, the colour of our eyes, our stature, the weight and fineness of our brain, and everything about us could, with full knowledge, be traced with absolute certainty to somewhere. If we had the pedigree it could be traced just the same in a boy as it could in a dog . . .

If it did not come that way, then . . . if he had been understood, if he had been trained as he should have been it would not have happened.

If there is a responsibility anywhere, it is back of him; somewhere in the infinite number of his ancestors, or in his surroundings, or in both. And I submit, Your Honor, that under

2. 'What Means This Freedom?', *Determinism and Freedom in the Age of Modern Science* ed. Sidney Hook (New York: New York University Press, 1958).

3. Darrow, 'Attorney for the Damned' *Philosophy: Paradox and Discovery,* ed Arthur J Minton (New York: McGraw-Hill, 1976) pp 302-304.

every principle of . . . right, and of law, he should not be made responsible for the acts of someone else.[3]

Darrow was successful in his plea: Leopold and Loeb were sentenced to life imprisonment.

Hard determinists, like Hospers and Darrow, are not saying that criminals should not be sent to prison, since evidently society must be protected from them; nor are they saying that the courts should altogether cease to blame the criminal and praise the innocent. These are, after all, devices which may cause the individual to become a different kind of person. What they do question, however, is the common assumption that criminals are morally responsible for what they do.

Morality is concerned with what people ought and ought not to do; but if what they do could not have been otherwise, if they do not possess the freedom to choose what to do, then it does not make much sense either to tell them that they ought to have done differently or to punish them for what they did. The challenge of determinism, therefore, is that it speaks of the illusion of freedom and thus of the absence of moral blame.

Exercise 1

Assuming that a person should be blamed for his actions only when he has freedom of choice, in which of the following cases do you think the person involved is blameworthy? Explain your answers.

a	The soldier for saving his life by collaborating with the enemy
b	The spy for giving away secrets under torture
c	The butcher for bleeding animals to death before selling them
d	The kleptomaniac for stealing
e	The boy for stealing food when he is starving
f	The motorist for speeding to save a life
g	The motorist for speeding because he is drunk
h	The foreigner for speeding because ignorant of the speed limit
i	The husband for murdering his adulterous wife
j	The father for beating his child for cheating
k	The mother for hiding her criminal son from the police
l	The surgeon for not knowing the latest treatment
m	The linguist for failing the maths exam
n	The bank manager for handing over the money to the armed robber
o	The hypnotised woman for undressing in public
p	The drug addict for stealing from the chemist
q	The Catholic unmarried mother for having an unwanted baby
r	The Muslim, living in Manchester, for bigamy
s	The IRA activist for killing the British cabinet minister
t	The psychopath for raping the woman

2. Libertarianism

It would appear that, if we wish to retain the idea of moral responsibility, we must reject determinism and accept that a person can, when confronted with the choice between right and wrong, act as a free agent. This view is known as *libertarianism*. This is not to say that libertarians reject determinism altogether: in general they agree that the inanimate world is mechanistic - that all events in it are mechanically caused and thus predictable - and that the mechanical chains of cause and effect may extend even to the animate world. What they deny is that the principle of universal causation applies also to *human action* and that accordingly human behaviour is predictable. It may well be that the kleptomaniac, left alone in a shop, will steal; but one can never be certain that he will. Physiological and psychological conditions may well dispose him towards stealing, but he may well choose to do otherwise; and in the making of this choice, says libertarianism, lies his freedom.

In presenting this argument, libertarians often distinguish between a person's formed character or **personality** and his or her **moral self**. Personality is an empirical concept, governed by causal laws, capable of scientific explanation and prediction, and known through observation of behaviour and psychoanalysis. The personality one has, formed by heredity and environment, limits the choices one has, and makes us more likely to choose certain kinds of actions and not others. A youth, accustomed to violence, is more likely to decide on a career of violence than someone brought up to condemn it. But however likely this may be, it is not inevitable. For if the youth is aware of the significance of his actions, it is possible that his *moral self* will counteract the tendencies of his personality and cause him to do something else: he may become a policeman instead! The moral self, therefore, is not an empirical but an ethical concept, operative when we decide what to do in situations of moral choice. Most commonly, this involves deciding between self-interest and duty, between, say, stealing and not stealing; and here the moral self is quite capable of making a *causally undetermined choice*, of subduing the inclinations of upbringing and temperament, and of deciding, through an effort of will, to do something that is not self-interested but which satisfies the sense of moral duty. In this respect, says the libertarian, the moral agent overcomes the pressures exerted upon him by his own personality and becomes morally responsible for what he does. It is this capacity which distinguishes men from animals: the former are capable of moral choice, the latter are not. Thus C A Campbell writes:

> *Here, and here alone, so far as I can see, in the act of deciding whether to put forth or withold the moral effort required to resist temptation and rise to duty, is to be found an act which is free in the sense required for moral responsibility; an act of which the self is sole author, and of which it is true to say that 'it could be' (or, after the event, 'could have been') 'otherwise' . . .*

> *There is X, the course which we believe we ought to follow, and Y, the course towards which we feel our desire is strongest. The freedom which we ascribe to the agent is the freedom to put forth or refrain from putting forth the moral effort required to resist the pressure of desire and to do what he thinks he ought to do . . .*

> *. . . the very function of moral effort, as it appears to the agent engaged in the act, is to enable the self to act against the line of least resistance, against the line to which his character as so far formed strongly inclines him. But if the self is thus conscious here of combatting his formed character, he surely cannot possibly suppose that the act, although his own act, issues from his formed character? I submit, therefore, that the self knows very well indeed, from the inner standpoint, what is meant by an act which is the self's act and which nevertheless does not follow from the self's character . . . the 'nature' of the self and what we commonly call the 'character' of the self are by no means the same thing. The 'nature' of the self comprehends, but is not without remainder reducible to, its 'character'; it must, if we are to be true to the testimony of our experience of it, be taken as including also the authentic creative power of fashioning and refashioning 'character'.[4]*

4. 'On Selfhood and Godhead' *Philosophy: Paradox and Discovery,* ed Arthur Minton (New York: McGraw-Hill, 1976) pp 342-343, 345-346.

For the determinist, this argument is very unsatisfactory. If it is admitted that my personality may be determined by such things as heredity and environment, why is it not also accepted by the libertarian that my moral attitudes may be conditioned in precisely the same way? Why is it agreed that a person is free to choose between duty and desire but not free in any other choices that he or she makes? The libertarian, in other words, has assumed the existence of free will in situations of moral choice but has provided no evidence for it.

The libertarian's reply is commonly composed of three additional arguments. In the first he makes a straightforward appeal to the facts of experience. Each of us frequently has the direct and certain experience of being a self-determining creature. We have this experience when we decide to drink tea rather than coffee, to read this book and not that, to wear a brown jacket and not a green one - and so on. This experience is common to all of us, and extends also to those whose choices are sometimes restricted (eg, the alcoholic or drug addict). For while, within a particular range of activities, they cannot help what they do, generally speaking they still have the immediate experience of decision; of making a choice, of deciding, for example, whether or not to take the dog for a walk or whether to go to Spain for their holidays. In these areas they do not feel any special difficulty in making up their minds, and indeed are able to compare these situations with those over which they have no control. Thus, although recognizing the limits of their freedom, they still have sufficient other experiences to sustain their general belief in the existence of free will.

An appeal to the facts of experience is also involved in the libertarian's second argument. This concerns an analysis of the way in which we make our decisions: **the act of decision-making**. All of us do this at some time or other and the process can be of varying length and benefit; but *that* we all do this demonstrates that each of us possesses free will. This is because we can only make decisions about what to do if

(a) we do not already know what we are going to do and;

(b) if it is in our power to do what we are thinking of doing.

Suppose, for example, that a student is wondering whether to pay her residence fees. She may take into consideration the size of her room, the quality of her meals, and so on. Now if she decides to pay, she makes a decision: she has weighed up the pros and cons. Significantly, this would still be an act of decision even if, unknown to her, she had no money in the bank. In this case she would simply be considering what to do with money that, in her ignorance, she thought she possessed. But what she could not do is decide whether to pay or not, *knowing* that she had no money. She could not decide what action to take if she knew beforehand that only one action was open to her. Thus for someone to make a decision about something, they must believe they have a real choice, that they are capable of doing either A or B; and if they cannot do either A or B, they cannot make a choice between them. The libertarian therefore concludes that, since we all do often make decisions, we must all believe that we can make choices, that we are free. In this way determinism, which rejects the existence of free will, is itself rejected by the universal experience of decision-making.

To this the determinist has a ready reply. No one disputes that people believe they are free and that this belief is supported by the experience of decision-making; but this is not to say that we actually are free. After all, a man can, on the evidence of certain experiences, believe many things - that the sun is shining, that his wife is faithful, that the world will end on Thursday; but believing these things does not mean that they are true. In the same way, the evidence of decision-making can deceive us into believing that free will exists. Benedict Spinoza (1632-1677) puts the point succinctly:

> *Thus the infant believes that it is by free will that it seeks the breast; the angry boy believes that by free will he wishes vengeance; the timid man thinks it is with free will he seeks flight; the drunkard believes that by a free command of his mind he speaks the things which when sober he wishes he had left unsaid. Thus the madman, the chatterer, the boy, and others of the same kind, all believe that they speak by a free command of the mind, whilst, in truth, they have no power to restrain the impulse which they have to speak, so that experience itself, no less than reason, clearly teaches that men believe themselves to be free simply because they are conscious of their actions, knowing nothing of the causes by which they*

are determined . . . Consequently, those who believe that, who believe that they speak, or are silent, or do anything else from a free decree of the mind, dream with their eyes open.[5]

The libertarian's third argument is designed to meet this objection, and it employs an important philosophical distinction. This is a distinction between two kinds of knowledge and, accordingly, between two kinds of truths or propositions which may be known to be true or false. Consider the following lists:

List A

All bachelors are unmarried
Black cats are black
You cannot simultaneously be in the room and out of it

List B

This table is brown
It is raining
George has one eye

The statements in **List A** are said to be **necessarily true**. This is because they could not possibly be false and because their truth is established independently of sense experience. So, for example, being an 'unmarried man' is precisely what is meant by the concept of 'bachelor': it is a type of proposition which is true *by definition* and which requires no empirical verification. The statements in **List B** are said to be **contingently true** because these are verified by sense experiences and because they may conceivably be false (given the possibility that these experiences may deceive me). So however certain I may be that George has one eye, this does not mean that he has. My own eyesight may be misleading me.

Another example will make this distinction clearer. If A, B and C are three positive numbers, and if A is greater than B, and B greater than C, then it is necessarily true to say that A is greater than C. This is true by definition and its negation necessarily false. If, however, A, B and C are three runners, and A has always beaten B, and B has always beaten C, it does *not* follow that A must necessarily beat C. Our experience may lead us to predict that he will, but he may be wrong. On the day of the race, A may damage a tendon and lose. From this we conclude that, in our observation of the world around us, it is impossible to achieve complete knowledge; that, in the world of contingent events, the possibility of error always exists.

5. Spinoza, *Ethic*, translated by W Hale White and revised by Amelia Hutchinson Stirling (London: T Fisher Unwin, 1894) pp 111-112.

Exercise 2

Which of the following statements are necessarily true (or false) and which contingently true (or false)?

a	2 + 2 = 4
b	2 trees + 2 trees = 4 trees
c	A straight line is the shortest distance between two points
d	Napoleon was Emperor of the French
e	All men die
f	If A knows B, and if B knows C, then A knows C
g	If A precedes B, and if B precedes C, then A precedes C
h	It is cold at the top of Everest
i	No object can be red and green all over
j	A triangle is a three-sided figure
k	A man cannot walk on water
l	Every man has a mother
m	I am reading this sentence
n	Skyscrapers are tall buildings
o	Time moves forwards, not backwards
p	Something exists

This distinction between necessary truth and contingent truth forms the basis for the libertarian reply to the determinist. The determinist, we remember, has argued that the evidence in support of free will - the experience of deliberation - while admissable as evidence for the *belief* in free will, is not admissable as evidence for the *existence* of free will. It is always possible, he says, that our experience may deceive us and that no such free will exists. In that case, replies the libertarian, the determinist is saying no more than that this experience, like all other experiences, belongs to the realm of contingency and is subject to error. One can say the same of the experience that I am sitting in this room or that last Thursday I got married: in either case it remains logically possible that I am hallucinating or that a clever hypnotist has been at work. The question to ask, therefore, is not whether I can be deceived by my experiences - this is now seen to be a truism - but whether the possibility of deception means that I cannot accept these experiences as *sufficient evidence for the truth of my beliefs*. For example, it is clear that I could be imagining things when I say 'I have a pen in my hand'; but does this mean that I have no good reason for saying that a pen is actually in my hand? Certainly not, says the libertarian, because the truth of this belief is justified by the immediate and direct evidence of sense experience itself. So overwhelming is this experience that I do not deny its basis in fact. Admittedly, the evidence for the pen's being there is insufficient when matched against the requirements of necessary truth, which excludes error; but it is not insufficient when matched against the requirements of contingent truth, which accepts error. For contingent truth is precisely that which is reached on the basis of corrigible evidence: it is something which, although fallible, I can still accept as being beyond reasonable doubt and view with certainty.

This, then, is the libertarian's case against the determinist. If the experience of deliberation is to be rejected as evidence for the existence of free will because this experience could deceive us, then *any evidence whatsoever*, so long as it is based on experience, must be rejected for the same reason. We must reject, for example, those experiences from which we deduce that there are material objects, that there are other minds besides our own, that there are such things as past events. We must discard, in other words, the *standard of evidence* which belongs to the realm of contingency and adopt instead a position of almost total scepticism, which few can accept and in which no valid or certain judgements can ever be reached about ourselves and our world. To put the matter more bluntly, if the act of deliberation is incompatible with the theory of determinism, and if this act must be counted among the certain facts of our experience, then this act must take priority over the theory, and the theory of determinism must be rejected.

3. Soft Determinism

It would seem then, that we must choose between, the belief in universal causation and, on the other hand, the belief in the existence of free will, it being accepted by both determinists and libertarians that these two beliefs are incompatible. This incompatibility is, however, rejected by the third party to the dispute, which says that human freedom and moral responsibility, far from being incompatible with determinism, is incomprehensible without it. This is the position taken by the so-called *soft determinists* or *compatibilists*.

The assumption that determinism is inconsistent with free will is, says the soft determinist, the result of considerable confusion about what precisely we mean when we say we are free. It is certainly true that freedom is incompatible with *fatalism*, the view that human beings are powerless to change the cause of events and that 'what will be, will be'; but it is not incompatible with determinism - the theory of universal causation - *if among the choices that determine our actions we count our own choices and desires*. To clarify this point, consider the following cases[6]:

A

Gandhi fasting because he wanted to free India
Stealing bread because one is hungry
Signing a confession because one wanted to tell the truth
Leaving the office because one wanted one's lunch

B

The man fasting in the desert because there was no food
Stealing because one's employer threatened to beat one
Signing because the police beat one
Leaving because forcibly removed

Now it is clear that the actions in column **A** conform to what the libertarian would call free actions; and indeed, with the exception of the last example, to what he would call moral actions. These are, to use Campbell's terminology, *causally undetermined choices*, in which the person involved, through an effort of will, subdues his natural inclinations and decides for duty rather than self-interest. Thus the moral self overcomes the dictates of his personality. These actions, however, are clearly distinguishable from those in column **B**, which are causally determined choices. These are actions controlled by antecedent conditions, and any appearance of freedom that they might possess is, says the hard determinist, an illusion.

But is it true, asks the soft determinist, that the actions in column **A** are uncaused? Take the case of Gandhi. To say that 'Gandhi fasted in order to free India' is the same as saying 'Gandhi's *desire* to free India *caused* him to fast'; and this desire, we may presume, was the result of other causes, such as his previous education and upbringing, the teaching of his Hindu faith, his experiences of British rule, and so on. In other words, while the precise causal explanation of Gandhi's fast may be difficult to establish - and here the historian and psychologist will help us - it is nevertheless accepted by the soft determinist that such an explanation is theoretically possible and that, if known, it would provide us with a complete and true account of why Gandhi did what he did. The conclusion is, therefore, that the actions in group **A** are no less determined than those in group **B**, and that *all* human actions, whether free or not, are wholly governed by causes.

6. Given by W T Stace *Religion and the Modern World* (New York: Harper & Row, 1952).

If all the events in columns **A** and **B** have causes, what is the difference between them? The difference, continues the soft determinist, lies in whether these events have *internal* or *external* causes. If you leave the country because you want a holiday, you leave of your own free will (ie voluntarily). If you leave because expelled by the authorities, you are forced to go (ie involuntarily.) But in each case your action is caused. When you leave freely, the cause is your desire to go abroad; when you leave unfreely, the cause is the force exerted upon you by the government. When, therefore, the cause is internal (ie the result of your own wishes or desires), you acted voluntarily and of your own free will; but when the cause is external (ie contrary to your wishes or desires) you acted involuntarily and under ocmpulsion.

According to the soft determinist, this distinction between internal and external causes explains why freedom (and so moral responsibility) is not only compatible with determinism but actually requires it. *All* human actions are caused. Here determinism is right. For if these actions were uncaused, they would be completely unpredictable, capricious, and therefore irresponsible. Thus when we say a person acted freely, we do not mean that his or her action was uncaused but rather that they were not compelled to do it, that they were under no kind of 'external' pressure, that they themselves chose to act in this manner. Here they act as free agents, even though their actions are just as much caused as those that are unfree. Similarly, when we say that a person is responsible for their actions, we still presuppose that they are free agents; but the freedom presupposed does not deny causal antecedents but rather accepts that freedom has causes, albeit causes of a particular kind. These causes proceed from the desires, beliefs and characters of those concerned: they are, that is, the 'internal' causes and the consequence of the particular psychological condition of each individual. This freedom, then, is the ability of every human being to act in accordance with his or her own wishes; and the more we know of these wishes, the more we are able to predict what each individual would do, if not what they will do.

If determinism is compatible with freedom in this last sense - if one's wishes and desires may be counted among the causes of one's actions - then it is also compatible with moral responsibility. If X could not have acted otherwise because of some 'external' physical constraint, if Smith's inability to swim prevented him from saving the drowning child, then clearly no moral responsibility is involved and X is not to blame. But if not being responsible means that X could not have acted otherwise because of certain 'internal' constraints - that Smith did what he did because of certain wishes or desires on his part - then this is the same as saying that X *was* responsible. What he did was of his own doing, freely undertaken, and the result of his character; that it was precisely his being X (and not Y) that caused, and was responsible for, his action.

Questions: Determinism and Free Will

1. Give examples from your own experience to support the thesis of determinism. Can you offer any alternative interpretations of these examples?

2. 'On Darrow's argument, all crooks get off.' Discuss.

3. Is it true to say that criminals have no more control over their behaviour than the sick have over their state of health? If it is true, what are the implications for our judicial system?

4. What argument, based on the immediate experience of decision-making, is introduced by the libertarians as evidence of free-will?

5. Give examples from your own experience to support Campbell's distinction between personality and moral self. How would a hard determinist assess these examples?

6. Does soft determinism adequately overcome the problems posed by hard determinism?

7. What premise, common to both libertarians and hard determinists, is rejected by soft determinists? On what grounds do they reject it?

8. Explain the libertarian claim that hard determinists are guilty of an unscientific assessment of the nature of evidence. Do you agree?

9. Analyse the following argument: In urging us to accept their theory as true, determinists provide a disproof of that theory. For the decision whether to accept the theory or not implies free will. There is no point in urging us to accept a theory if our choice is determined anyway.

10. Read the following account by A S Neill of his school, Summerhill. Do you think the absence of rules achieves the desired effect? What rules, if any, do you think essential for the education of children?

Summerhill began as an experimental school. It is no longer such; it is now a demonstration school, for it demonstrates that freedom works.

*When my first wife and I began the school, we had one main idea: to **make the school fit the child** - instead of making the child fit the school.*

I had taught in ordinary schools for many years. I knew the other way well. I knew it was all wrong. It was wrong because it was based on an adult conception of what a child should be and of how a child should learn. The other way dated from the days when psychology was still an unknown science.

Well, we set out to make a school in which we should allow children freedom to be themselves. In order to do this, we had to renounce all discipline, all direction, all suggestion, all moral training, all religious instruction. We have been called brave, but it did not require courage. All it required was what we had - a complete belief in the child as a good, not an evil, being. For almost forty years, this belief in the goodness of the child has never wavered; it rather has become a final faith . . .

What is Summerhill like? Well, for one thing, lessons are optional. Children can go to them or stay away from them, for years if they want to. There is a timetable, but only for the teachers.

The children have classes usually according to their age, but sometimes according to their interests. We have no new methods of teaching, because we do not consider that teaching in itself matters very much. Whether a school has or has not a special method for teaching long division is of no significance, for long division is of no importance except to those who **want** *to learn it. And the child who* **wants** *to learn long division* **will** *learn it no matter how it is taught.*

Children who come to Summerhill as kindergarteners attend lessons from the beginning of their stay; but pupils from other schools vow that they will never attend any beastly lessons again at any time. They play and cycle and get in people's way, but they fight shy of lessons. This sometimes goes on for months. The recovery time is proportionate to the hatred their last school gave them. Our record case was a girl from a convent. She loafed for three years. The average period of recovery from lessons aversion is three months.[7]

Bibliography: Determinism and Free Will

* indicates text referred to or extracted in main text

Berofsky, Bernard (ed) *Free Will and Determinism* (New York: Harper & Row, 1966) A comprehensive anthology.
Campbell, C A 'On Selfhood and Godhead',* *Philosophy: Paradox and Discovery*, ed Arthur J Minton (New York: McGraw-Hill, 1976)
Darrow, Clarence, 'Attorney for the Damned',* *Philosphy, Paradox and Discovery*, ed Arthur J Minton (New York: McGraw-Hill, 1976) An excellent general anthology.
Dworkin, G (ed) *Determinism, Free Will and Moral Responsiblity* (Englewood Cliffs, NJ: Prentice-Hall, 1970)
Honderich, T (ed) *Essays on Freedom of Action* (London: Routledge & Kegan Paul, 1973)
Hospers, John 'What Means This Freedom?'* *Determinism and Freedom in the Age of Modern Science*, ed S Hook (New York: New York University Press, 1958) The volume contains papers given at a New York symposium.
Neill, A S *Summerhill: A radical approach to child rearing** (London: Victor Gollancz, 1962)
Pears, D F (ed) *Freedom and the Will* (London: Macmillan, 1963)
Spinoza, Benedict de *Ethic*,* trans W Hale White, and revised by Amelia Hutchinson Stirling (London: T Fisher Unwin, 1894)
Stace, W T *Religion and the Modern World** (New York: Harper & Row, 1952)
Thornton, Mark *Do we have Free Will?* (Bristol: Bristol Classical Press, 1989) Very readable introduction to the major issues.
Watson, G (ed) *Free Will* (Oxford: Oxford University Press, 1982)

---

7. A S Neill, *Summerhill: A radical approach to child rearing* (London: Victor Gollancz, 1962) pp 4-5.

Discussion: Behaviourism

According to the libertarian model of man, all human beings have the capacity to act freely, the existence of free will being a matter of immediate experiential fact. Having acted in one way the individual feels certain that he could have acted in another. Man therefore achieves intellectual and moral maturity only after a long struggle: he is responsible for his victories, for which he deserves praise, and he is responsible for his failures, for which he deserves blame. This view of human beings is, however, rejected by **behaviourism**. There are many versions of behaviourism, all of which employ the principles of determinism, but the two most important are **psychological behaviourism** and **bio-behaviourism**.

Psychological Behaviourism

The origins of psychological behaviourism are generally attributed to the opening paragraph of an essay published in 1913 by John B Watson (1878-1958), the so-called 'father' of this branch of the behavioural sciences:

John B Watson

Psychology as the behaviorist views it is a purely objective experimental branch of natural science. Its theoretical goal is the prediction and control of behavior. Introspection forms no essential part of its methods, nor is the scientific value of its data dependent upon the readiness with which they lend themselves to interpretation in terms of consciousness. The behaviorist, in his efforts to get a unitary scheme of animal response, recognizes no dividing line between man and brute. The behavior of man, with all its refinement and complexity, forms only a part of the behaviorist's total scheme of investigation.[1]

Watson's suggestion that behaviour can be predicted and controlled follows from the determinist doctrine of universal causation. If everything in the universe is bound to the law of cause and effect, then it is possible to predict, once a certain event X has occurred, that it will have a particular result Y. By the same token, if I can set up certain conditions such that X occurs, then I have controlled the appearance of Y. Thus Watson and his followers maintain that man operates within a wholly determined and orderly world and that all human behaviour, including man's moral decisions, are governed and controlled by causal processes which are in principle knowable. Imperfect prediction of human events and decisions is thus due to imperfect knowledge. What are regarded as free actions are no more than those actions which an embryonic science of human behaviour has not as yet explained.

Less familiar to us is Watson's rejection of what he calls 'introspection' and 'consciousness'. We are all sufficiently aware of our thoughts (or consciousness) that we can, after a process of interior analysis (or introspection) report them to others. The trouble is, says Watson, that these reports are so varied, and the thoughts they describe so private, that no reliable classification of

1. 'Psychology as the Behaviorist Views it', *Psychological Review*, (March 1913), 20, p 158.

these inner sensations is possible. For example, after a process of self-examination, X may conclude that he is in love with Y, and even tell Y that he is; but there is no means whereby an outsider, even Y, can conclusively check that X really does feel like this. Thus Watson rejects introspection as unscientific: he does not deny the existence of so-called 'mental events' but maintains that, because the evidence available cannot be observed by any one except the subject, it cannot provide the data of psychology. Some of Watson's followers go even further:

> *The simplest and most satisfactory view is that thought is simply behavior - verbal or non-verbal, covert or overt. It is not some mysterious process responsible for behavior but the very behavior itself in all the complexity of its controlling relations, with respect to both man the behaver and the environment in which he lives. The concepts and methods which have emerged from the analysis of behavior, verbal or otherwise, are most appropriate to the study of what has traditionally been called the human mind.[2]*

What, then, does determine the behaviour of men? Watson believed that two factors were decisive. There is *heredity*, which involves merely the inheritance of a body and certain physiological features: one does not inherit intelligence, talents, or instincts. There is also the effect of one's *environment*. By the manipulation of man's surroundings, so Watson contends, the behaviour of man can be decisively altered, and even quite complicated activities - like driving a car, solving a problem, falling in love - can be broken down into a series of learned responses. This is clear from Watson's famous remark:

> *Give me a dozen healthy infants, well-formed, and my own specified world to bring them up in and I'll guarantee to take any one at random and train him to become any type of specialist I might select - doctor, lawyer, artist, merchant-chief and, yes, even beggar-man, and thief, regardless of his talents, penchants, tendencies, abilities, vocations, and race of his ancestors.[3]*

The process whereby environment affects behaviour Watson called 'conditioning'. His theory of conditioning was influenced by the pioneering work of the Russian physiologist Ivan Pavlov (1849-1936.) During his research into the digestive glands of dogs, Pavlov noticed that, while all dogs salivate when eating, the secretion of saliva also occurred before: it was enough for them to see the food or even hear the sound of their keeper's footsteps. In his research, Pavlov carried this to the point where his animals would react to a particular stimulus that did not normally cause salivation (ie the dogs would salivate on hearing a musical note played before feeding.) Because food invariably causes salivation, Pavlov calls food an 'unconditional stimulus' and the salivation an 'unconditioned response'. A musical note, on the other hand, because it does not usually produce salivation, is called a 'conditioned stimulus'. In Pavlov's experiments, the dogs had so associated the conditioned stimulus (music) with the unconditional stimulus (food) that it produced the unconditioned response (salivation). When this occurs, says Pavlov, the unconditional response may be called a 'conditioned response'. According to him, a conditioned stimulus always results in a conditioned response.

Classical or Pavlovian conditioning, to which Watson is indebted, explains a type of learning familiar to us all. Schoolchildren, for example, associate bells with food and the beginning of lessons, while at other times such sounds may denote danger. This form of conditioning cannot however account for all human behaviour. Hungry children (or dogs) will not sit patiently all day waiting for a bell to be rung: if no food appears, they will seek it for themselves. People, in other words, are not always conditioned by their environment but will often operate on it to get what they want. Such actions are called *operant behaviours* and they are learned by *operant conditioning*.

2. B F Skinner, *Verbal Behavior* (New York: Appleton-Century-Crofts, 1957) p 449.
3. J B Watson, *Behaviorism* (London: Kegan Paul, 1925) p 82.

The notion of operant conditioning is associated with the work of B F Skinner (b 1904), whom many regard as the foremost behaviourist of our day. What is being conditioned here is not a reflex response (like salivation) but any kind of spontaneous behaviour that the animal performs without specific stimulus. Operant conditioning therefore changes *voluntary* behaviour and thus is sometimes known as *behaviour modification*. If a rat in a 'Skinner box' accidentally hits a lever that produces food, it will eventually associate the lever with the food and press the one to get the other: it has learnt a new voluntary behaviour. The most important step in operant conditioning is to arrange the environment so that the desired behaviour occurs. To achieve this, the behaviour must be *reinforced*. Reinforcement that is pleasant (like rewarding or praising) Skinner calls **positive reinforcement**. For pushing the lever the rat is rewarded with food, the diligent student with high marks, the industrious worker with increased pay, and so on.

Negative reinforcement, on the other hand, acts to remove an unpleasant stimulus, which is a reward in itself. So the rat, suffering from electric shocks, will hit the lever to switch off the current. In human affairs this same technique can be seen in the government's threat of punishment to achieve obedience - in the pain, humiliation or discomfort it may and does inflict on the individual. Reinforcement distinguishes between those things we *have* to do to avoid punishment and those we *want* to do for rewarding consequences. Both methods increase the probability that an action or behaviour will be repeated.

Bio-Behavourism

The second form of conditioning is for many people the more alarming and potentially danger-ous of the two. This is achieved through bio-behavioural control, otherwise known as 'genetic engineering' or **eugenics**, which seeks to maintain or improve the genetic makeup of the species. As first used by the English geneticist Francis Galton in the late 19th century, the term 'eugen-ics' stood for a blatantly racist and class-orientated programme, his intention being to allow the more suitable races a better chance of prevailing over the less suitable.

> *It may seem monstrous that the weak should be crowded out by the strong, but it is still more monstrous that the races best fitted to play their part on the stage of life, should be crowded out by the incompetent, the ailing, and the desponding.*
>
> *The time may hereafter arrive, in far distant years, when the population of the earth shall be kept as strictly within the bounds of number and suitability of race, as the sheep on a well-ordered moor or the plants in an orchard-house; in the meantime, let us do what we can to encourage the multiplication of the races best fitted to invent and conform to a higher and generous civilization, and not, out of a mistaken instinct of giving support to the weak, prevent the incoming of strong and hearty individuals.*[4]

While subsequent eugenicists have denounced Galton's prejudices, many still share his belief that mankind is in a state of progressive genetic decline and that some form of eugenics is necessary to halt it. With Crick and Watson's discovery in 1953 of DNA (deoxyribonucleic acid) - the code which determines each individual's genetic structure - this is now a genuine possibility, allowing for the direct improvement of genotypes and the reduction of genetic deficiencies through genetic surgery.

Human eugenics can be divided into two types, positive and negative. **Positive eugenics** involves the planned breeding of so-called superior men and women to improve the genetic pool and to create new inherited capacities for future generations. This parallels techniques already used successfully in agriculture for the production of new hybrid breeds of cattle and other food

---

4. *Hereditary Genius* (London: Macmillan, 1870) p 343.

stuffs. The most famous example of positive eugenics is the sperm-bank proposed by Hermann J Muller, the leading eugenicist of recent years. The sperm of selected men, chosen for their intellectual and social desirability, would be collected, frozen and stored in sperm-banks, and then used in the full-scale insemination of large numbers of women. This, Muller contends, would significantly improve the human genetic stock. Indeed, Muller goes so far as to suggest that certain specific qualities could be eugenically produced by this method: 'a genuine warmth of fellow feeling and a cooperative disposition, a depth and breadth of intellectual capacity, moral courage and integrity, an appreciation of nature and art, and an aptness of expression and of communication'.[5]

Muller's programme is not altogether far-fetched, particularly if we take into account recent developments in so-called *recombinant DNA research*. This research provides the means for freely transferring genetic information (DNA) from one cell into a cell of a different genetic background, and thus allows the gene to produce the same product regardless of the cell in which it is used. This is not cloning - which requries the transfer of all genetic material from one cell into a cell whose DNA has been removed - but it does open up the possibility of altering the genetic makeup of a test-tube embryo prior to implantation in the womb. By this means parents could decide the physical characteristics of their offspring before birth.

Not surprisingly, positive eugenics has been subject to many criticisms. One is that, in making more people genetically alike, it will reduce the evolutionary advantages of genetic variation, which allows species to be more adaptable to any drastic environmental changes that may occur. Another is the notorious difficulty of fixing those characteristics considered valuable by society. We may consider intellect and beauty desirable, but there is no guarantee that our children will. Muller himself, in an early list of valuable sperm-donors, includes Marx, Lenin and Sun Yat Sen; but in subsequent lists these names are excluded and replaced by Einstein and Lincoln! But perhaps the most questionable eugenic assumption is that these desired qualities have a genetic rather than environmental basis. While it may be true that some characteristics can be genetically engineered, it is false to suppose that *all* can be eugenically acquired. This, indeed, is to underestimate the claims of behaviourists like Watson and Skinner, who argue that the desired characteristics are more probably controlled by environment. However strong the genetic predisposition may be to act in a certain way, it is, they argue, the effect of behavioural conditioning that is more likely to produce the desired result.

Negative eugenics is preventative genetic medicine: it has the laudable objective of eliminating or treating those genes carrying disease or disability. The most widely practised example of this is *amniocentesis*, leading to therapeutic abortion. By obtaining cells from the amniotic fluid surrounding the unborn child, parents with chromosomol translocations can be told of the high risk of producing children who are mentally retarded or who possess congenital malformations. This procedure is generally regarded as a major beneficial advance in biomedical technology. Other precedures involve voluntary or involuntary sterilization.

Negative eugenics shares all the criticisms of positive eugenics, not least the problem of deciding what is genetically good and bad and the problem of deciding who makes that decision. Its major difficulty, however, is that faced by all preventative medicine: How far can the programme of prevention be extended? This appears when we move from the treatment of particular individuals (or foetuses) to the treatment of whole populations. In the particular case it may well be a clear-cut teleological judgement for doctor and parent alike that a badly handicapped child should be aborted; but to give this decision normative ethical significance - to say that foetuses with this genetic defect ought always to be aborted - is to make a further teleological judgement about the place of retarded or physically defective individuals in our society: to judge them, in other words, according to the principle of social utility. But how far can

---

5. 'Should we strengthen or weaken our genetic heritage?' *Daedalus*, 90, No 3 (Summer, 1961) p 445.

this principle be extended? Does it immediately legitimate the compulsory sterilization of retarded individuals? Does it require that marriages between people of reduced intelligence should be disallowed? Does it mandate the screening of whole populations for particular biochemical defects that can be detected *in utero*? And in all these questions another ethical dilemma is presupposed: the question of the invasion of privacy, and what one does with the information beyond giving it to the individuals concerned.

Of the three following extracts, two present persuasive arguments for psychological and bio-behavioural control. The first is taken from Skinner's futuristic novel *Walden Two* (1948). Here Skinner (in the guise of the creator of Walden Two, Frazier) argues that, if the terrifying problems of the present world are to be overcome, we must reorientate our values in such a way as to ensure the survival of the species. This involves above all sacrificing the 'myth' of freedom for designed control. In *Walden Two*, the country of the future, the behavioural analyst applies the principles of operant conditioning primarily to the rearing and education of children, shaping them 'with due regard for the lives they are going to lead.'

The second extract is taken from an article by Joseph Fletcher. In the 1960s Fletcher achieved considerable fame as the leading exponent of so-called 'situation ethics', a moral viewpoint which was receptive to the liberal and permissive tone of the time. According to Fletcher, the most important aspect of the moral life is not a blind adherence to legalistic-deontological maxims - what he calls the *a priori* approach - but rather to the spirit of 'loving concern' which should always underpin them. This loving concern is expressed in the pragmatic desire to meet and fulfil human needs. Anything, therefore, that contributes to the improvement of the human situation, such as bio-behavioural control, should be enthusiastically supported.

It is perhaps appropriate that the last extract should belong to Aldous Huxley, the author of *Brave New World*. In that book Huxley warned against the dangers of all forms of totalitarian control. In his *Brave New World Revisited* (1959) Huxley reasserts his earlier criticism and points to the great impersonal forces that now menace freedom, among them being the modern techniques of psychological and biological manipulation. His final remarks provide a salutary, if ultimately pessimistic, assessment of the capacity of modern man to prevent the final disappearance of freedom altogether.

1. B F Skinner: Walden Two [6]

'Isn't it time we talked about freedom?' I said. 'We parted a day or so ago on an agreement to let the question of freedom ring. It's time to answer, don't you think?'

'My answer is simple enough,' said Frazier. 'I deny that freedom exists at all. I must deny it, or my program would be absurd. You can't have a science about a subject matter which hops capriciously about. Perhaps we can never *prove* that man isn't free; it's an assumption. But the increasing success of a science of behavior makes it more and more plausible.'

'On the contrary, a simple personal experience makes it untenable,' said Castle. 'The experience of freedom. I *know* that I'm free.'

'It must be quite consoling,' said Frazier.

'And what's more, you do, too,' said Castle hotly. 'When you deny your own freedom for the sake of playing with a science of behavior, you're acting in plain bad faith. That's the only way I can explain it.' He tried to recover himself and shrugged his shoulders. 'At least you'll grant that you *feel* free.'

'The "feeling of freedom" should deceive no one,' said Frazier. 'Give me a concrete case.'

'Well, right now,' Castle said. he picked up a book of matches. 'I'm free to hold or drop these matches.'

'You will, of course, do one or the other,' said Frazier. 'Linguistically or logically there seem to be two possibilities, but I submit that there's only one in fact. The determining forces may be subtle but they are inexorable. I suggest that as an orderly person you will probably hold -ah! you drop them! Well, you see, that's all part of your behavior with respect to me. You couldn't resist the temptation to prove me wrong. It was all lawful. You had no choice . . . '

'That's entirely too glib,' said Castle. 'It's easy to argue lawfulness after the fact. But let's see you predict what I will do in advance. Then I'll agree there's a law.'

'I didn't say that behavior is always predictable, any more than the weather is always predictable. There are often too many factors to be taken into account. We can measure them all accurately, and we couldn't perform the mathematical operations needed to make a prediction if we had the measurements. The legality is usually an assumption, but none the less important in judging the issue at hand.'

'Take a case where there's no choice, then,' said Castle. 'Certainly a man in jail isn't free in the sense in which I am free now.'

'Good! That's an excellent start. Let us classify the kinds of determiners of human behavior. One class, as you suggest, is physical restraint, handcuffs, iron bars, forcible coercion. These are ways in which we shape human behavior according to our wishes. They're crude, and they sacrifice the affection of the controllee, but they often work. Now, what other ways are there of limiting freedom?'

Frazier had adopted a professorial tone and Castle refused to answer.

'The threat of force would be one,' I said.

'Right. And here again we shan't encourage any loyalty on the part of the controllee. He has perhaps a shade more of the feeling of freedom, since he can always "choose to act and accept the consequences," but he doesn't feel exactly free. He knows his behavior is being coerced. Now what else?'

I had no answer.

'Force or the threat of force - I see no other possibility,' said Castle after a moment.

'Precisely,' said Frazier.

'But certainly a large part of my behavior has no connection with force at all. There's my freedom!' said Castle.

'I wasn't agreeing that there was no other possibility - merely that *you* could see no other. Not being a good behaviorist - or a good   Christian, for that matter - you have no feeling for a tremendous power of a different sort.'

'What's that?'

6. B F Skinner, *Walden Two* (New York: Macmillan, 1948; edition used, 1970) pp 257-264.

'I shall have to be technical,' said Frazier. 'But only for a moment. It's what the science of behavior calls "reinforcement theory". The things that can happen to us fall into three classes. To some things we are indifferent. Other things we like - we want them to happen, and we take steps to make them happen again. Still other things we don't like - we don't want them to happen and we take steps to get rid of them or keep them from happening again.'

'*Now*,' Frazier continued earnestly, 'if it's in our power to create any of the situations which a person likes or to remove any situation he doesn't like, we can control his behavior. When he behaves as we want him to behave, we simply create a situation he likes, or remove one he doesn't like. As a result, the probability that he will behave that way again goes up, which is what we want. Technically it's called "positive reinforcement".

B F Skinner

'The old school made the amazing mistake of supposing that the reverse was true, that by removing a situation a person likes or setting up one he doesn't like - in other words by punishing him - it was possible to *reduce* the probability that he would behave in a given way again. That simply doesn't hold. It has been established beyond question. What is emerging at this critical stage in the evolution of society is a behavioral and cultural technology based on positive reinforcement alone. We are gradually discovering - at an untold cost in human suffering - that in the long run punishment doesn't reduce the probability that an act will occur. We have been so preoccupied with the contrary that we always take 'force' to mean punishment. We don't say we're using force when we send shiploads of food into a starving country, though we're displaying quite as much *power* as if we were sending troops and guns. . .' .

'Now that we *know* how positive reinforcement works and why negative doesn't . . . we can be more deliberate, and hence more successful, in our cultural design. We can achieve a sort of control under which the controlled, though they are following a code more scrupulously than was ever the case under the old system, nevertheless *feel free*. They are doing what they want to do, not what they are forced to do. That's the source of the tremendous power of positive reinforcement - there's no restraint and no revolt. By a careful cultural design, we control not the final behavior, but the *inclination* to behave - the motives, the desires, the wishes.

'The curious thing is that in that case *the question of freedom never arises*. Mr Castle was free to drop the matchbook in the sense that nothing was preventing him. If it had been securely bound to his hand he wouldn't have been free. Nor would he have been quite free if I'd covered him with a gun and threatened to shoot him if he let it fall. The question of freedom arises when there is restraint - either physical or psychological . . .

'We have no vocabulary of freedom dealing with what we want to do,' Frazier went on. 'The question never arises. When men strike for freedom, they strike against jails and the police, or the threat of them - against oppression. They never strike against forces which make them want to act the way they do. Yet, it seems to be understood that governments will operate only through force or the threat of force, and that all other principles of control will be left to education, religion, and commerce. If this continues to be the case, we may as well give up. A government can never create a free people with the techniques now allotted to it.

'The question is: Can men live in freedom and peace? And the answer is: Yes, if we can build a social structure which will satisfy the needs of everyone and in which everyone will want to observe the supporting code. But so far this has been achieved only in Walden Two. Your ruthless accusations to the contrary, Mr Castle, this is the freest place on earth. And it is free precisely because we make no use of force or the threat of force. Every bit of our research, from the nursery through the psychological management of our adult membership, is directed toward that end - to exploit every alternative to forcible control. By skillful planning, by a wise choice of techniques we *increase* the feeling of freedom.

'It's not planning which infringes upon freedom, but planning which uses force. A sense of freedom was practically unknown in the planned society of Nazi Germany, because the planners made a fantastic use of force and the threat of force.

'No, Mr Castle, when a science of behavior has once been achieved, there's no alternative to a planned society. We can't leave mankind to an accidental or biased control. But by using the principle of positive reinforcement - carefully avoiding force or the threat of force - we can preserve a personal sense of freedom.'

Questions: Skinner

1. Give examples of positive and negative reinforcement operating today. Do you think Skinner is right in his measurement of their effects?

2. Do you agree with Frazier that Walden Two is the 'freest place on earth?'

3. To what extent do you think our quality of life would be increased or diminished in Walden Two? Give examples.

2. *Joseph Fletcher: Ethical Aspects of Genetic Controls* [7]

The ethical question . . . is whether we can justify designed genetic changes in man, for the sake of both therapeutic and nontherapeutic benefits. We are able to carry out both negative or corrective eugenics - for example, to obviate gross chromosomal disorders - and positive or constructive eugenics - for example, to specialize an individual's genetic constitution for a special vocation. Like all other problems in ethical analysis, the morality of genetic intervention and engineering comes down to the question of means and ends, or of acts and consequences. Can we justify the goals and the methods of genetic engineering?

. . . Leaving aside technical philosophical conventions, let me suggest that when we tackle right-wrong or good-evil or desirable-undesirable questions there are fundamentally two alternative lines of approach. The first one supposes that whether any act or course of action is right or wrong depends on its consequences. The second approach supposes that our actions are right or wrong according to whether they comply with general moral principles or prefabricated rules of conduct . . . The first approach is consequentialist; the second is *a priori*.

This is the rock-bottom issue, and it is also (I want to suggest) the definitive question in the ethical analysis of genetic control. Are we to reason from general propositions and universals to normative decisions, or are we to reason from empirical data, variable situations and human values to normative decisions? Which? One or the other.

. . . The more commonly held ethical approach is a . . . pragmatic one - sometimes sneered at by *a priorists* and called a 'mere morality of goals'. This ethics is my own, and I believe it is implicit in the ethics of all biomedical research and development as well as in medical care. We reason from the data of each actual case or problem and then choose the course that offers an optimum or maximum of desirable consequences.

For those whom we might call situational or clinical consequentialists results are what counts, and results are good when they contribute to human well-being. On that basis the real issue ethically is whether genetic change in man will, in its foreseeable or predictable results, add to or take away from human welfare. We do not act by *a priori* categorical rules nor by dogmatic principles, such as the religious-faith proposition that genetic intervention is forbidden to human initiative or the metaphysical claim that every individual has an inalienable right to a unique genotype - presumably according to however chance and the general gene pool might happen to constitute it. For consequentialists, making decisions empirically is the problem. The question becomes, 'When would it be right, and when would it be wrong?'.

What, then, might be a situation in which constructive or positive eugenics would be justified because the good to be gained - the proportionate good - would be great enough? . . . Take cloning of humans, for example, as a form of genetic engineering . . . There might be a need in the social order at large for one or more people specially constituted genetically to survive long periods outside bathyspheres at great marine depths, or outside space capsules at great heights. Control of a child's sex by cloning, to avoid any one of 50 sex-linked genetic diseases, or to meet a family's survival need, might be justifiable. I would vote for laboratory fertilization from donors to give a child to an infertile pair of spouses.

It is entirely possible, given our present increasing pollution of the human gene pool through uncontrolled sexual reproduction, that we might have to replicate healthy people to compensate for the spread of genetic diseases and to elevate the plus factors available in ordinary reproduction. It could easily come about that overpopulation would force us to put a stop to general fecundity, and then, to avoid discrimination, to resort to laboratory reproduction from unidentified cell sources. If we had 'cell banks' in which the tissue of a species of wild life in danger of extinction could be stored for replication, we could do the same for the sake of endangered humans, such as the Hairy Ainu in northern Japan or certain strains of Romani gypsies.

If the greatest good of the greatest number (ie, the social good) were served by it, it would be justifiable not only to specialize the capacities of people by cloning or by constructive genetic engineering, but also

---

7. 'Ethical Aspects of Genetic Control', *New England Journal of Medicine,* 185, 1971, pp 776-783. Reprinted in *Ethics in Medicine*, ed S J Reiser, A J Dyck and W J Curran (Massachusetts: The MIT Press, 1977) pp 387-393.

to bio-engineer or bio-design para-humans or 'modified men' - as chimeras (part animal) or cyborg-androids (part prosthetes). I would vote for cloning top-grade soldiers and scientists, or for supplying them through other genetic means, if they were needed to offset an elitist or tyrannical power plot by other cloners - a truly science-fiction situation, but imaginable. I suspect I would favor making and using man-machine hybrids rather than genetically designed people for dull, unrewarding or dangerous roles needed none the less for the community's welfare - perhaps the testing of suspected pollution areas or the investigation of threatening volcanos or snow-slides.

Ours is a Promethean situation. We cannot clearly see what the promises and the dangers are. Both are there, in the biomedical potential. Much of the scare-mongering by whole-hog or *a priori* opponents of genetic control link it with tyranny. This is false and misleading. Their propoganda line supposes, for one thing, that a cloned person would be a 'carbon copy' of his single-cell parent because the genotype is repeated, as if such genetically designed individuals would have no individuating personal histories or variable environments. Personalities are not shaped alone by genotypes.

Furthermore, they presume that society will be a dictatorship and that such designed or cloned people people would not be allowed to marry or reproduce from the social gene pool, nor be free to choose roles and functions other than the ones for which they had a special constitutional capability. But is this realistic? Is it not, actually, a mood or additudinal posture rather than a rational or problematic view of the question? . . . The danger of tyranny is a real danger. But genetic controls do not lead to dictatorship - if there is any cause-and-effect relation between them it is the other way round - the reverse. People who appeal to *Brave New World* and *1984* and *Fahrenheit 451* forget this, that the tyranny is set up first and then genetic controls are employed. The problem of misuse is political, not biological.

. . . Needs are the moral stabilizers, not rights. The legalistic temper gives first place to rights, but the humanistic temper puts needs in the driver's seat. If human rights conflict with human needs, let needs prevail. If medical care can use genetic controls preventively to protect people from disease or deformity, or to ameliorate such things, then let so-called 'rights' to be born step aside. If research with embryos and foetal tissue is needed to give us the means to cure and prevent the tragedies of 'unique genotypes', even though it involves the sacrifice of some conceptuses, then let rights take a back seat . . .

Owing to the work of microbiologists and embryologists we are already able to produce babies born from parents who are separated by space or even by death; women are already able to nourish and gestate other women's children; one man can 'father' thousands of children; virgin births or parthenogenesis (for that is what cloning is) are likely soon to be feasible; by genetic intervention we can shape babies, rather than only from the simple seed of our loins; artificial wombs and placentas are projected by biochemists and pharmacologists. All this means that we are going to have to change or alter our old ideas about who or what a father is, or a mother, or a family. Francis Crick, co-describer of DNA, and others are quite right to say that all this is going to destroy to some extent our traditional grounds for ethical beliefs.

Questions: Fletcher

1. What kind of society would you like to see established today? Using the techniques of bio-behaviourism, how would you set about achieving it?

2. Assess Fletcher's remark that 'the problem of misuse is political, not biological.'

3. Will developments in bio-behavioural techniques 'destroy our traditional grounds for ethical beliefs'? Give examples.

3. Aldous Huxley: Brave New World Revisited [8]

(We) find ourselves confronted by a very disquieting question: Do we really wish to act upon our knowledge? Does a majority of the population think it worth while to take a good deal of trouble, in order to halt and, if possible, reverse the current drift towards the totalitarian control of everything? In the United States - and America is the prophetic image of the rest of the urban-industrial world as it will be a few years from now - recent public opinion polls have revealed that an actual majority of young people in their teens, the voters of tomorrow, have no faith in democratic institutions, see no objection to the censorship of unpopular ideas, do not believe that government of the people by the people is possible, and would be perfectly content, if they can continue to live in the style to which the boom has accustomed them, to be ruled, from above, by an oligarchy of assorted experts. That so many of the well-fed young television-watchers in the world's most powerful democracy should be so completely indifferent to the idea of self-government, so blankly uninterested in freedom of thought and the right to dissent, is distressing, but not too surprising. 'Free as a bird', we say, and envy the winged creatures for their power of unrestricted movement in all the three dimensions. But, alas, we forget the dodo. Any bird that has learned how to grub up a good living without being compelled to use its wings will soon renounce the privilege of flight and remain forever grounded. Something analogous is true of human beings. If the bread is supplied regularly and copiously three times a day, many of them will be perfectly content to live by bread alone - or at least by bread and circuses alone. 'In the end', says the Grand Inquisitor in Dostoevsky's parable, 'in the end they will lay their freedom at our feet and say to us, "Make us your slaves, but feed us."' And when Alyosha Karamazov asks his brother, the teller of the story, if the Grand Inquisitor is speaking ironically, Ivan answers: 'Not a bit of it! He claims it as a merit for himself and his Church that they have vanquished freedom and done so to make men happy.' Yes, to make men happy; 'for nothing', the Inquisitor insists, 'has ever been more insupportable for a man or a human society than freedom.' Nothing, except the absence of freedom; for when things go badly, and the rations are reduced and the slave drivers step up their demands, the grounded dodos will clamour again for their wings - only to renounce them, yet once more, when times grow better and the dodo-farmers become more lenient and generous. The young people who now think so poorly of democracy may grow up to become fighters for freedom. The cry of 'Give me television and hamburgers, but don't bother me with the responsibilities of liberty', may give place, under altered circumstances, to the cry of 'Give me liberty or give me death'. If such a revolution takes place, it will be due in part to the operation of forces over which even the most powerful rulers have very little control, in part to the incompetence of those rulers, their inability to make effective use of the mind-manipulating instruments with which science and technology have supplied, and will go on supplying, the would-be tyrant. Considering how little they knew and how poorly they were equipped, the Grand Inquisitors of earlier times did remarkably well. But their successors, the well-informed, thoroughly scientific dictators of the future, will undoubtedly be able to do a great deal better. The Grand Inquisitor reproaches Christ with having called upon men to be free and tells Him that 'we have corrected Thy work and founded it upon miracle, mystery and authority'. But miracle, mystery and authority are not enough to guarantee the indefinite survival of a dictatorship. In my fable of *Brave New World*, the dictators had added science to the list and thus were able to enforce their authority by manipulating the bodies of embryos, the reflexes of infants, and the minds of children and adults. And instead of merely talking about miracles and hinting symbolically at miracles, they were able, by means of drugs, to give their subjects the direct experience of mysteries and miracles - to transform mere faith into ecstatic knowledge. The older dictators fell because they could never supply their subjects with enough bread, enough circuses, enough miracles and mysteries. Nor did they possess a really effective system of mind-manipulation. In the past free-thinkers and revolutionaries were often the products of the most piously orthodox education. This is not surprising. The methods employed by orthodox educators were and still are extremely inefficient. Under a scientific dictator education will really work - with the result that most men and women will grow up to love their servitude and will never dream of revolution. There seems to be no good reason why a thoroughly scientific dictatorship should ever be overthrown.

---

8. *Brave New World Revisited* (London: Chatto and Windus, 1959) pp 161-164.

Meanwhile there is still some freedom left in the world. Many young people, it is true, do not seem to value freedom. But some of us still believe that, without freedom, human beings cannot become fully human and that freedom is therefore supremely valuable. Perhaps the forces that now menace freedom are too strong to be resisted for very long. It is still our duty to do whatever we can to resist them.

Questions: Huxley

1. 'There seems to be no good reason why a thorough scientific dictatorship should ever be overthrown.' Do you agree with Huxley's conclusion?

2. 'The power of man to make himself what he pleases means . . . the power of some men to make other men what *they* please' (C S Lewis.) Discuss in the light of Huxley's remarks.

3. To what extent does the way we live now increase or decrease our freedom to act? Give examples.

Questions: Behaviourism

1. 'The definition of utility will change as our political and social needs change.' Do you consider this an argument for extending or limiting behavioural control?

2. How do you think Skinner or Fletcher would reply to the question: Who controls the controllers? How would you reply?

3. What moral difficulties do you see in the creation of genetic data-banks, which would help select those most suitable for different types of job?

4. Read the following extract. What conditioning techniques would you employ to sell a product? Give examples when you would consider such techniques justified and unjustified. Are there any products that you would never sell?

> *A firm specializing in supplying 'education' material to schoolteachers in the form of wall charts, board cutouts, teachers' manuals made this appeal to merchants and advertisers: 'Eager minds can be molded to want your products! In the grade schools throughout America are nearly 23,000,000 young girls and boys. These children eat food, wear out clothes, use soap. They are consumers today and will be the buyers of tomorrow. Here is a vast market for your products. Sell these children on your brand name and they will insist that their parents buy no other. Many farsighted advertisers are*

cashing in today . . . and building for tomorrow . . . by molding eager minds' thorugh Project Education Material supplied to teachers. It added reassuringly: 'all carrying sugar-coated messages designed to create acceptance and demand for the products . . .' In commenting on this appeal Clyde Miller, in his The Process of Persuasion, *explained the problem of conditioning the reflexes of children by saying, 'It takes time, yes, but if you expect to be in business for any length of time, think of what it can mean to your firm in profits if you can condition a million or ten million children who will grow up into adults trained to buy your product as soldiers are trained to advance when they hear the trigger words "forward march."* '[9]

Bibliography: Behaviourism

* denotes text referred to or extracted in main text

Beauchamp, T L (ed with J F Childers *Principles of Biomedical Ethics* (Oxford: Oxford University Press, 1983) An application of general ethical theories to specific medical situations.
Cox, Harvey (ed) *The Situation Ethics Debate* (Philadelphia: The Westminster Press, 1968)
Fletcher, Joseph 'Ethical Aspects of Genetic Control',* *New England Journal of Medicine*, 285, (1971) pp 776-783. Reprinted in *Ethics in Medicine*, ed S J Reiser, A J Dyck and W J Curran (Massachusetts: The MIT Press, 1977) pp 387-393;
    Situation Ethics (London: SCM Press, 1966)
Galton, Francis *Hereditary Genius** (London: Macmillan, 1870)
Huxley, Aldous *Brave New World Revisited** (London: Chatto & Windus, 1959)
Lear, John *Recombinant DNA: The Untold Story* (New York: Crown Publishers, 1978) A readable but often sensational account.
Muller, Hermann J 'Should we strengthen or weaken our genetic Heritage?'* *Deedalus*, 90, No 3 (Summer, 1961) pp 432-450.
Packard, Vance *The Hidden Persuaders* (New York: David McKay, 1957)*
Ramsey, Paul *Fabricated Man: The Ethics of Genetic Control* (New Haven & London: Yale University Press, 1970)
Richards, John (ed) *Recombinant DNA: Science, Ethics, and Politics* (New York & London: Academic Press, 1978)
Skinner, B F *Verbal Behavior** (New York: Appleton-Century-Crofts, 1957);
    Walden Two* (New York: Macmillan, 1948)
Simmons, Paul D *Birth & Death: Bioethical decision-making* (Philadelphia: The Westminster Press, 1983) A discussion of abortion, euthanasia and genetic engineering from the biblical perspective.
Singer, Peter (ed with William Walters) *Test-tube Babies* (Oxford: Oxford University Press, 1982)
Watson, John B *Behaviorism** (London: Kegan Paul, 1925;
    'Psychology as the Behaviorist Views it',* *Psychological Review* (March 1913), 20, pp 158-177.
Zilinskas (ed with B K Zimmerman) *The Gene-Splicing Wars: Reflections on the Recombinant DNA Controversy* (London: Collier Macmillan, 1986)

---

9. Vance Packard, *The Hidden Persuaders* (New York: David McKay, 1957) pp 158-159.

APPENDIX

META-ETHICS

In seeking to understand the meaning and function of ethical terms like 'good' and 'bad', Meta-ethics has produced a great number of different theories. These can be usefully classified under three general headings: 1)**Ethical Naturalism** (also known as Definism); 2)**Ethical Non-naturalism** (or Intuitionism); and 3) **Ethical Non-cognitivism** (or Emotivism).

1. Ethical Naturalism

This theory holds that all ethical statements can be translated into non-ethical ones, more specifically into verifiable *factual* statements. For example, consider the difference between 'Adolf Hitler committed suicide in 1945' and 'Adolf Hitler was an evil man'. The first statement is a factual statement, the truth or falsity of which can be determined by evidence. The ethical naturalist holds, however, that the second statement is also verifiable (or falsifiable) in much the same way. We can find out whether Hitler was evil either by establishing if, in his personal behaviour, he was for example cruel, deceitful or cowardly; or by determining whether his actions had evil consequences. If we find evidence that he was like this, or that his actions did have these results, then we have verified the statement that 'Adolf Hitler was an evil man'. If the evidence points in the opposite direction, then this statement is false.

Another form of ethical naturalism reduces all ethical statements to expressions of approval or disapproval, whether personal or general. So, if I say 'Mother Theresa is good', I am not saying anything about the nature or quality of the woman herself but merely that 'I approve of Mother Theresa', or that 'The majority of people approve of Mother Theresa'. Again, these statements can be conclusively verified or falsified, this time by an estimate of my and other people's psychological response to Mother Theresa. Both are verifiable (or falsifiable) by observation of oneself or by a statistical account of whether this view is shared by others.

Of the many objections to ethical naturalism, the most obvious is that it appears to prevent us from settling, or even engaging in, any kind of moral dispute. If 'A is good' simply refers to the disposition of the speaker - that he or she approves of A - then this judgement can never be wrong (except when the person concerned has misread his own feelings); it can never be disputed by another person, since it is sufficient for me to be right that I approve of it; and it will be logically compatible with any judgement that I, or anyone else, may subsequently hold. If I now hold that 'Slavery is wrong', but tomorrow hold that 'Slavery is right', both positions will be valid in so far as they accurately describe a change in my attitude. If someone else should hold that 'Slavery is wrong', this position is also valid since it is merely the expression of his or her disapproval. Nor can the discovery of any factual evidence make my position false and the other person's true (or vice versa). Although we might both change our minds when this evidence comes to light, our original claims would still be correct as expressions of our differing attitudes at a particular moment in time.

However, the most famous objection to ethical naturalism comes from G E Moore (1873-1958). In his book *Principia Ethica*[1] Moore argues that all forms of ethical naturalism, by seeking to define moral words like 'good', 'bad' and so on in non-moral terms, commit what he calls 'the naturalistic fallacy'. His argument is based on a technique he devised for testing when proposed definitions were correct or incorrect. He called this 'the open question technique'. The word 'brother', for example, has the definition 'being male and being a sibling'. This definition makes the question, 'I know George is a brother, but is he male and a sibling?' pointless because the first part of the sentence has already supplied the answer to the question. It is what Moore calls a 'closed question': the properties denoted by the words 'male' and 'sibling' represent a necessary condition for anyone to be a brother. But if I then ask the question, 'I know George is a brother, but is he a teacher at Harvard'? this is not a senseless question since the definition of George as a brother says nothing about whether he teaches at Harvard. This is what Moore calls an 'open question'; the properties denoted by the words 'teacher at Harvard' do *not* represent a necessary condition for anyone being a brother. Moore concludes that a definition is correct when the question asked is closed and incorrect when the question is open. Asking an open question, in other words, means that the two expressions being used do *not* mean the same thing.

Now, since Moore maintains that all naturalistic definitions of ethical terms will result in 'open questions', his claim is that no ethical term can be defined solely in terms of any naturalistic property. To suppose otherwise is to commit the 'naturalistic fallacy'. Thus, the proposition 'Hitler was evil' cannot be substantiated by evidence of his cruelty because I can still ask the open question. 'I grant that Hitler was cruel, but nevertheless *is* cruelty evil?'

---

1. *Principia Ethica* (Cambridge: Cambridge University Press, 1903) pp 5-21.

The legitimacy of this question means that being evil cannot be defined by the fact of cruelty. And the same can be said of the identification of 'good' with 'I approve of it'. While it would be ridiculous to ask the closed question: 'I approve of it, but do I approve of it?', it would not be silly to ask the open question: 'I approve of it, but is it good?' Hence the identification of good with my approval cannot be supported.

According to Moore, then, any attempt to define ethical language by means of naturalistic terms (eg, 'good' as 'pleasure', 'happiness', 'desire', 'approval', 'virtue', 'knowledge' and so forth) is mistaken. For any theory which argues that the good life is identical with any natural property is guilty of the naturalistic fallacy, which assumes that goodness is something that can be grasped by an act of direct observation.

2. Ethical Non-naturalism

Having exposed the naturalistic fallacy inherent in all forms of ethical naturalism, Moore now proceeds to his own moral theory. This is known as *ethical non-naturalism*. If ethical language can never be reduced to factual statements, then, as we have seen, it can never be regarded as true or false on the basis of observable evidence. Does this mean that ethical statements can never be considered true or false? Moore denies this. We do possess another method of verification, in which we decide whether an ethical proposition is true or false through a process of *moral intuition*. Here it becomes *self-evident* to us that something is good or not. For example, if we say 'Mother Theresa is good', this statement is not verifiable by observation and experience. Yet nevertheless we say that the statement *is* true - and *correctly* say that it is - because we can immediately see that a property of moral goodness does belong to this woman. But what is this property? It is, says Moore, a unique and indefinable quality, something which, although it cannot be analysed, we can recognize is possessed by somebody or not. In this sense it is like the colour 'yellow': it is what Moore calls a 'simple notion', which you cannot explain to anyone who does not already know it; but, unlike 'yellow', which is a *naturalistic* quality that can be observed, 'goodness' cannot be so perceived. 'Goodness', then, is a *non-natural* property, the presence of which cannot be decided by the senses but is know intuitively none the less.

> . . . *If I am asked 'What is good?' my answer is that good is good, and that is the end of the matter. Or if I am asked 'How is good to be defined?' my answer is that it cannot be defined,and that is all I have to say about it . . .*
>
> *'Good', then, if we mean by it the quality which we assert to belong to a thing, when we say that the thing is good, is incapable of any definition, in the most important sense of that word. The most important sense of 'definition' is that in which a definition states what are the parts which invariably compose a certain whole; and in this sense 'good' has no definition because it is simple and has no parts. It is one of those innumerable objects of thought which are themselves incapable of definition, because they are the ultimate terms by reference to which whatever is capable of definition must be defined.[2]*

There are many difficulties with this theory, not the least being that it appears, like ethical naturalism, to rule out the possibility of moral disagreement. If good is a non-natural property that cannot be analyzed through the normal procedures of observation and investigation, then what exactly is it that Moore is claiming to *know* by intuition? This becomes difficult to establish once we realize how notoriously hard it is to decide between intuitions. If I intuit that 'The President will be assassinated tomorrow' and you intuit that he won't be, then tomorrow we can decide which of our intuitions was correct; but this, be it noted, has been decided by sense-experience and not by intuition. If, however, sense-experience is disallowed, where shall we turn to decide between our intuitions? If they contradict each other, both cannot be right; but each *will* be right for the person whose intuition tells him so. It seems, then, that we are forever prevented from knowing which intuition is true (or false) since, on Moore's theory, the only method of verification common to intuitionism is the self-evidence of the intuition itself.[3]

3. Ethical Non-cognitivism

Ethical naturalism and ethical non-naturalism are both *cognitive* theories of meta-ethics; they both maintain that ethical propositions communicate a type of *knowledge*. Ethical naturalism argues that this knowledge can be scientifically verified or falsified. Ethical non-naturalism denies this and claims instead that ethical propositions ascribe a certain indefinable quality to objects and actions and that these propositions will be deemed true or false by the process of intuition. *Ethical non-cognitivism* rejects both these positions. Naturalism is denied because, as Moore demonstrated, it commits the naturalistic fallacy; and Moore's own position is rejected because there exists no simple, unanalyzable quality called 'good' disclosed by intuition; because indeed, ethical propositions are *non-cognitive*, communicating no knowledge whatsoever and containing nothing therefore that can be rendered true

---

2. *op. cit*, pp 6, 9-10.

3. For further criticisms of Moore's position, see G C Field, "The Place of Definition in Ethics", *Proceedings of the Aristotelian Society*, XXXII (February, 1932) pp 79-94; and W K Frankena, "The Naturalistic Fallacy", *Mind*, XLVIII (October, 1939) pp 464-477. Both articles are reprinted in *Readings in Ethical Theory*, ed W Sellars and J Hospers (New York: Appleton-Century-Crofts, 1952) pp 92-102, 103-114.

or false. The assertion 'George is a liar' does say something which is either true or false; but the ethical statement 'Lying is wrong' asserts nothing at all, not even that the speaker disapproves of lying. Thus ethical statements, although they may look as if they are communicating some information, are in fact cognitively meaningless.

What, then, is the function of ethical statements according to ethical non-cognitivism? For the English philosopher, A J Ayer, in his book *Language, Truth, and Logic*,[4] their function is purely 'emotive': either to express the feelings and emotions of those who employ them - and to this extent they are more like screams, groans or grunts of pleasure - or to arouse feelings in others or to stimulate action, primarily through commands. Consider, for example, the difference between someone who says 'I am in pain' and another who says 'Ouch!' The first person is *asserting* or *describing* that he is in pain (and this assertion or description is true if he is in pain and false if he isn't). The second person is not asserting or describing anything at all. The word 'Ouch!' is merely expressing or displaying their pain, something they could equally well express by their posture, facial expression or other kind of non-verbal action. In the same way, a mother who commands her child to 'Always tell the truth' is expressing not so much her own feeling towards truthfulness but her desire to develop this particular feeling in her offspring. According to Ayer, just as one would not say that a cry of pain or a command is true or false, so it is also incorrect to say that ethical judgements, which express feelings and issue commands, are true or false. If Carol says 'Stealing is right' and Mary says 'Stealing is wrong', this is equivalent to shouting 'Hurrah for stealing' and 'Boo to stealing'. They are expressing a feeling, a feeling of approval or disapproval; but they are not describing these feelings or even asserting that they have them (although one might be able to infer from their exclamations that they do have them). This distinguishes the theory from the theory of ethical naturalism. There, the speaker was stating a proposition which could be scientifically tested (that he or she had or had not a particular attitude); but here all that is being expressed is the feeling itself or the desire to arouse this feeling in others.

Ethical non-cognitivism does, however, share with ethical naturalism the criticism that, if ethical statements make no cognitive claims, no contradiction between conflicting claims is possible and no moral disagreement can take place. To meet this objection, a less extreme version of the non-cognitive theory has been suggested by C L Stevenson in his book *Ethics and Language*.[5] Stevenson argues that moral disagreements about what is right and wrong are possible because they very often turn out to be 'disagreements in attitude', and that these disagreements in attitude are themselves based on 'disagreements in belief'. The point to note is that disagreements in belief *can* be resolved by evidence. For example, A may express the moral attitude that 'Drivers ought to wear seat-belts'. Let us say that A's attitude is here supported by his belief that government statistics about fatal accidents are correct. If, however, B can demonstrate that these statistics are incorrect, then it is possible that A will change his mind and withdraw his original moral claim. Here B has refuted A and changed A's attitude. Stevenson concludes that to say that the difference between A saying 'X is right' and B saying 'X is wrong' is always merely a difference in approval, and that neither can be invalidated, is incorrect. For A's approval of X may, in many instances, be founded on a belief which evidence can show is unjustified.

One final amendment of ethical non-cognitivism should be mentioned. This is the theory of *Prescriptivism* proposed by R M Hare in his book *The Language of Morals*. For Hare, the primary function of the statement 'X is good' is not only to express an attitude or produce one in others but to *commend*, that is, 'to guide choices, our own or other peoples', now or in the future.'[6] Hare readily admits that this commendation or prescription of action is the non-cognitive component of ethical sentences, but such sentences also contain cognitive elements. For in commending X we are saying two things: first, that X actually possesses certain characteristics or properties that make it good; and second, that we know these characteristics are good because they conform to the standards or criteria of goodness that we commonly appeal to when we make judgements of this sort. For example, if I say 'That motor-car is a good one', I am, first, commending it as the sort of car that would be good to buy; and second, commending it because it has particular qualities that make not only it commendable but any motor-car that possesses them commendable:

> when I commend a motor-car I am guiding the choices of my hearer not merely in relation to that particular motor-car but in relation to motor-cars in general. What I have said to him will be of assistance whenever in the future he has to choose a motor-car or advise anyone else on the choice of a motor-car or write a general treatise on the design of motor-cars (which involves choosing what sort of motor-cars to advise other people to have made). The method whereby I give him this assistance is by making known to him a standard for judging motor-cars.[7]

---

4. *Language, Truth and Logic* (London: Victor Gallancz, Ltd, 1946) pp 102-114. Ayer restates his position in "On the Analysis of Moral Judgments", which appears in his *Philosophical Essays* (London: Macmillan, 1954) pp 231-249.
5. *Ethics and Language* (New Haven: Yale University Press, 1943) See also Stevenson's "The Emotive Meaning of Ethical Terms", *Mind,* XLVI (January 1937) pp 14-31. Reprinted in Sellars and Hospers *op. cit*, pp 415-429.
6. *The Language of Morals* (Oxford ; The Clarendon Press, 1952) p 126.
7. Hare, *op. cit*, p 132.

This example shows why Hare believes that ethical non-cognitivism is wrong in two important aspects:

1. Non-cognitivism does not recognize that a cognitive element is necessary for the support of moral judgements. For in saying 'X is good', reasons must be given for supposing that X contains 'good-making characteristics'; and whether it does or does not contain them can be factually established. In other words, when I say 'John is good', I am commending John as a model for imitation because I believe he possesses certain qualites, like courage and honesty; and whether I am right or wrong in this, whether he is actually courageous and honest, can be independently established.

2. Non-cognitivism fails to see that all moral judgements, far from referring to individual approval, function also as universal guides to choice: that anything else like X, having the same 'good-making characteristics' - will also be good and will be commended as such. We imply, in other words, that there are not just private reasons for asserting 'John is good' - that he is good merely because I approve of him - but that this statement also has universal application; that *any man of this type* will be deemed good and commended as such.

It is worth mentioning one further point made by Hare. If it is the case that we justify our moral judgements by some moral standards or criteria - those which decide, for instance, that courage and honesty **are** 'good-making characteristics' - what do we do when someone else rejects them? In that case, says Hare, we make a *decision of principle*: we appeal to those principles that have guided our choices and decisions and try to give good reasons why these principles, and not others, are the correct ones to adopt. We thus engage in an analysis of rival principles. What these principles are, and how we decide between them is the business of ***Normative Ethics.*.**

Bibliography: Meta-ethics

* denotes text referred to or extracted in main text

Ayer, A J *Language, Truth, and Logic** (London: Victor Gollancz, 1946);
        'On the Analysis of Moral Judgements', *Philosophical Essays* (London: Macmillan, 1954)
Ewing, A C *The Definition of Good* (London: Routledge & Kegan Paul, 1947) Preliminary study of meta-ethics.
Foot, Philippa (ed) *Theories of Ethics* (Oxford: Oxford University Press, 1967) An important collection of essays by Stevenson and Frankena (on Moore), Ormson and Mabbott (on Mill), Rawls and J J C Smart.
Frankena, William K *Perspectives on Morality** ed K E Goodpaster (Notre Dame & London: University of Notre Dame Press, 1976) Includes Frankena's important essays on Moore.
Hancock, Roger N *Twentieth Century Ethics* (New York & London: Columbia University Press, 1974) Useful introductory sections on Moore, Ross, Ayer, Hare and Rawls.
Hare, R M *The Language of Morals** (Oxford: The Clarendon Press, 1962)
Hospers, John & Sellars, W (eds) *Readings in Ethical Theory* (New York: Appleton-Century-Crofts, 1952) An extensive collection of texts, containing the important criticisms of Moore by G C Field and W K Frankena.
Hudson, W D *Modern Moral Philosophy* (London: Macmillan, 1970) Excellent introduction to meta-ethics.
McGrath, Patrick *The Nature of Moral Judgements* (London: Sheed & Ward, 1967) Contains separate chapters on Ayer, Stevenson and Hare.
Moore, G E *Principia Ethics** (Cambridge: Cambridge University Press, 1903)
Olthuis, James H *Facts, Values and Ethics* (Assen, the Netherlands: Koninklijke Van Gorcum, 1968) Critique of Moore and the movements that followed him.
Stevenson, C L *Ethics and Language** (New Haven: Yale University Press, 1943);
        'The Emotive Meaning of Ethical Terms', *Mind*, XLVI (January 1937) pp 14-31. Reprinted in Sellars and Hospers, *op. cit*, pp 415-429.
Toulmin, Stephen E *The Place of Reason in Ethics* (Cambridge: Cambridge University Press, 1950) Close to the emotive theory, but laying greater emphasis on the cognitive content of moral judgements.
Warnock, Mary *Ethics since 1900* (London: Oxford University Press, 1960) Chapters 1-4 contain useful short accounts of Moore, intuitionism and emotivism.

INDEX

Abortion
and the Right to Life, 48
Judith Thomson, 'A Defense of Abortion' (extract), 52-4
Questions, 55
Bibliography, 62
Act-Utilitarianism, 111, 113-114
Animal Rights
and the Right to Life, 51
Peter Singer, 'All Animals are Equal' (extract), 59-60
Questions, 61
Bibliography, 62
Anscombe, Elizabeth, 141
'War and Murder' (extract), 123-4
Questions, 124
Appollodorus, 16
Aquinas, St. Thomas
on the morality of war, 118-119
'Summa Theologiae' (extract), 119, 128
Anytus, 15
Aristophanes, 15
Aristotle, 9
Asclepius, 21
Ayer, A.J., 158

Baier, Kurt, 41-42
Baldwin, Stanley, 127
Behaviourism, 143-7
Questions, 154-5
Bibliography, 155
See also Psychological Behaviourism and Bio-Behaviourism
Bio-Behaviourism, 145-7
Bentham, Jeremy, 63, 75-6, 85
his principle of utility, 64-5, 114
his hedonic calculus (extract), 66-7
and Rule-utilitarianism, 111
Mill's criticism of, 69
Questions, 68
Broad, C.D., 11

Campbell, C.A., 135, 139, 141
Categorical Imperative, 99-102, 113
Civil Disobedience, 22-9
John Rawls on, 23-4
Henry Thoreau on, 25-6
Peter Kropotkin on, 27-9
Questions, 30-1
Bibliography, 32
Compatibilism. See Soft Determinism
Conditioning, 144-5
Contingent Truth, 137-8
Crick, Francis, 145
Crito, 15-16, 20, 22, 33
extract from, 17-20
Critobulus, 16

Dahl, Roald, 83
Darrow, Clarence, 133, 141

DNA (deoxyribonuleic acid), 145
Definism. See Ethical Naturalism
Determinism,
and Free Will, 131-140
Questions, 141-2
Bibliography, 142
Deontological ethics, 33, 47, 114
definition of, 11-12
and Kant, 95
and Ross, 109, 111
Dostoyevsky, Fyodor, 76
'Crime and Punishment' (extract), 79
Questions, 80

Echecrates, 21
Egoism
general definition, 34-5
Questions, 45
Bibliography, 46
See also Ethical Egoism and Psychological Egoism
Eichmann, Adolf, 93
Einstein, Albert, 146
Epicurus, 35, 41, 45, 70
Ethical Egoism
defined, 40
criticisms of, 41-2
Ethical Naturalism, 156-7, 158
Ethical Non-naturalism, 156, 157
Ethical Non-cognitivism, 156, 157-8
Emotivism. See Ethical Non-cognitivism
Eugenics, 145-6
Euthanasia
and the Right to Life, 49-50
voluntary and involuntary, 50
direct and indirect, 50
active and passive, 50-1
James Rachels, 'Active and Passive Euthanasia' (extract), 56-8
Questions, 58
Bibliography, 62
Extended Rule-utilitarianism
ethical theory of, 114

Fair Play, duty of, 22, 23-4
See also Rawls
Fatalism, 139
Fletcher, Joseph, 147
'Ethical Aspects of Genetic Control' (extract), 151-2
Questions, 152, 154
Franks, Bobby, 133
Free Will
and Determinism, 131-140
Questions, 141-2
Bibliography, 142
Galton, Francis, 145
Gandhi, Mohandas K., 120, 139
'Non-violence' (extract), 121-2

Questions, 122
Good Will, 97-9
Gyges, myth of (extract), 43

Hannibal, 77
Hard Determinism, 131-4
and punishment, 132-4
reply to Libertarianism, 136, 139
Hare, R.M., 159
Hedonic Calculus, 66
Hedonism
and Epicurus, 35
and Bentham, 64
and Mill, 69
Heine, Heinrich, 96
Hegesius, 45
Hitler, Adolf, 49, 67
Hobbes, Thomas, 40
Hospers, John, 132, 134
Hugo, Victor, 103
Huxley, Aldous, 76, 147
'Brave New World' (extract), 81
Questions (1), 82
'Brave New World Revisited' (extract), 153-4
Questions (2), 154

Instrumental Good, 35, 65
Intrinsic Good, 35, 65
Intuitionism. See Ethical Non-naturalism

Kant, Immanuel, 104, 108, 112, 115
ethical theory of, 95-102
on morality of war, 118
'Groundwork of the Metaphysic of Morals' (extract), 100-1
Criticisms, 105-7
Questions, 115-116
Bibliography, 117
Kepler, 79
King, Martin Luther, 22, 30
Kropotkin, Peter, 22
'Law and Authority' (extract), 27-9
Questions, 29
Bibliography, 32

Lackey, Douglas, 120
'Ethics and Nuclear Deterrence' (extract), 125-6
Questions, 127
Lenin, 146
Leon, 15
Leopold, Nathan, 133
Lewis, C.S., 86
'The Humanitarian Theory of Punishment' (extract), 89-90
Questions, 90, 154
Libertarianism, 131, 135-8
reply to Hard Determinism, 136-8

for Questions and Bibliography, see Determinism
Lincoln, Abraham, 37
Locke, John, 132
Loeb, Richard, 133
Lycon, 15
Lycurgus, 79

Machiavelli, Niccolo, 76
'The Prince' (extract), 77
Questions, 78
Mahomet, 79
Marx, Karl, 146
Menninger, Karl, 86
'The Crime of Punishment' (extract), 87-88
Questions, 88
Meta-ethics, 156-9
Mill, John Stuart, 86
utilitarian theory of, 69-72
'The Greatest Happiness Principle' (extract), 70-1
Questions (1), 74
Critiscisms, 75-6
'In Favour of Capital Punishment' (extract), 91-2
Questions (2), 92
Moore, G.E., 156-8
Morse, Senator Wayne, 31
Mozart, Wolfgang Amadeus, 72

Muller, Hermann J., 146

Napoleon, 79
Naturalistic fallacy, 156-7
Necessary truth, 137-8
Negatice eugenics, 145-7
Negative reinforcement, 145, 149
Neill, A.S.
'Summerhill' (extract), 141
Newton, Sir Isaac, 79
Noninterference, duty of, 49
Normative Ethics,
defined, 9, 11
Questions, 14

Operant conditioning, 144-5

Plato, 9
'Crito' (extract), 17-20
'The Apology', 16
'Phaedo', 20-1
'The Republic' (extract), 43
Pasteur, Louis, 67
Pavlov, Ivan, 144
Positive eugenics, 145-6
Positive Reinforcement, 145, 149
Prescriptivism, 159
Prima facie duty, 108-110, 113
Psychological Behaviourism, 143-5
Psychological egoism, 131
defined, 37
criticisms of, 38-40
Punishment
utilitarian theory of, 85
retributive theory of, 85

theory of rehabilitation, 85-6
Karl Menninger on, 87-8
C. S. Lewis on, 89-90
J. S. Mill on, 91-2
and Hard Determinism, 132-4
Questions, 93
Bibliography, 94
Purtill, Richard, 109

Quinlan, Karen, 51

Rachels, James, 47
'Active and passive euthanasia' (extract), 56-8
Questions, 58
Rand, Ayn, 68
'The Fountainhead' (extract), 44-5
Randolph, A. Philip, 31
Rawls, John, 22, 30
'The duty of fair play' (extract), 23-4
Questions, 24
Bibliography, 32
Recombinant DNA, 146
Right to Life, 47-62
Bibliography, 62
See also Abortion, Euthanasia, Animal Rights
Ross, W.D.,
ethical theory of, 108-9
criticisms of, 109-110, 113
and rule-utilitarianism, 111
Rule-utilitarianism
ethical theory of, 111-114
Bibliography, 117

Satyagraha, principle of, 120-1
Schlage, Bruno, 93
Seneca, Lucius, 104
Service, duty of, 49
Shaw, G.B., 115
Shawcross, Sir Hartley, 128
Singer, Peter, 47, 51
'All Animals are Equal' (extract), 59-60
Questions, 61
Situation ethics, 147
Skinner, B.F., 144, 146-7
'Walden Two' (extract), 148-150
Questions, 150, 154
Socrates, 9, 20, 22, 33-4, 71
biography, 15-16
in Plato's dialogue 'Crito', 17-20
Questions, 21
Bibliography, 21
Soft Determinism, 131, 139-140
for Questions and Bibliography, see Determinism
Solon, 79
Spinoza, Benedict, 136
Stauffenberg, Claus von, 67
Stevenson, C.L., 158-9
Sun Yat Sen, 146

Teleological ethics, 33, 47, 114, 146
definition of, 11
and utilitarianism, 64

and Kant, 95
and Ross, 109, 111
Thayer, William Sidney, 115
Theresa, Mother, 67
Theseus, 16
Thomson, Judith, 47-8
'A Defense of Abortion' (extract), 52-4
Questions, 55
Thoreau, Henry, 22
'In the Duty of Civil Disobedience' (extract), 25-6
Questions, 26
Truman, President Harry S., 67
'Presidential papers' (extract), 129

Universalizability, principle of, 99-100
and Rule-utilitarianism, 111
Utilitarianism
defined, 63-5
Bentham's version of, 63-7
Mill's version of, 69-71
criticisms of, 75-6
and the theory of punishment, 85
and the morality of war, 118
Questions, 83
Bibliography, 84

War, morality of
Kantian theory of, 118
utilitarian theory of, 118
Aquinas on, 118-119
Bibliography, 129
Questions, 129
Watson, James, 145
Watson, John B., 143-4, 146